UNDERGROUND
ARCHITECTURE

Overleaf **Eric Aumonier's Archer statue at East Finchley.**

Above **Direction sign at Manor House, 1932.**

Below **Designs for the reconstruction of Finchley Central as a four platform station were undertaken by Reginald Uren for Charles Holden during 1937-39. Tall, narrow towers over stairwells to the low level ticket hall would adjoin the road bridge. Plans were progressively rationalised to leave the towers as the main elements. London Transport and the LNER could not agree over the cost and the project was shelved. Further designs were prepared in 1947 but no work carried out. This is an early sketch for the station by Charles Holden.**

UNDERGROUND ARCHITECTURE

David Lawrence

Capital Transport

ACKNOWLEDGEMENTS

Many individuals and organisations have rendered invaluable help during this book's preparation. I would especially like to record the assistance and encouragement offered by Charles Hutton, who allowed me to borrow from his uncompleted biography of Charles Holden; Desmond Croome, Mike Horne and Alan A. Jackson for checking the text; Dr Neil Bingham, Robert Elwall, Alison Felstead, Fiona Kirk, Tim Knox, Angela Mace and Julian Osley of the RIBA British Architectural Library and Drawings Collection; Sheila Taylor, Patricia Austin, Hugh Robertson, Simon Murphy and other staff of the London Transport Museum for their help.

I am also indebted to the local history collections of the London Boroughs of Ealing, Enfield, Hammersmith & Fulham, Kensington & Chelsea, Hillingdon, Hounslow, Islington, Redbridge and Richmond, the Cities of London and Westminster, and to the following individuals: Finch Allibone; R.Y. Ames Ltd; Martin Angus; Elizabeth Argent; the Codrington Library, All Souls College, Oxford; Edward Armitage; the Art Workers Guild; Winifred and Freda Aumonier; Nick Bailey; Peter Bancroft; Sheelagh Barton; Hazel Berriman – Royal Cornwall Museum; Tony Bilbow; Jo Bossányi; Alan Brookes Associates/ Alan Brookes/ Andrew Fursdon/ Matthew Bedward; Gordon Buck; Michael Carlton; Vivien Castle; Stephen Chaplin; Trevor Chinn, Archivist – Gordon Russell Ltd; Gaye Chorlton; John Cornforth; Philip Coverdale; Darkside; Robyn Denny; Design Research Unit/ Jim Williams/ Chris Ellingham; Trata Drescha; M.L. Duffie; David Easton; Tom Eckersley; W.P.N. Edwards; Dr M.M. Figgis; Nigel and Sylvia Figgis; Finsbury Library; Alan Fletcher; Malcolm R. Ford; Margaret Foreman; June Fraser; Geoffrey Fouquet; Abram Games; Barry Gaskin; David Gentleman; A.H. Gerrard; Michael Goj; A. Stuart Gray; Angela Green; Oliver Green; Philip Greenslade; the Guildhall Library; Henry Haig; W.D.C. Hall; Sydney Hardy; Birkin Haward senior; W.R. Headley; Ruth Heaps; Peter Heaps; John Helps/ The Building Crafts Training School; Dr Geoffrey Hick; Jack and Penny Howe; Paul Huxley; Lotte and Joan MacIver; J. Jarvis & Sons plc; Martin Johnson/AHP Partnership; David Johnstone; Gwyn Jones; Eitan Karol; A. Bernard Kaukas; John (Chas) Kennett; Bob Kindred; Margaret Kriesis; Duncan M. Lamb; Sean Lander; Brian and Hilary Lewis; John Mason; Alexandra McFall; John Measures; Dr David Mellor; Kenneth Millard; R.L. Moorcroft; The National Art Library Archive of Art and Design; Christopher Nell; Sir Eduardo Paolozzi; Margaret Perry; Pilkington plc; Asha Quinn; Sam Rabin; John Ramsay; John Reed; Alfred Reeves; Dr Ruth Richardson; Royal Academy; Royal Society of British Sculptors; Judy Russell; Pat Schleger; Peter Sedgley; K.J.H. Seymour; Wendy Sheridan; South London Art Gallery; Keith and Pearl Spedding; Margery and Gordon Stewart; V.L. Stubbs; Cassidy Taggart Partnership – Michael Cassidy; David F. Taylor; Shirley Tyler; Andrew Wallace; George Woolliscroft & Sons Ltd; the Worshipful Company of Goldsmiths; Roy Turner; James Wyatt; Ben Yuri Gallery.

I am also grateful for the assistance of Roland Paoletti and the staff of the Jubilee Line Extension Project Office, and the several architectural practices working on the Jubilee Line Extension: William Alsop and Jan Störmer/ John Smith; Sir Norman Foster & Partners/ Katy Harris, Gerard Evenden; Herron Associates at Imagination/ Ron Herron; Michael Hopkins & Partners/ David Selby; MacCormac Jamieson Pritchard/ Ian Logan; Ian Ritchie Architects/ Gordon Talbot; Troughton McAslan/ Piers Smerin; van Heyningen & Haward Architects/ Birkin Haward; Weston Williamson/ Chris Williamson.

Finally, I would like to remember with affection Ruth Bucknell and Roy Neate for their kindness and support so freely given.

D.L.

Left **Pre-war dreams of a transport interchange neighbouring a planned airport at Fairlop.**

Right **Foster Associates were commissioned in 1977 to redevelop the Hammersmith station island site. The architects' scheme provided for office blocks on the perimeter around a large open space with shopping and recreational facilities above the rail and bus terminal, sheltered by a canopy of Teflon-coated fibreglass. Fears voiced about the cost of the work led to the abandonment of plans in 1979. Sir Norman Foster and Partners are now working on a station for the Jubilee line extension.**

CONTENTS

For Simon and Sylvia Lawrence,
and for Gaye.

First published 1994

ISBN 185414 160 0

Published by
Capital Transport Publishing
38 Long Elmes, Harrow, Middlesex

Printed by
Bath Midway Press
Midlands Industrial Estate
Holt, Wiltshire

© David G. Lawrence 1994

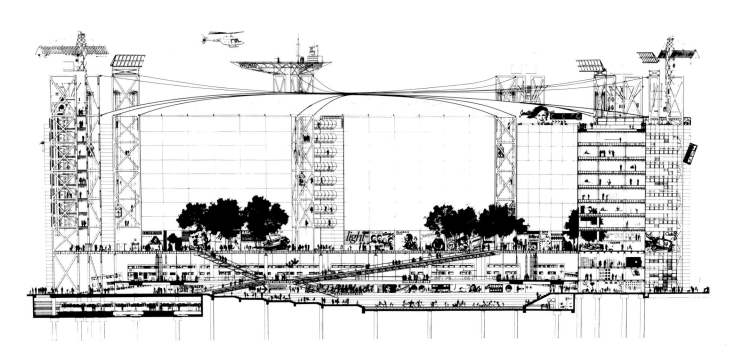

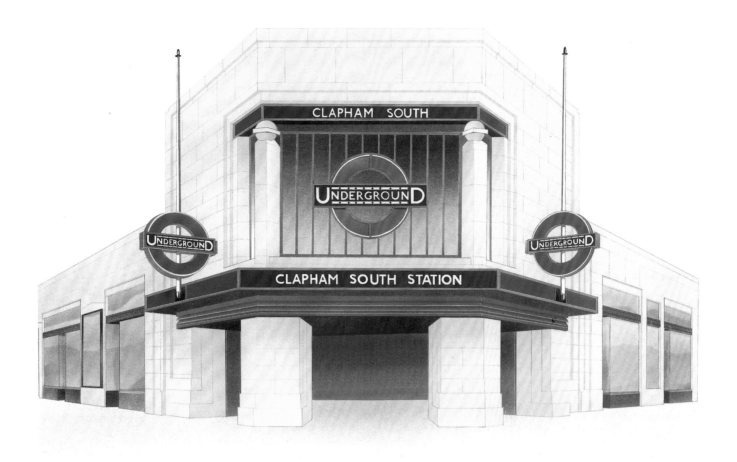

FOREWORD

by Christopher Nell, Environments Manager, London Underground Ltd

Change can be seen throughout the Underground system; it is there in layers and the historian or enthusiast can read it like a book. They can do this because not only have the designers, architects and engineers left their mark through their knowledge and expertise but they have also left something of their personality. These people have turned London's Underground into something unique, even idiosyncratic, as different as it can be from the underground railways of Paris, Brussels, New York or even Glasgow.

The Underground also reflects the nation's fortunes and aspirations. The confidence of the Victorian engineer to build a passenger railway underground as a means of reducing the pressure on the city's road traffic was both remarkable and visionary. Compare the scepticism with which some still view the idea of travelling under the Channel despite the advances of 150 years of design engineering and construction.

In architecture Leslie Green and Holden are the giants; Green for his prolific architectural output and for developing a style of building which unified the system, making its station architecture unique in the streetscape and effectively branding the transportation offer. I find Holden and his contemporaries the most interesting, for their clarity of design and for stripping away the decorative excesses of the period in return for space and clear volumes. Holden brought new materials into the system and used them for their physical qualities without regard to their cost. The window glass, for example, was the cheapest he could find, yet in use it gives a pleasant, obscuring effect whilst filtering the light. Holden's stations have stood the test of time and, despite the additional layers of alteration and changes in requirements, their original clarity is still evident.

I am pleased that David Lawrence has written this book because it provides the enthusiast with a well researched authoritative reference on the Underground's development in addition to providing the amateur with a well presented and illustrated history of the capital's favourite means of transport.

As new stations are built and existing ones refurbished, I hope to influence a return to seeing the clarity of the structure expressed, and signing and other hardware contrasted against a calm and neutral background. This will indicate to the public that London Underground is a well managed and confident transport system that London can be proud of.

INTRODUCTION

Beneath our feet, below the streets and buildings of this teeming metropolis, there runs a complex network comprising many miles of tunnels. While the roads above throng with traffic, hundreds of trains run through these iron and concrete arteries, carrying millions of night workers, commuters, shoppers, tourists and theatre or cinema-goers from the suburbs into and around the city – keeping it alive.

How do we know the railway is there: how can we catch a train? This is the function of the station: to advertise, to attract and welcome travellers, and to offer all the facilities necessary for making a journey. It serves as a shopfront and entrance to the system, and must make the transition from street to train safe and comfortable. As far back as the Euston Arch, designers have been concerned with the concept of the station as gateway and urban focus.

I began this book by photographing the stations that appealed to me visually. As I looked closer I began to see the wealth of architectural and design history present on the Underground, which by its relative compactness has retained much of the integrity the main line railway has lost. The Underground was an early pioneer of what is now called corporate identity to unite its many parts and it forms a total environment created by the co-ordination of good design, materials, signs, furniture and equipment.

Underground stations may be seen as a modern continuation of the great railway tradition adapted specifically to suit the peculiar needs of a modern mass-transit system. The best of the architecture has preserved the identity of the railway station whilst setting an innovative example through inspired patronage, providing both public and staff with clean and bright facilities enhanced by good design and accessible art.

In this book many official photographs from the London Transport Museum photographic archives are supplemented by drawings prepared from original plans to give an impression of preliminary and unbuilt designs. Towards the back of the book an appendix contains biographical details of the main architects and some artists employed on Underground projects.

It has not been the intention to offer a gazetteer of stations, nor a protracted architectural criticism of the buildings discussed in this book, but to present an objective historical account. A great many buildings still survive and the interested reader could do no better than to spend an afternoon visiting the stations and enjoying them at first hand.

Twickenham, October 1994   DAVID LAWRENCE

THE FIRST UNDERGROUND RAILWAYS

Bishop's Road, Paddington — western terminus of the Metropolitan Railway in 1863 — from an engraving in the *Illustrated London News*. This site was redeveloped in 1933.

The first underground passenger railway in the world was opened by the Metropolitan Railway on 10th January 1863; with a steam operated line running nearly four miles between Bishop's Road, Paddington and Farringdon Street.

From this short line, extensions were made which would eventually be linked to form the present Circle line, and branches radiating outward from the centre were opened to tap traffic from the developing suburbs in south-west, west and north-west London.

The stations on the original railway were all single-storey structures faced with white Suffolk brick and cement rendering to simulate rusticated stonework; at Edgware Road 'Ransome's Artificial Stone' was used for dressings. Ironwork was painted to look like bronze. For the most part the railway was built under public roads to avoid demolition of property and the paying of easements to private landowners. Intermediate stations were provided at Edgware Road, Baker Street, Portland Road (now Great Portland Street), Gower Street (now Euston Square) and King's Cross.

Sir John Fowler was engineer-in-chief for the Metropolitan, and Thomas Marr Johnson (1826-1874) the resident engineer, but it has been suggested that the original Metropolitan surface buildings were designed by the architect John Hargrave Stevens. Stevens had been appointed surveyor to the Bayswater, Paddington and Holborn Bridge Railway (shortly to be incorporated as the North Metropolitan) in January 1853 to carry out preliminary surveys for the route of the line. This work was done and Stevens paid for his services, but it is recorded that subsequent station plans were submitted by Fowler himself for approval.

The Metropolitan works were received with mixed comments, *The Building News* reporting that there was 'very little architectural character in any of the stations, but a wonderful amount of engineering skill and good workmanship,'[1] and *The Builder* remarked that 'the stations are less remarkable externally, and in architectural details, than they are for their disposition of plan, and the clever construction of some of them.'[2] It can be said that the station buildings — decorated in the Italianate styling popular during this period — were considerably overshadowed by the great accomplishment of the engineers who used the latest available technology to build this innovative railway.

Bishop's Road occupied an awkward position between the main-line station and the Great Western Railway coal depot alongside Paddington canal basin, further restricted by an approach road to the Great Western goods depot. Bishop's Road bridge was partially demolished to make room for the station building, set back behind a forecourt for cabs and omnibuses. The structure had a gable at each end with high pavilion roofs and balustered parapets. Platforms were built in a cutting between blind-arcaded brick retaining walls, beneath a bow girder and plate glass roof of 62ft span. Stairways and offices were set into the walls at platform level and a footbridge stood towards the east end of the platforms. From the westbound side there was a subway to the Great Western station. The station was completely rebuilt in 1933 to become a suburban annex of Paddington main-line terminus.

Baker Street station began as two side platforms (now those serving the Circle line numbered 5 and 6) in a single tunnel with two running lines. Small station buildings — one for each platform — were located on the north and south corners of Marylebone Road at Baker Street. Each building had a separate entrance and exit with booking office between them; stairs descended through archways to the platforms. Basement rooms were given over to parcel offices, stores and lavatories. Similar buildings were provided at Gower Street. The railway tunnel was widened to 45ft for the platforms, and the arches of the retaining walls were carried outward and upward to form skylights emerging at either side of the main road in the front gardens of houses. The shafts were lined with white glazed earthenware tiles and capped by thick sheets of glass with iron gratings for ventilation. Lighting was by means of gas lamps in large glass spheres. The Metropolitan locomotives were intended to give out little exhaust, but from contemporary accounts the smoky conditions below ground were far from comfortable. *The Building News* described Baker Street as having a 'gloomy, catacomb-like appearance.'[3]

Top **Contemporary engraving of Portland Road; the domes were removed during 1869-70 to relieve the smoky tunnel atmosphere.**

Above **Side elevation of Portland Road based on the architect's drawings, station offices on left.**

Impression of platform tunnel at **Baker Street** showing arches for light and ventilation. Tracks were laid to both standard and broad gauges, the latter to suit **GWR** locomotives and rolling stock.

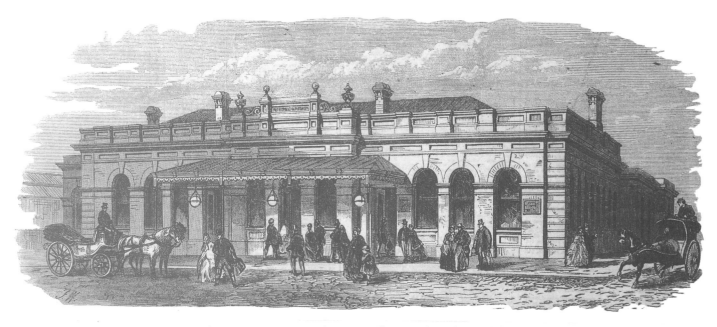

Farringdon as rebuilt in 1865. Part of this structure is still extant behind the new building of 1923.

An unsavoury area of narrow alleys and yards used for the slaughter of animals from the nearby Smithfield live-meat market was cleared to build a temporary 'City' terminus with a station located at the corner of Farringdon Road and Cowcross Street. For the Metropolitan Railway extension to Moorgate Street, opened on 23rd December 1865, a new building was erected at Farringdon, fronting onto New Charles Street east of the temporary terminus. Within the white Suffolk brick structure, ticket halls and booking offices for the various railway companies serving the station were placed each side of a refreshment room — the first such facility to be operated for the Metropolitan by the catering firm of Spiers & Pond. At the rear the halls were linked by a circulating area with doorways onto the departure gallery for the island and two side platforms. To the north west of this was a separate exit gallery (since removed), the ends of which were aligned with stairs and walkways in the cutting retaining walls, giving access on the southbound side direct to Turnmill Street and on the northbound side back through the station building to Charles Street. Independent galleries for departing and arriving passengers were also a feature of the early District Railway stations. Passengers were sheltered from the elements by a twin-arch elliptical wrought-iron roof with eleven bays each 22ft-long.

The original Paddington station of 1868 which stood on Praed Street opposite the main-line terminus.

On 1st October 1868 the Metropolitan Railway opened an extension from Praed Street Junction (west of Edgware Road) to Gloucester Road. Stations were again designed under the supervision of John Fowler and described by The Builder as 'very light, graceful and effective structures.'[4] Intermediate stations were opened at Praed Street (now Paddington), Bayswater, Notting Hill Gate and High Street Kensington. The extension now forms a western segment of the Circle line.

Buildings were of white Halsey perforated bricks with stone dressings, the windows and doorways set within high arches, and entrances sheltered by iron and glass verandahs. To reduce the noxious atmosphere which had been experienced in the first subterranean Metropolitan stations the platforms on this extension were built in open cuttings adjoining roads, protected by semi-elliptical overall roofs with decorative end windscreens and supported on cast-iron brackets. The windscreens were apparently never fitted with glass, and were later removed. Bayswater survives in essentially original condition to give an impression of these early stations.

Land stretching from the village of Old Brompton up to Hyde Park was used for the growing of fruit, vegetables and flowers, and the joint Metropolitan and District South Kensington station which opened on Christmas Eve 1868 stood on the site of Harrison & Bristow's nursery. The area had been renamed in the 1860s when it was felt that an association with Kensington might be beneficial to housing development then spreading into the locality; it is now known chiefly for its large museums.

The Metropolitan had extended its line east from Gloucester Road to meet the first part of the District Railway running between this point (initially to be called Brompton Exchange) and Westminster Bridge (now Westminster) with intermediate stations at Sloane Square, Victoria and St James's Park. The railway companies financed the extension of Exhibition Road south to the station. John Fowler and T. Marr Johnson were also engineers for the District, and the stations for this line were completed in the Italianate style used by the Metropolitan Railway at this time. Façades were later obscured by large enamel publicity signs.

Gloucester Road differed from other stations on the 1868 extension in having a second storey, and wings set back at either side. This building has recently been restored and despite some later additions retains much that is original.

A pre-opening view of the spacious trainshed at Kensington (High Street). The unglazed windscreen is seen at the far end.

District trains used the Metropolitan platforms at South Kensington until additional platforms to the south came into use on 10th July 1871, after thirty houses in Pelham Street had been demolished for the enlargement; the District station (on early plans shown as 'Cromwell Road') was completed on 19th July the same year. For a brief period during 1895 the District campaigned for South Kensington to be the terminus of the projected but unrealised London & South Wales Railway.

The Metropolitan used a side platform and island with bay line accessed from the west; two further islands and another side platform were served by District trains. In all there were three tracks and four platform faces for Metropolitan trains, and three tracks with three platform faces for District trains. (The platform usage established when two separate companies operated through the station was altered to improve running in 1957, and in 1967-69 the layout was rearranged again so that all trains now serve a single island platform made from two formerly separate islands.) A 485-yard subway was opened on 4th May 1885 to provide a covered route for passengers to the exhibition grounds south of the Albert Hall, and was later rebuilt to serve the museums along Exhibition Road.

From Gloucester Road the District Railway constructed an extension to West Brompton, with a terminus alongside a station of the West London Extension Railway. Trains worked by the Metropolitan from Gloucester Road commenced on 12th April 1869 and District through trains ran between Blackfriars and West Brompton from 1st August 1870.

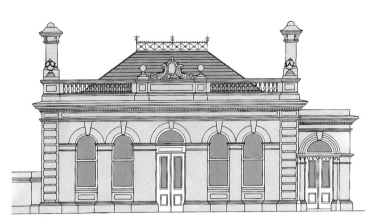

The structure at West Brompton remains largely as originally built, with white Suffolk brick walls and a slate pavilion roof surrounded by a parapet wall, now without its ornamental urns. Twin iron footbridges built for departing and arriving passengers both survive, although the exit footbridge is no longer linked directly with the street. The platforms are covered for a distance of some 66ft by an overall roof with wooden windscreen and supporting posts. The station ceased to be a terminus when the line was extended to Putney Bridge on 1st March 1880. Some rebuilding was carried out in 1928 when external mouldings were removed and the ticket hall rearranged; a former ladies' room on the right-hand side was rebuilt for retail space, altering the symmetrical façade. After World War II the frontage was painted cream and brown. Rebuilding was considered again in 1937 and 1959, but not carried out, and a repair and renovation programme was completed in 1990.

From Bishop's Road the Great Western Railway constructed a branch to Hammersmith via Notting Hill, exploiting the potential of feeder traffic from the western suburbs and more outlying districts. The line opened on 13th June 1864 and was operated jointly with the Metropolitan as the Hammersmith & City Railway from 1866. A wooden station on the Hammersmith Branch came into use at Westbourne Park on 1st February 1866 and was reconstructed to open as a joint station spanning the branch and Great Western main lines on 1st November 1871, thereby facilitating interchange for passengers between west London and the west of England without the need to travel into Paddington. The Hammersmith terminus of this line is also of interest architecturally. The present building was completed by the GWR Engineering Department with company Architect Percy Emerson Culverhouse (1872-1953) during 1907-09.

Top left **Elevation of the first South Kensington station. There were subsequently separate Metropolitan and District facilities on this site.**

Top right **West Brompton, seen here before alteration, was virtually identical to South Kensington, and remains as an example of these early stations.**

Above **Provision of a single structure for both Hammersmith and main west of England lines resulted in a long building on the overbridge at Westbourne Park, with pedimented pavilions as distinguishing features. In a common style for the period, the walls were of polychrome brick with inset moulded terracotta panels.**

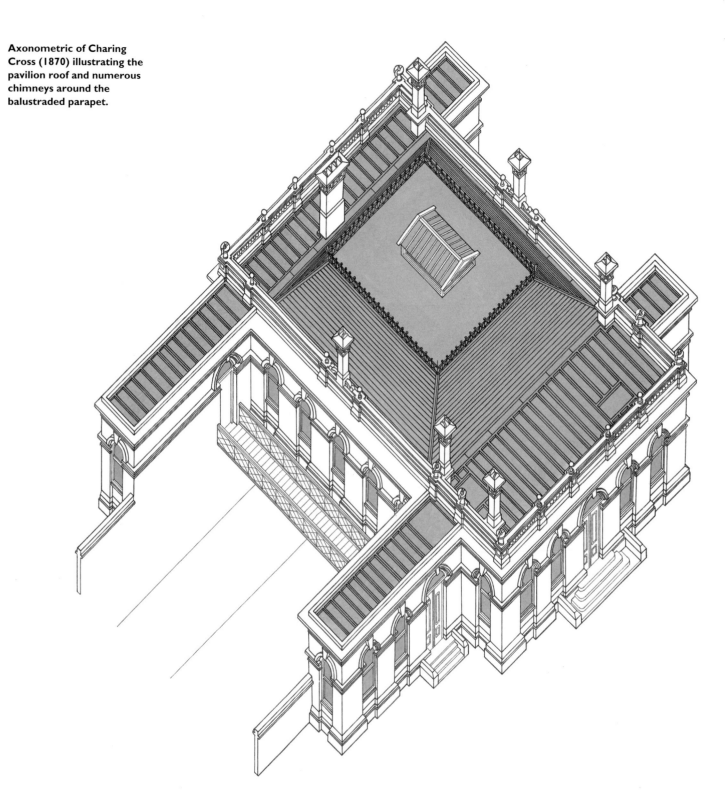

Axonometric of Charing Cross (1870) illustrating the pavilion roof and numerous chimneys around the balustraded parapet.

On 30th May 1870 the District Railway extended its tracks from Westminster Bridge (now Westminster) to Blackfriars, with intermediate stations at Charing Cross (now Embankment) and The Temple. Charing Cross station was built south of the main-line station at the foot of Villiers Street. The brick building featured elements of Renaissance detailing, such as the balustered parapet wall and decorative iron railings to the pavilion roof, employed on many of the early District and Metropolitan stations. A narrow ticket hall crossed the tracks between two entrance lobbies, with a refreshment room opposite the booking office. Access to the platforms was via separate departure and exit staircases enclosed in the side wings and linked by an open gallery. The platforms were built between piles supporting Hungerford Bridge, and beneath overall roofs which extended on each side of the station building.

Facilities at Blackfriars were not completed until 1873. Over the station itself, architect Frederick J. Ward designed an unusual structure described by *The Builder* as 'somewhat

bizarre . . . in the Oriental style,'[5] with Mooresque windows and minarets on towers rising over 100ft above the ground. During this period architects were influenced by building styles from many periods, and the use of polychromy (variously coloured materials) in architecture, put forward in the writings of John Ruskin (1819-1900), had been taken up by architects from the mid-nineteenth century. In addition to the white brick then in common use by the District Railway and many other builders, the Blackfriars station was dressed in Bath stone and decorated with blue and white tiles and dark red bricks. In front of the windows were balconies with gilded iron railings. The interior of Ward's building was fitted out for use as an hotel or restaurant. An adjoining block of shops and offices curving round from the station to meet Queen Victoria Street was completed by Ward in a similar style some time afterwards. The station superstructure was damaged by a bomb in 1940 and the area has since been redeveloped.

In their pursuit of opulent buildings Victorian designers revived many architectural styles, as seen here with Frederick Ward's Moorish fantasy for Blackfriars.

At Earl's Court the original wooden station opened on 30th October 1871 had burnt down on 30th December 1875, and a new permanent building on the west side of Earl's Court Road designed under the supervision of the District Railway's engineer-in-chief John (later Sir John) Wolfe-Barry was opened on 1st February 1878. By this time the District's style had changed: gone were the elaborate mouldings and parapets in favour of a generally plain – and also cheaper – white Suffolk brick structure. Distinguishing features were the corner chimneys and the setting out of bricks around doors and windows. Staff accommodation was contained in the two-storey wing adjoining the public facilities. An overall roof sheltered the two 500ft-long island platforms. In 1882 a fire at Hammersmith (opened 1874) required the provision of another new station building.

John Wolfe-Barry also supervised the design of stations on the District Railway extensions to Ealing and Putney Bridge made in 1879 and 1880 respectively. From a junction with the London & South Western Railway at Turnham Green a line was opened to Ealing Broadway on 1st July 1879, running via Acton Green (now Chiswick Park), Mill Hill Park (now Acton Town) and Ealing Common. The stations all had the same brick bands set out around doors and windows, and small lantern lights over the ticket halls. Similar stations were built at Boston Road (renamed Boston Manor 11th December 1911) and Osterley & Spring Grove on the branch to Hounslow Town which opened on 1st May 1883. The Fulham extension from West Brompton to Putney Bridge opened on 1st March 1880 with intermediate stations at Walham Green (now Fulham Broadway) and Parsons Green. Design of the stations themselves was carried out by a Mr Clemmence.[6]

The Earl's Court station of 1878, rebuilt in brick and in the stripped-down style John Wolfe-Barry adopted for his District Railway western extensions.

A suburban station on the Ealing branch of 1879, with station master's house on the right and characteristic lantern light to booking office.

Putney Bridge station when new; note the bold simple detailing and lettering set into the brickwork.

T.P. Figgis designed his modest stations for the City & South London Railway with simple classical details. Stockwell, the then southern terminus, is seen when new in 1890.

The City & South London Railway (C&SLR) opened to passengers between Stockwell and King William Street on 18th December 1890, and was both the first standard gauge tube and the first railway to employ electric traction in London. To avoid disturbance of surface buildings the tube was shield-driven at deep level, and much of the work was done via shafts at station sites which later contained the passenger lifts.

The five original surface buildings on the line at Great Dover Street (now Borough), Elephant & Castle, Kennington New Street (now Kennington), Kennington Oval (now Oval), and Stockwell were all designed by Thomas Phillips Figgis with elements of early Arts and Crafts and neo-classical detailing. The structures were made distinctive by a lead-covered dome with cupola lantern and weathervane which housed some of the lift equipment; the main part of the building was of red brick with white stone or cement dressings. At the north end, the King William Street terminus was constructed under an existing property.

Design details varied from site to site: a round-fronted entrance at Stockwell (rebuilt circa 1924), and various pediment treatments at Kennington and Oval. Side walls were pierced by mullioned windows between brick pilasters.

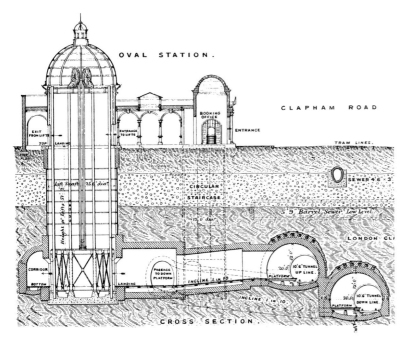

OVAL STATION.

CLAPHAM ROAD

CROSS SECTION.

Left **Cross-section of Oval** showing the arrangement of lift shaft and dome, with brick lined platform tunnels (cast-iron segments were later used to avoid damage from settlement) at different heights to obviate the need for steps. Below **Oval** (now rebuilt). Bottom **Patterned tile frieze** used in the passage and platform walls.

Left and above **T.P. Figgis's station and C&SLR company headquarters at Moorgate.** The influence of Arts & Crafts styling can be found in the carved stonework to the ground floor façade.

Left **Impression of his Bank station by Sidney Smith, with St Mary Woolnoth church behind.**
Below **Left-hand entrance of building, recently demolished.**

An extension of the C&SLR to Angel on 17th November 1901 included intermediate stations at City Road (closed from 9th August 1922) and Old Street, seen in 1915. The three stations were carried out by T.P. Figgis: City Road and Angel featured shaped parapet walls above comparatively plain brick elevations (see page 53), and the larger Old Street included Figgis's recurring motifs of rustication and stone strings. Old Street was provided with three lifts, superseded by escalators from August 1925. This station was completely rebuilt in 1968.

From a point north of Borough the City & South London Railway was extended to Moorgate on 25th February 1900 and the terminus at King William Street abandoned. Intermediate stations were provided at London Bridge and Bank.

The building at Moorgate on the corner of Moor Place and Moorgate itself is by far the largest structure designed by T. Phillips Figgis for the C&SLR, and in addition to the station facilities the upper floors contained the railway company's general offices. Portland stone was used to face the ground floor, with some carved work including foliage details in the Arts and Crafts style, and the company's crest over the office entrance. Upper walls were of red brick with stone bands and green slates to the roof, the general arrangement suggesting comparisons with Norman Shaw's Allied Assurance offices, St James's Street (1881-83) and his New Scotland Yard building (1897-90). The ticket hall interior was finished in polished teak and tiles, and four lifts carried passengers down to the platforms. In the 1930s the entrances were rebuilt, and other alterations include the blocking of former window voids. The building was listed on 10th November 1977.

At Bank, Nicholas Hawksmoor's St Mary Woolnoth church of 1727 had been acquired by the railway company for demolition, but when it sought renewal of construction rights the authorities insisted that the church be preserved. Engineers Sir Benjamin Baker, David Hay and Basil Mott with architect Sidney R.J. Smith (designer of the Tate Gallery, Millbank) carried out the complex work of underpinning the structure and building a sub-surface station with upper lift landings partly where the crypt had been. A subway was provided to the Central London Railway's Bank station.

Over stairwell entrances on King William Street against the side of the church Smith built a granite and Portland stone façade with classical detailing, including the reclining figure of Mercury. New ornamental iron railings and gates were put up in front of the church itself. The left hand screen wall was demolished in 1992 and the centre of the façade rebuilt as an InterCity travel office, but it still gives access to the station and via lifts to the tube platforms.

With the northward projections it was viable to consider a southern branch, and on 3rd June 1900 a new section was brought into use between Stockwell and Clapham Common via Clapham Road (now Clapham North). Architectural work was again undertaken by T.P. Figgis, these late designs having heavier detailing than the original C&SLR stations but no lift domes. Island platforms were provided in single tunnels. The high structure on the right in the Clapham Common view housed an institute for railway staff. Both stations were rebuilt during 1922-24 (see page 52).

Above **Oxford Circus in original form with cherub figure over pediment. The superstructure of this building is in typical Harry Bell Measures style with ornate gables and decorative finials.**

Below left and right **Shepherd's Bush, which is still extant despite plans to redevelop it in 1968, and Lancaster Gate, rebuilt in 1961. Similar façade treatments were to be found in shop fronts designed by Measures.**

After several years of planning and construction the Central London Railway opened to the public on 30th July 1900 with a 5¾ mile line between Shepherd's Bush and the Bank – the first tube line of the new century.

Intermediate stations were provided at Holland Park, Notting Hill Gate, Queens Road (Queensway from 1st September 1946), Lancaster Gate, Marble Arch, Bond Street (opened 24th September 1900), Oxford Circus, Tottenham Court Road, British Museum (now replaced by Holborn), Chancery Lane and Post Office (St Paul's from 1st February 1937).

Surface buildings at each station were designed by Harry Bell Measures and had pinkish-brown unglazed terracotta façades. The use of terracotta as a building material increased considerably in the latter half of the nineteenth century. It is a durable facing material resistant to the harsh city atmosphere, and can be mass-produced in moulded blocks for later assembly like a kit of parts when a number of similar façades are required to be constructed at reasonable cost. It appears that the particular terracotta used by Measures was only partly fired to achieve the required colour: this caused the material to deteriorate prematurely.[7] Measures' choice of a single distinctive material served to identify the stations, and at the

same time his designs fitted in comfortably with the contemporary styling of shopfronts. Lift equipment was housed in the basement, permitting the construction of single storey stations to allow commercial development above. Frontages were based on a series of segmental arches, between which pilasters were carried up to an architrave and had superimposed corbels and narrow pediments above roof level; a small 'grotesque' was set below each corbel. The frieze itself was bellied out and decorated with swags of fruit. Additional mouldings were sometimes included, as at Lancaster Gate, and at Oxford Circus and Notting Hill Gate Measures took the assemblage of decorations a stage further, adding a high triangular pediment surmounted by a cherub figure. (The cherub at Oxford Circus was removed in October 1952.)

What little coverage the stations received in the contemporary architectural press was less than enthusiastic. *The Builders Journal and Architectural Record* described them as 'inoffensive combinations of buff terracotta with red brick',[8] and subsequently included the comment of one correspondent: 'wretched terracotta structures, apparently cast from one badly detailed mould'.[9]

Above **Harry Measures made extensive use of florid detailing in the terracotta work of many buildings including his CLR stations. Whilst the Oxford Circus cherub was displaced some time ago, a near relative looks down over the entrance to Arlington House, Camden.**

Below left **ticket office at Shepherd's Bush.**

Below right **Platforms were lined with plain white tiles and the station name shown on enamelled iron boards.**

TOWARDS A UNIFORM ARCHITECTURE

Above **Impression of a typical exterior. The wrought-iron grille is believed to be a later addition based on a design used in lift shaft ventilators at these stations.**

Four tube railway companies, forming the basis of the present Bakerloo, Northern and Piccadilly lines, built lines in the first decade of the twentieth century: the Baker Street & Waterloo Railway (BS&W); the Charing Cross, Euston & Hampstead (CCE&H); the Brompton & Piccadilly Circus (B&PC); and the Great Northern & Strand (GN&S).

Charles Tyson Yerkes (1837-1905), a dynamic American financier, formed the Underground Electric Railways Company of London Ltd (UERL, commonly called the Underground Group) as a holding company, acquiring control of the Metropolitan District Railway to electrify it and entering into agreements with the tube companies to construct and equip their lines.

The B&PC changed its name to Great Northern, Piccadilly & Brompton Railway (GNP&B) in 1902 and absorbed the GN&S, thereby uniting the two central portions of the present Piccadilly line. The first section of the BS&W opened on 10th March 1906 between Baker Street and Kennington Road (now Lambeth North) and was extended to Elephant & Castle on 5th August the same year; the GNP&B opened on 15th December 1906; the CCE&H on 22nd June 1907. In 1907 two westward projections of the BS&W (by this time known as the Bakerloo) were made: the first to Great Central (now Marylebone) on 27th March and thence to Edgware Road on 15th June.

Above left **Brompton Road, between Knightsbridge and South Kensington, closed 1934.**

Above **Piccadilly Circus, with cornice set out for bay in building above, both now demolished.**

Below **Oxford Circus in the original pattern of BS&WR stations.** A frieze runs above the ground floor openings; for the Piccadilly and Bakerloo buildings this was usually oxblood coloured with gilded script lettering. All the stations of the CCE&HR, and certain stations of other Underground Group tubes, had a white lower frieze with black grotesque characters. Above the arches there was generally a second frieze to match the lower one. The BS&WR used gilded metal letters on the oxblood ground, and the GNP&BR and CCE&HR either plain oxblood or white. King's Cross and Euston had no upper frieze. As early as 1908 façades were being altered to incorporate the 'UndergrounD' device (see Chalk Farm page 30): that at Oxford Circus has recently been replaced by a facsimile of the original lettering.

For the railways in Underground Group control the first steps could now be taken towards adopting a style of architecture which would unite the various parts. The design of stations for the BS&W, CCE&H and GNP&B railways was carried out by Leslie W. Green, and the reconstruction of District Railway stations after electrification by that company's architect, Harry W. Ford. Both Green and Ford used a flamboyant classical style to project a confident and progressive image and make potential passengers aware of the new electric train services.

That Leslie Green designed more than 40 stations and other structures for the Underground Group in some three years with his assistants Stanley A. Heaps and Israel Walker is perhaps remarkable. Despite the standardised pattern of building, each one was adapted to its site and no two designs were wholly alike. Green was born in 1875 – the same year as Charles Holden – and one may speculate on how different London's later tube stations might have been had he not died at the young age of 33.

For his surface buildings Green adopted features similar to Harry Bell Measures' stations, including the practice of using moulded terracotta blocks, this time heavily glazed (and known as faience) in a deep ruby red colour described as 'sang de boeuf' – oxblood. Brightly coloured faience was coming into use at this time, and here it ensured the buildings stood out from their neighbours and helped to create a uniform appearance by which the Tube companies' stations could be easily identified. The ground floor of each building housed the booking office and upper lift landing. A mezzanine floor contained the lift gear and in many cases office accommodation. Staff facilities were usually provided in the basement with access from the emergency staircase. The façade comprised one or more arches carried up around windows in the mezzanine floor, ranging from one arch at Gillespie Road (now Arsenal), to six at Holloway Road. If the building was on a corner site the combined frontages could have as many as fourteen arches, as at Chalk Farm. Christian Barman claimed in his book 'An Introduction to Railway Architecture' that the original pattern for Green's stations was Lewis Isaacs' (1829-1908) Holborn Viaduct station (completed 1873); it may be more than coincidence that Lewis Isaacs was Chairman of the GNP&B and a director of the District. Stanley Heaps stated in 1927 that the unitary arrangement of piers and arch was derived from the original sample structures erected at Lillie Bridge Underground depot by three contractors.[1] Heaps commented that the façades 'savoured too much of mass-production'.[2]

Below **Elephant & Castle** station shortly after completion. Later generations of critics have considered these stations gaudy and ungraceful, and others fought to preserve their unique identity. To the railway attempting to update its system the most difficult problem they have presented is the high cost of rebuilding them to install modern equipment.

Left **Leicester Square. Advantage** was taken of the corner site for this large building serving the Theatreland area of the West End.

Below **Chalk Farm**, an impressive structure, with the longest façade of a Leslie Green tube station. The 'Underground' lettering was added circa 1908 as part of a comprehensive signing scheme.

Above left **York Road, between King's Cross and Caledonian Road, was closed in 1932 but the building still stands.** Above right **Holloway Road is regarded as one of the best examples of the Leslie Green stations and is a Grade II listed building.**

Below left **Underground Electric Railways cartouche on a corner of Oxford Circus station, incorporating the company's initials.** Below centre **At the point where two arches sprang from the frieze together was also placed a cartouche – based on a form of heraldic device; several patterns have been noted.** Below right **A simpler corner cartouche and a typical design of keystone.**

Below **Smaller windows in the mezzanine floor were usually either of the 'oeil de boeuf' type with prominent hood-mould, or rectangular with a pediment. At King's Cross the arches were separated by venetian windows. This arrangement appears to be unique among Green's stations.**

Above **The exteriors were lit with Maxim arc lamps and incandescent lamps with wrought-iron brackets. Canopies – some with wrought-iron embellishments and clocks – were later added over entrances. Flat roofs were provided for future development above the stations. In this view of Mornington Crescent taken by Bedford Lemere, workmen are seen putting signs on the lift exit doors prior to opening day.**

Besides Knightsbridge, non-standard façades were to be found at **Holborn**, below left, **Waterloo**, below right, where there was a passageway to the ticket hall; and **Marylebone**, with lifts at basement level. (The former has now been rebuilt, the latter two demolished.) Embankment, Tottenham Court Road, Trafalgar Square and Regent's Park had no surface buildings whatsoever, the latter station being identified by decorative signs mounted over the stairwells on Marylebone Road. There has been some dispute over the material used to clad the central sections of the main and side station frontages at Holborn; examination of contemporary photographs indicates that a coloured granite was used, probably red, set into the Portland stone surround. Mouldings were of a simplified pattern throughout the elevations, consistent with the reduced amount of carving practical in the harder facing material.

In the main, the exteriors of Leslie Green's stations were composed of blocky Edwardian classical features, presenting a solid and reliable image. Brightly coloured glazing served to make the stations immediately recognisable as part of a single entity. Exterior details and the interior decoration showed the influence of Arts and Crafts and Art Nouveau styles – the lettering to friezes, iron grilles in entrances and ventilation spaces, and leaf motifs in the ticket hall tiling and lift door fretwork. Green made this new art accessible to all by applying it to these public buildings. Knightsbridge featured the most clearly Art Nouveau inspired decoration – perhaps to complement the opulent surroundings. Between and on either side of the arches large floral designs were moulded in low-relief, and the frontage was set back at each side with upper edges following the flowing shapes. The arches themselves were without mouldings and the pilasters capped by volutes beneath pulvinated frieze. An arcade led to the ticket hall and continued to a similarly embellished entrance at the rear, now an entrance to the Basil Hotel.

Right **Booking office at South Kensington showing the faience ticket window surrounds and pomegranate motif tile frieze.**

Opposite from top, left to right **Camden Town, Holborn; Belsize Park, Tottenham Court Road, Caledonian Road, King's Cross (half panels shown); South Kensington, Russell Square; Highgate, Brompton Road, Lambeth North, Piccadilly Circus (half panels).**

Above **Panelled tiling in two colours at Russell Square.**

Right **Decorated lift doors and position indicators at Hampstead.**

Below **A second pattern of tile frieze, this one based on the acanthus leaf.**

Bottle green tiles lined the ticket hall walls up to a frieze of green majolica tiles at shoulder height moulded with an acanthus leaf or pomegranate design (omitted in stations constructed towards the end of the period such as Hampstead, Edgware Road and Strand). Upper walls were of white painted plaster or tiled in cream and green. Booking windows were styled classically as miniature aedicules (the arrangement of base, columns and pediment surrounding an opening), and fabricated from faience blocks or fire resistant wood.

Lifts were manufactured by the Otis Elevator Company. The cars were panelled in teak and there were decorative wrought-iron grilles over the entry doors. There were also indicator devices giving the relative position of the lift in the shaft, as in the view of Hampstead, which has the deepest platforms on the Underground at 192ft below the surface. Wherever possible separate landings and passageways were provided at each level so that passengers entered the cars on one side and left them on the other, moving forwards in each case to clear the lift for passengers travelling in the opposite direction. By maintaining the flow in this way the cars could be emptied and reloaded faster and without causing congestion. At street level the lift exit lobbies often opened directly onto the street.

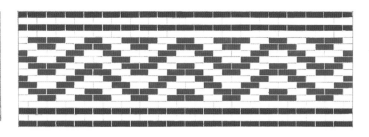

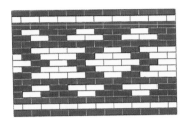
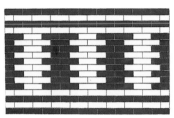
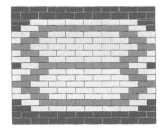
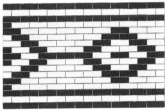

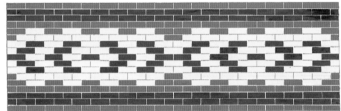

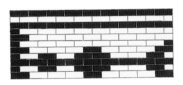
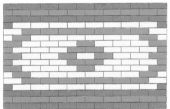
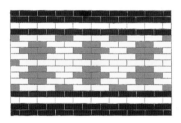
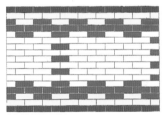

Station platform tunnels were 21ft 2in diameter; BS&W platforms were nominally 291ft long, and those for the other two tubes 350ft. At Aldwych the platforms were somewhat shorter at 250ft. Tiling had been proved durable as a lining to the platform tunnel walls, and enhanced the reflection of light. To improve upon plain white walls and aid station recognition, the designers introduced geometric patterns with coloured tiles which varied between stations. To what extent the design was carried out by the architects or left to the contractors to settle on site is difficult to ascertain, but their joint achievement was a considerable number of different patterns. Fixed in modules of varying length to suit each platform, coloured tiles were arranged in horizontal, vertical and diagonal motifs on a white or cream ground; coloured bands ran the full length of the walls at waist and frieze height, and vertical bands or rings were placed at regular intervals and in pairs either side of entrances. Simpler horizontal banding was continued throughout the lower passages and emergency stair shafts. The station name was fired into the tiles, and fixed at three points along the platform. Adjoining the entrances and exits, flat representations of aedicules carried direction information; other signs in the tiling guided passengers to trains or lifts.

The tiling schemes were a considerable innovation for a railway company at this time, but *The Electrical Times* remarked that rather than the different designs it would have been better to repeat the station name like 'the pattern of a wallpaper'.[3] This far-sighted suggestion would not be taken up until 30 years later when station name friezes were first introduced. Unfortunately no provision was made for the display of large posters on platform walls, and over the years the patterns disappeared under panels of advertisements.

Harry W. Ford's stations were mostly built on existing and relatively spacious sites, and instead of carrying superstructures they were built a full two storeys high, with offices on the first floor and much decorative detail at roof level. Whilst not using the oxblood glaze, Ford's frontages were no less colourful than Green's: in addition to the honey brown self colour of the faience, mouldings and lettering would be picked out in green, white or dark brown.

The District Railway widened its trackbed between West Kensington and Hammersmith to accommodate the additional running lines of the Great Northern, Piccadilly & Brompton Railway, and a joint station to Ford's designs was opened at Barons Court on 9th October 1905, with a tube service from 15th December 1906. Arches were segmental rather than the semi-circular pattern adopted for the tube stations, and over the doorways broken-apex pediments displayed the station name in glazed brown lettering. A District Railway monogram is moulded into the faience blocks on the chamfered corner of the building. Shop units each side of the main entrance originally had stained glass in their upper windows.

The ticket hall is faced to full-height with mid-green tiles, and mouldings in dark green. A frieze of majolica tiles decorated with a patera motif combining the two shades of green is placed around the upper walls. Faience blocks are also used as a surround to the booking windows. Small booking offices were provided on each side of the entrance passage, the right hand one being demolished to enlarge the ticket hall circa 1930.

On the platforms are unusual wooden seats with enamelled iron station nameboards fixed to the backrests. A London Transport programme announced in 1969 included proposals for the development of both Barons Court and Earl's Court station sites to provide office accommodation, but no work was carried out and both stations are now listed buildings.

In 1906 Harry W. Ford rebuilt Earl's Court station as a joint District and GNP&B facility with a new façade to Earl's Court Road. Coloured details add interest to the light brown clearglazed faience frontage: arch keystones are green, and a green frieze bears the station name and railway companies' name in white.

The main part of the ticket hall was panelled with wood. Steps at the rear led down to a concourse with the four Piccadilly line lifts on the right and further stairs to the two District island platforms. On 4th October 1911 the first escalators on the Underground were installed to carry passengers from beneath the eastbound island to the Piccadilly platforms, and Earl's Court was also the location for the first automatic lifts on the Underground, commissioned in 1932.

Hammersmith became the western terminus of the Great Northern, Piccadilly & Brompton Railway when it came into operation on 15th December 1906. The joint station (now redeveloped) was rebuilt by Ford in a similar style to Earl's Court. Pilasters were partly coloured green and arch keystones were white. On the Piccadilly side of the station two tracks served an island platform, flanked to the north by a side platform and to the south by a second island which at one time was partitioned down the middle and also functioned as the eastbound District platform.

Similar treatments for the other two District stations rebuilt by Ford in conjunction with the Piccadilly tube opening. The lettered frieze and some detailing from the Hammersmith façade has been retained and re-erected in the new ticket hall of 1993. Earl's Court remains in basically original form.

Above **Sidney Smith's original scheme for Euston.** Above right **The station as executed. Lifts descended to the single C & SLR island platform. A subway was opened to the main line terminus on 18th May 1907, and from 22nd June that year a low level passage linked the C & SLR and CCE & HR platforms. The C & SLR top station was permanently closed on 30th September 1914. The building was demolished in 1934.**

Below right **The station at Maida Vale was completed in 1915 by Stanley Heaps after the style of Leslie Green.**

A northern extension of the City & South London Railway (C&SLR) was made from Angel, Islington, to Euston on 12th May 1907. On the corner of Eversholt and Drummond Streets, opposite the main-line station, a surface building designed by Sidney R.J. Smith was erected. The building was similar in plan to the contemporary tube stations of the Underground Group. As a cladding to the steel frame, Smith used white and green Doulton's Carrara-ware faience with florid detailing: the segmental arches had projecting voussoirs and swags decorated the pilasters. A further four storeys containing offices were planned but not completed.

The Bakerloo was continued north-west from Paddington, via Warwick Avenue and Maida Vale, to gain Kilburn Park on 31st January 1915; a final section opened on 11th February 1915 from Kilburn Park to Queen's Park, where a link was made with the London & North Western Railway's new suburban line to Watford. Maida Vale was not completed until 6th June 1915. The design is based on the format established by Leslie Green and is believed to have been executed by his assistant Stanley Heaps, who had been appointed Architect to the Underground in 1910 following Green's death. Heaps would later become Chief Architect to London Transport and held the post until 1943.

A major change influenced the design of the Maida Vale building; for the first time escalators were installed from the start, and as the escalator machinery was entirely below ground it was possible to omit the mezzanine floor. Escalators have the advantage over lifts that they carry a continuous flow of traffic and are safer – passengers cannot be trapped between levels as might happen if a lift mechanism failed. It was later found that the installation of escalators at locations where lifts had formerly operated increased the number of passengers using the station.

The sang-de-boeuf faience façade differed in detail from the earlier Green stations: pilasters were carried the full height of the wall through the springing of segmental arches and decorated with pendant blocks. Mouldings were simplified: there was no plinth, and the architrave was reduced to short sections on the pilasters; arch keystones were omitted. Faience mullions divided the windows into three segments, and transoms with dentils beneath split them into upper and lower sections. Upper window lights were framed with wrought-iron glazing bars in a diagonal arrangement. The original iron lamp brackets are still in place.

Separate entrance and exit stairs linked street-level with the basement ticket hall, crossing each other part way down. The stairwell was decorated with two mosaic bullseye symbols. Ticket hall walls were tiled in white up to a green and white chequered band. Two escalators descend 34ft 6in to a landing between the platforms. A three-storey office block over the station was proposed in 1975 but not carried out. The station is now a listed building.

More space was available at Kilburn Park, where the building was completed in similar style to the Maida Vale design but with a ticket hall at street level.

Above **At Kilburn Park a long canopy formerly extended towards the road for the benefit of bus passengers.**

Below left **The ticket hall at Kilburn Park, showing the chequered banding which was a feature of stations on this extension.**

Below right **Bullseye nameboards, then a recent development, were mounted at alternate heights to improve visibility for both seated and standing passengers.**

METROPOLITAN AND DISTRICT RECONSTRUCTIONS

Top left **An early view of the arcade at High Street, Kensington.**

Top right **Attractive wrought iron grilles for George Sherrin's South Kensington, rebuilt in 1907.**

Below **Great Western Railway architect P.E. Culverhouse reconstructed the terminus of the Hammersmith & City Railway during 1907-09, designing a sizeable red brick building housing shops and staff rooms around a concourse with central booking office.**

Increasing property values prompted the Metropolitan and District railways to capitalise on their street frontages by relocating station facilities below ground and erecting premises for letting as retail spaces. George Sherrin – architect to the Metropolitan – rebuilt several stations with arcades during 1905-1909, including those at Victoria (between Victoria Street and Terminus Place) and Liverpool Street, completed by his son Frank Sherrin in 1911/12.

At High Street, Kensington, Sherrin laid out an arcade with glass roof from the High Street to an octagonal hall containing the ticket office, with direct access to Pontings' and Derry & Toms' stores. Beyond this, widened stairways led to and from the platforms, replacing the separate departure and arrival footbridges. Work was completed in 1907. London Transport built a new ticket hall beyond the octagon in 1937-39, but Sherrin's elegant arcade survives.

For South Kensington – shared with the District Railway – a new basement ticket hall was entered through an arcade with stucco façades flanked by Ionic columns and with decorative iron grilles in the archways at each end. The iron and glass roof was supported on trusses encased with fibrous plaster enrichments. In the ticket hall a round fronted booking office (removed circa 1951) stood between two stairways down from the arcade.

Harry W. Ford replaced the 1880 station at Walham Green (now Fulham Broadway) during 1910 with a steel-framed structure clad in clear-glazed terracotta of a pale buff colour. Ford chose to style the façade like a 'Queen Anne' town house rather than use the arcaded frontage he had employed at Earl's Court and Hammersmith. Ionic pilasters and a festoon of fruit frame the mullioned sash windows of the first floor restaurant. Above the cornice a parapet formerly displayed the station name in a recess flanked by swags.

The terracotta facing is continued into the ticket hall with its arcade of five bays and glass roof. Corbels are embellished with the District Railway monogram. Above a dado of 'antique' dark green tiles the booking office front was panelled with oak. Opposite the ten booking windows were shops and a J. Lyons & Co tea room. South of the footbridge on the Putney side a second flight of stairs lead up to a separate road exit for arriving spectators to Chelsea F.C. ground, and beyond the ticket hall arcade a path for returning football crowds continues directly to the northbound platform. The canopy over the entrances is a later addition. The building was listed in February 1985 and has since been restored. A similarly styled building was erected by Ford at Ealing Broadway in 1911 and one at Aldgate East in 1914.

Above left **Exterior and interior details at Walham Green (now Fulham Broadway).**

Above **Ford's exterior with moulded lettering.**

Below **The ticket hall arcade with booking office to left.**

Two further stations by Harry Ford for the District Railway: Ealing Broadway of 1911 in Portland stone (the building survives although not in railway use); Aldgate East of circa 1915, demolished after resiting the station in 1938. A noteworthy detail is Ford's inclusion of the word UndergrounD in addition to the railway companies' initials: Ford claims to have originated the feature of enlarged first and last letters which became widely used throughout the organisation.

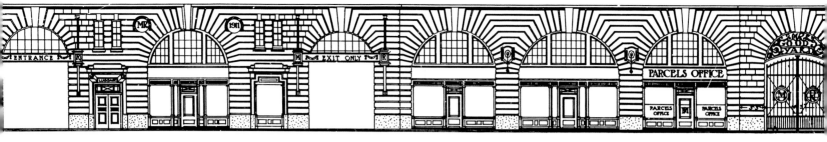

As traffic increased, better facilities became desirable and the Metropolitan Railway decided that Baker Street would be the location of its centralised headquarters and a 'flagship' station. The Metropolitan Railway Act 1902 provided for various improvements at the station, and in 1911 the company embarked on a comprehensive rebuilding programme, envisaging a combined Circle and Metropolitan station, an hotel development, new general offices over the 'East station' platforms, and a separate block of residential flats to the north. Based on original drawings of 1907-11 prepared by Frank Sherrin, the work was designed and carried out by Charles W. Clark, architect of all Metropolitan works from 1911 to 1933.

On a new approach road alongside Marylebone Road, a station building was erected in a restrained classical style, with a rusticated Portland stone façade and high arches containing the doorways and mezzanine floor windows. The ticket hall and concourse were laid out in the basement, with a ladies' room, buffet, lost property store and bookstall among the facilities. Walls were lined with granite and off-white faience, and the ceiling decorated with fibrous plaster laurel wreaths. Stairs led down to the Metropolitan platforms and also to a second concourse adjoining the Circle platforms at sub-basement level. Several lifts were installed for the movement of goods. By constructing the station below ground the surface was freed for other revenue-earning purposes, and here a restaurant was opened. At the east end of the building was a parcels office and loading dock.

A triangular structure at the corner of Upper Baker Street with subsurface booking office replaced the two original 1863 Circle buildings, and a reinforced concrete footbridge – claimed to be the first of its kind in London – linked the booking office with the westbound Circle platform. The bridge was completed in 1911 and the surface building in 1913. (This Circle office was closed in the late 1950s and rebuilt as a subway entrance during 1966-67).

Fronting onto Allsop Place a new seven-storey office building was partially suspended on piers over the Metropolitan platforms. The steel and reinforced concrete structure was clad in faience in a style described by the Metropolitan as 'Neo-Grec', with decorative cast-iron panels depicting various objects related to the railway such as signal posts, buffers and coupling chains. Two cherubs over the central entrance supported the company's armorial bearings. On the ground floor were the offices of the Chairman, General Manager and Chief Engineer. The boardroom walls were lined with brown Liberty canvas and the windows had stained glass leaded lights. The general office staffs were installed in the building on 1st January 1914.

Above **Front elevation of Baker Street by Charles W. Clark completed in 1911.**

Bottom left **The head offices in Allsop Place at time of completion.**

Bottom right **Interior of Baker Street ticket hall.**

Below **Coat of Arms over the central entrance of the head offices, now known as Selbie House.**

Harry W. Ford rebuilt Charing Cross (the present-day Embankment) following preliminary work by his colleague Howard Chatfeild Clark (1860-1917) undertaken in 1909. The original structure had been covered in publicity signs for some years and was described by one newspaper as a 'hideous erection'. In 1912 Ford had designed a five-storey block for office or hotel use in red brick with stone dressings. The elevation to Villiers Street would 'resemble Wren's additions to Hampton Court Palace.' Parliamentary restrictions prevented this development and Ford revised his plans. The construction of a single-storey steel, brick and concrete Portland stone-clad building was completed in 1914.

Entrances were flanked by paired Doric columns carrying a pediment with the Underground bullseye device in mosaic tesserae (removed when the station was refurbished in 1950-51). Similar mosaic bullseyes were used at Maida Vale and Wood Lane stations during this period. The arcade ticket hall layout was maintained and an enlarged booking office installed. Cream Doulton's Carrara-ware faience encased the roof-supporting columns. Arrival stairs behind the booking office opened onto a separate right of way through the building.

Shown on early plans as 'Norfolk Street', The Temple station opened on 30th May 1870 (the prefix was later dropped), named after the area which until the fourteenth century was occupied by the Knight's Templars and afterwards leased to lawyers who still have rooms there. To comply with the wishes of the Metropolitan Board of Works and the Duke of Norfolk, a local landowner, section 45 of the Metropolitan District Railway Act 1868 required that most of the station be unobtrusively below street-level; the low single-storey brick station building was set against Temple Place with steps down to the entrance. The flat roof promenade was opened to the public but closed at the instigation of the Police in 1873 as it had become a haunt of prostitutes. It is recorded that a small restaurant was included in the design but never opened.

The ticket hall was enlarged circa 1896 and the entire station rebuilt by Harry W. Ford 1914-15. To match Somerset House the 280ft-long structure was clad in natural and reconstructed Portland stone, with an arcaded façade of seventeen bays to Victoria Embankment. The rebuilding provided for a restaurant and two shops. Duncan Carse painted a watercolour of Ford's station and this was exhibited at the Royal Academy architecture exhibition for 1915. Circa 1928 a passimeter was installed and the booking office converted into a kiosk; the entrance from Victoria Embankment has since been closed for the installation of a wall-type booking office. The roof is once again available for public use.

Ford is also believed to have been responsible for new station buildings on the Hounslow branch at Hounslow Town (now Hounslow East) in 1909, Heston-Hounslow (now Hounslow Central) and Acton Town (both 1910) and Northfields (1911). Of these, only the structures at Hounslow Central and Hounslow East still stand.

Top **Temple from the Victoria Embankment; the bulk of the station building taken up by office accommodation.** Above **Watercolour impression of Temple by Duncan Carse.** Left **Acton Town as rebuilt by Ford. The 'Underground' sign seen on the left was displayed at stations from 1908 until the bullseye device (attributed to Harry Ford) was developed as a universal house symbol.**

SUBURBAN CLASSICAL

Above **The elaborate Italian villa-style of Edgware chosen by Stanley Heaps to enclose all the station and retail facilities within one structure around a bus yard.**

Below **Brent in the late 1930s.**

The Trade Facilities Act of 1921 enabled the Underground, which had been formulating a plan of new works before the 1914-18 war, to give practical consideration to the modernisation of its system and extensions to serve the developing suburbs and London County Council housing estates. It was to Frank Pick (1878-1941), the then Joint Assistant Managing Director of the Underground Group, that the task of planning these extensions fell, and the Underground now began to take an earnest interest in the design of its station buildings, under the care of in-house architect Stanley A. Heaps and his assistant Thomas Bilbow.

Work started on the extension of the Hampstead Railway from Golders Green to Edgware in 1922; the line opened as far as Hendon Central on 19th November 1923 with an intermediate station at Brent (now Brent Cross), and the second section to Edgware came into use on 18th August 1924 with stations at Colindale and Burnt Oak.

For the intermediate stations Heaps produced buildings of Georgian character with low-pitched pyramidal roofs and Portland stone colonnades of coupled Doric columns before the entrances. Detailing of the stonework was kept simple. The main building enclosing the ticket hall was steel-framed with a cladding of narrow red Dorking bricks, and red Italian tiles covered the upper roof with its projecting eaves. Heaps later commented that the building style was chosen with consideration for the suburban surroundings, and mindful of the fact that the public would become aware of this surface line without the use of 'buildings that blatantly advertised the railway' but which were 'sufficiently dignified to command respect, and sufficiently pleasing to promote affection.'[1]

Above **Hendon Central** before a development of flats was built above the station.

Below left **Vestibule at Hendon Central.**

Below right **Ticket hall at Brent** showing the clerestory windows and wooden 'passimeter' ticket booth.

At Brent the colonnade was set out at each end over the entrances, but the arrangement was varied for Colindale (since rebuilt) where the central portion stood forward. Bronze lettering on the frieze showed the station name, and a decorative wrought iron balustrade with enamel bullseye sign stood on top of the stone parapet. Wood and glass doors gave onto the double-height ticket hall with its eight mullioned windows for clerestory lighting. Walls up to the architrave were finished in silver-grey tiles framed with green bands, and joinery was of polished oak. Black and white floor tiles were laid in a chequerboard pattern.

The ticket halls were essentially concourses around which all facilities were grouped; this was based on American and Continental practice and would be continued for Holden's stations of the 1930s. From the outset tickets were issued from a wooden passimeter in the centre of the hall. All stations had island platforms accessed either by footbridge or subway. Shelter from the elements was afforded by deep wood and steel canopies. At Burnt Oak, built to serve the London County Council's new Watling Estate, a temporary wooden building was provided initially. This was superseded by a brick structure opened in August 1928, and here the colonnade was replaced by a canopy between two blocks containing kiosks giving a less grand appearance.

The original building at Colindale was destroyed by a bomb during World War Two.

The terminus of the line was built on the Edgware Manor Estate. Around a bus forecourt 100ft wide by 69ft deep, Stanley Heaps built an impressive station building with flanking wings to the north and south. The station building was made more imposing by giving the entrance colonnade its own tiled roof in place of the wrought-iron balustrade at other stations on the extension, and the general roof line was broken by small pyramidal roofs at each end of the wings. Both *The Builder* and *The Architect & Building News* commented that the pitch of the roofs was perhaps a little too steep. Floors in the colonnade were paved with red and buff tiles in a chequerboard pattern.

Roads, shops and houses soon followed, and the first resident of the new estate is reported to have been the novelist A.S.M. Hutchinson. A garage was built close to the station to provide vehicles for the feeder bus services. Despite attempts by the architects to preserve the building intact the balance of the three-sided colonnade was destroyed in 1938 with demolition of the north wing in preparation for a new station and the line's extension to Bushey Heath, a development halted by the war. The south wing was demolished in 1988 to provide access to a new bus station and garage, and an entrance/exit, designed carefully to match the original entrance, was opened in the south side wall.

Centre **Another view of Edgware. The north wing has since been rebuilt for retail spaces in a style approximating to the original.**

Bottom **Permanent station at Burnt Oak with simplified entrance design.**

DEVELOPING A CORPORATE STYLE

Architecturally, the Edgware line stations had broken no new ground, and although Leslie Green's stations for the three Yerkes' tubes, with their distinctive glazed terracotta façades, had been effective in identifying the Underground organisation, their design was no longer in keeping with contemporary architectural thinking and they were not suited to the changing traffic requirements without undergoing considerable rebuilding. The Underground company had before it the task of bringing order to the existing system and needed to create for itself a single identity in the public's eye: the increasing competition from other means of public transport demanded that the railways adopt a progressive image. The design of the stations would need to reflect the organisation's 'modern' spirit, and advertise that they were points where fast and comfortable trains were waiting to whisk the traveller to town. The authoritative air of the buildings would create the feeling that the city was but a short journey away, telescoping distances in the traveller's mind. The architecture should be attractive, but first and foremost functional, and there should be no doubt that the building was a railway station. As an Underground booklet of 1926 put it: 'what is a station? An inviting doorway in an architectural setting that cannot be missed by the casual pedestrian.'[1] With its successor London Transport, the Underground Group was arguably the only transport operator in this country to achieve this to any degree, and at the same time retain the integrity of the railway station as a building of distinctive type.

Of course, the Underground was in business to pay its dividends – to increase custom was to increase profit – but unlike other organisations driven purely by the profit motive, the Underground, through Frank Pick, sought to improve the quality of life of its customers through the provision of good facilities and more comfortable surroundings than were absolutely necessary for adequate functioning of the system. Pick saw that a new design approach was required to deal with the control of architecture as the system expanded into the suburbs, and it was Charles Holden of the architects' partnership Adams, Holden and Pearson that he appointed for the task. To consider how Pick and Holden met, a little background information may be useful.

The English Arts and Crafts movement – a number of architects, designers and craftsmen who came together with the aim of uniting all the arts – played an important part in the history of design from the latter half of the nineteenth century, and William Morris (1834-1896), one of their leading voices, preached the tenet of 'fitness for purpose' which was to be a recurring theme for the Functionalist movement in architecture from the second decade of this century. Inspired by the work of the British Arts and Crafts designers, the Deutscher Werkbund was formed by Herman Muthesius (1862-1927) in 1907 as a collective of 12 architects and designers (the membership would eventually rise to four figures) with the aim of reconciling the arts and crafts with industry.

A small group of English architects and designers visited Cologne in 1914 to see an exhibition staged by the Werkbund. Impressed by what they saw, they felt that an organisation should be set up in England along similar lines. In 1915 the Design and Industries Association (DIA) was founded, and it was through the Committee of the DIA that Frank Pick and Charles Holden met.

Holden's first commission for the Underground was to rebuild the side entrance of Westminster station. This small work, completed in 1924, pleased Pick and in the same year Holden was set to work on remodelling some stations in conjunction with enlargement of the City & South London Railway carried out during 1922-24. These included Angel, Old Street, Stockwell, Oval, and Clapham North, the last two named surviving as examples of the style adopted. Ticket halls were rebuilt after the installation of escalators and T.P. Figgis's station façades replaced with biscuit-cream faience slabs and black tile copings to the parapet walls. At Clapham Common access to a new subsurface ticket hall under the clock tower was gained via a small round entrance building of light brown and black faience, with a domed glass roof to light the stairwell inside. This structure was 'listed' on 27th March 1983.

Charles Holden's first Underground work – the riverside entrance to Westminster. The restrained handling and simple set backs look forward to the Morden line stations. Recent works have revealed that the rendered surfaces were applied over the original façade. This entrance has been lost during major reconstruction for the Jubilee line extension.

Borough after reconstruction by Holden during 1922-24 with a smooth light-brown faience cladding replacing T. P. Figgis's brick and stonework.

This compact stairwell entrance shelter at Clapham Common is now a listed structure. The diamond motif appearing on the metal frieze was used by Holden on several station canopies at this time.

Here was begun a special, and today perhaps unusual relationship: the direct working together of architect and client to achieve a common purpose. Pick was an autocrat – once described by Charles Holden as a 'benevolent dictator'[2] – and his strong persuasive manner enabled him to gain the acquiescence of his directors. Despite his sometimes strident nature, Pick was sensitive to the special knowledge of his managers and the designers that were commissioned; the work of committees was carried out after he and Holden had agreed their plans, and was not allowed to interfere with the vision and aims of the two men. With Pick's critical encouragement, Holden was given a more or less free hand, and Pick would often approve designs from a small sketch which Holden was able to infuse with the spirit of the design. Much time was saved by this direct process.

In 1924 Bond Street station was redesigned with the first of Holden's Portland stone frontages. The façade embodied all the basic features which would be carried through the design of the Morden stations: projecting canopy with fascia showing the station name in Johnston script and projecting signs to improve visibility from a distance, floodlighting to the façade, the vertical treatment of windows and a moulded stone lintel over the entrance voids. The rebuilding was completed in 1927, replacing the entrance by Harry Measures; it has itself now been demolished in conjunction with enlargement of the station.

Above **For Angel, on the northern section of the former C & SLR** rebuilt during 1922-24, a new streamlined façade was added in front of the original building of 1901.

Left the rebuilt exterior of **Bond Street** (since removed), precursor of Holden's stations for the Morden line.

The City & South London Railway was connected to the Hampstead and Highgate lines at Camden Town, modernised and rebuilt to take bigger rolling stock between 1922 and 1924. With the Edgware extension, the increased capacity made possible the projection of the line further southward. The Underground Group at first proposed a connection to their previously authorised Wimbledon & Sutton Railway, but this was later truncated to a terminus at Morden by agreement with the Southern Railway who would take over the Wimbledon & Sutton. Work on the five-mile tube extension from Clapham Common to Morden began on 31st December 1923.

With this project Charles Holden had his first opportunity to design wholly new Underground buildings. Most of the stations were to be built at road interesctions, and Holden was required to develop a format of façade which would be flexible enough to suit the approaches at each location. This he did by taking the basic flat frontage with set-backs tried at Westminster, and dividing the elevation into three parts: a centre portion to face the corner or main roadway, and two side wings whose angles could be varied according to the peculiarities of the site. Miniature and full-scale prototypes were built in an exhibition hall at Earl's Court to evaluate the design. To see how the solution was applied, one can compare the stairwell entrance at Tooting Bec (formerly Trinity Road), which represents the most acutely angled frontage, with the curved front of South Wimbledon and with the terminus at Morden, where the absence of side roads permitted a straight façade.

Underground officers visited the 1925 Paris Exposition Internationale des Arts Décoratifs et Industriels Modernes (from which came the term 'Art-Deco' to describe a particular style of design) to inspect the buildings, and saw there the unadorned geometric pavilions of some countries; this may have contributed to their faith in Holden's designs being the right way to progress, but the use of bold cubic forms can also be seen throughout Holden's work before this time, from the Incorporated Law Society extension of 1902-4 to the war cemetery pavilions at several locations in France and Belgium of the early 1920s.

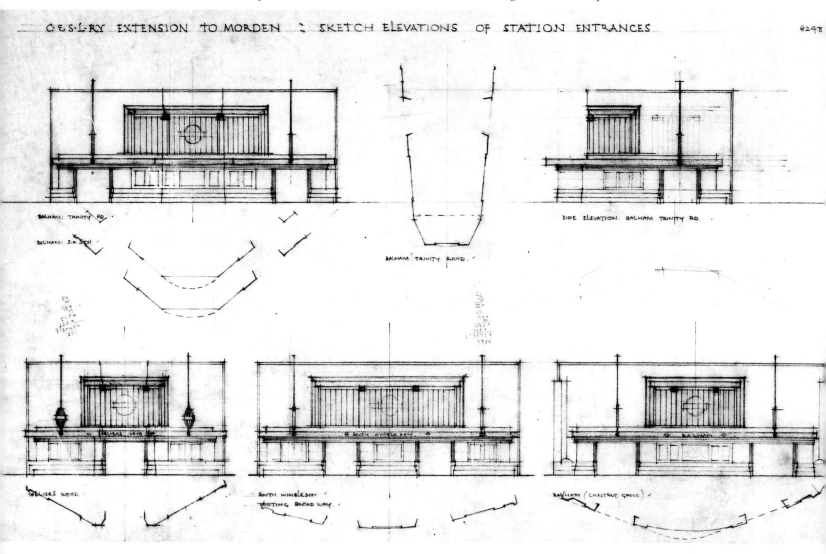

The external features were those which had been developed for the Bond Street reconstruction, adapted for the angled frontages. Portland stone was selected as the best material because it had a distinctive appearance and weathered well, and was the traditional building material of London; it also provided a light surface for floodlighting. The buildings were designed to support additional floors if necessary, and Portland stone would be compatible with a future brick or stone superstructure.

The plain nature of the elevation was determined by two factors. The Underground stipulated that the stonework be easily washed by the natural action of the rain, thus maintaining a good appearance without costly cleaning. The façade also had to be effective when floodlit at night: Holden gave careful consideration to the effect of shadows and the outcome was the simple, bold setbacks around the windows and wide entrances which took on a striking appearance in a raking light. The stone walls were not fully load-bearing: lintels over entrances and windows were supported by steel joists set in concrete and the main body of the structure was brick with a steel and concrete frame. Roofs were flat behind low parapet walls.

The need for an upper storey or mezzanine had been dispensed with after the adoption of the escalator, with its equipment entirely below ground, but Holden used a two storey frontage – with an upper floor of greater height – to incorporate the clerestory window, thus lighting the entrance vestibule by day and advertising the station at night, when the interior lighting would shine out through the large stained glass bullseye. The bullseye motif also served to unite the vertical and horizontal elements of the façade. The three windows were separated by stone pillars with spherical capitals – three dimensional representations of the bullseye motif – of little structural purpose, but serving as distinctive finials to the rectangular

Above **The weathered exterior of Tooting Broadway, showing clearly the stepped mouldings along the plinth and around the architraves.**
Left **An experiment in diffused lighting in the escalator shaft at Clapham South.**
Below **Chandelier design used at a number of stations on the extension.**

Above The angular form of one Trinity Road (now Tooting Bec) entrance produced in response to the restricted site. Here the ticket hall was built below ground. Opposite page upper **South Wimbledon at night, showing the dramatic effect of floodlighting on the stonework. These stations were among the first London buildings to use exterior lighting in this way.** Opposite below **A typical platform on the extension, with panels of white tiling in coloured borders, and station nameboards mounted at alternate heights. In 1976, as part of an experiment by Design Research Unit, exits were painted yellow and headwalls bright green. This use of colour to add emphasis was carried through to the Jubilee stations of 1979, but appeared somewhat out of place on the Morden line.**

uprights. Above the windows a blue enamel fascia displayed the station name, and this blue band was repeated in the entrance canopy, which also concealed the floodlighting units. The blue bands can be seen as a development of the bar on the Underground bullseye symbol, and they also stressed the horizontal line – a practice coming into vogue for new Continental architecture of the time. (Contemporary critics describing the Underground works saw the horizontal effect repeated in the design of rolling stock and even in the track itself.) Bullseye signs on 'Venetian' masts projected from the sides of the building to increase visibility from a distance. A moulded lintel – originally of stone but for later stations cast in concrete – was placed over the entrances.

A polygonal vestibule whose plan was derived from the angles of the façade was connected to the ticket hall by a passage or stairs. The walls of the vestibule were faced in black concave tiles and thin biscuit-cream fillets. A frieze of black faience blocks was moulded to match the profile of the lintel and above this was a row of biscuit-cream slabs (the first known use of the biscuit-cream glaze on the Underground) and a second black band below the windows. The upper walls and false ceiling were painted, the ceiling having a cornice with four wide, shallow steps. An iron chandelier with exposed bulbs lit the vestibule. Holden had not yet been given complete control over design of new stations and the Underground engineers specified the interior finishings.

As at other stations rebuilt by the Underground during this period, ticket hall and platform walls were faced with glossy silver-grey tiles, divided into panels by borders of green, grey, dark green and dark mauve-grey tiles. Escalators and fixed stairways were installed at all stations except Morden, where the platforms were in cutting and stairs only were required. Tickets were sold from passimeter booking booths.

The extension opened on 13th September 1926, and the stations were afterwards described by P. Morton Shand in the *Architectural Review* as 'prophetic beacons of the new age'.[3] A floodlight was mounted on the roof of some of the new stations for publicity purposes in December 1926. Mansion House and Post Office (now St Paul's) stations were rebuilt with similar stone frontages in 1929, with a granite facing introduced for the lower walls to reduce marking of the stone. Neither façade remains.

C.W. CLARK AND THE METROPOLITAN

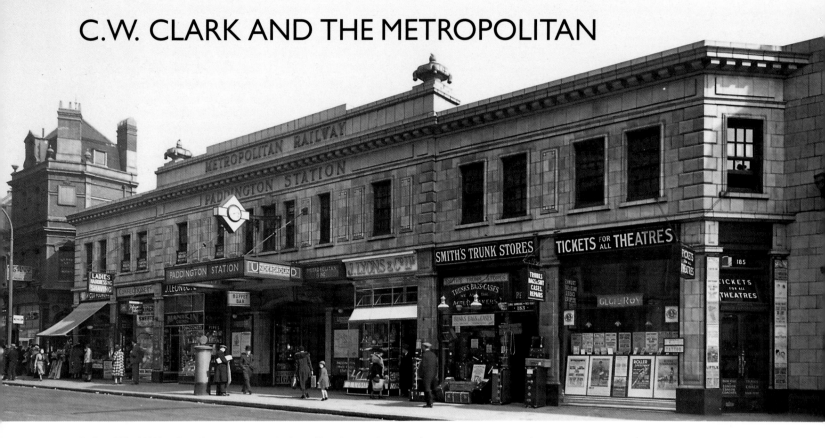

Before World War One the Metropolitan began rebuilding stations to update its image as the operator of new electric services. This classical style may have suited the period of its inception, but by the late 1920s the fussy details seemed dated alongside Holden's work for the Underground Group. Note the clock based on the diamond motif adopted by the Metropolitan.

With the official completion of reconstruction work at Praed Street (now Paddington) on 25th May 1914 the Metropolitan Railway had begun a programme for the modernisation of several existing stations. Metropolitan architect Charles W. Clark designed a new frontage in a classical style he had also employed for the company's general offices building at Baker Street in 1913, here using biscuit-coloured faience cast to simulate stonework. Railway company and station names were shown in green lettering on a frieze below the cornice and large urns were placed on top of the pediment. Plans were also made for Farringdon Street to be rebuilt, but progress was interrupted by the First World War.

When finances were sufficiently recovered after the war the scheme was resumed in stages, but rather than pursue contemporary trends in building design, Clark revived his pre-war style with minor detail changes. There was some simplification of the design for the buildings at Great Portland Street and Euston Square which were completed towards the end of the reconstruction programme. Stations rebuilt by the Metropolitan during this period were as

FARRINGDON & HIGH HOLBORN STATION

Above **Impression of name frieze and main cornice; in other examples the rectangular bosses were replaced by diamonds. The lettered frieze feature had been used by the Underground Group architects from 1906.**

Right **Lettering above the entrance at Farringdon.**

In this view of **Willesden Green** the mosaic ticket office facing can be clearly seen.

follows: Farringdon (1923); Willesden Green and St John's Wood Road (both 1925, the latter demolished); Aldgate (1926); Edgware Road and Notting Hill Gate (both 1928; the latter demolished); Swiss Cottage (1929 — demolished); Great Portland Street and North Harrow (both 1930); Euston Square (1931 — demolished).

The façade was varied to suit each location. In addition to the frieze the station name was displayed in stencils on the steel and glass entrance canopies, and was backlit at night. A marble or granite plinth ran around the base of the building. Metal casements with small leaded panes were fitted to upper windows and limited use was made of stained glass. Passenger and staff facilities occupied the ground floor, with provision for refreshment rooms or commercial office space on the storey above. For the interiors of these, and other Metropolitan stations altered during the period, much use was made of large mosaic tiles in shades of green and blue. Glossy rectangular tiles in various colours and patterns lined the passages and stairways.

Interior of **Farringdon & High Holborn** (Farringdon from 21st April 1936). A block of shops and offices was completed opposite the station in a similar style on 17th November 1923. The station was to have been rebuilt in 1947 and 1972-73 but has survived and was listed in 1977, although this did not prevent removal of the original booking office.

Both these stations survive in near-original form, although there are plans to redevelop the Edgware Road site. The backlit name stencils on the canopy edges may be noted. The raised lettering on the frieze was in red, green or gold at different locations.

By the time Euston Square (now demolished) and **Great Portland Street** were completed in 1930-31, detailing had been simplified. The segmented glass canopy at Euston Square was also used by Clark at Chiltern Court, and is reminiscent of the Paris Metro.

The stations at Croxley and Watford. The line stopped a mile outside Watford town centre and the terminus served the Cassiobury Park area.

To suit the more rural surroundings of the Watford Branch opened in 1925 Clark designed stations at Croxley and Watford in the vernacular style of the Arts and Crafts domestic revival houses. Of note are the tall chimney stacks indicating the presence of solid fuel fires: compare this with the contemporary gas and electrically heated stations by Stanley Heaps for the Underground Group. The entrance canopies appear somewhat heavy with their cast-iron supporting columns.

Charles W. Clark's largest single work, and the swansong of the Metropolitan Railway as an independent organisation, is the Chiltern Court block built over Baker Street station. This had originally been intended as an hotel, for which site clearance was carried out between 1915 and 1917, but after the war it was decided to construct a block of flats and shops. An elaborate port-cochére erected in front of the 1911 block was completed on 17th March 1924, and the remaining 200 feet of Portland stone façade built across the parcels depot. The proprietors of Madame Tussaud's Waxworks proposed a subway from the station concourse into the basement of their rebuilt museum, but the Metropolitan declined to pursue this suggestion.

Construction of Chiltern Court was begun on 2nd August 1927 and completed in 1930. The building would have frontages of 400ft to Marylebone Road, 300ft to Upper Baker Street, and 200ft to Allsop Place. In a review of the works *Building* said that 'this immense block will strike a harmonious note in the solid symphony of Marylebone Road.'[1] Except for the brick-faced Allsop Place wing, the elevations were of Portland stone, with artificial stone above the main cornice. A feature was made of four projecting bays in the facade and decorative balconettes above the ground floor arches. There were 198 flats, ranging in size from a 'three-room bachelor flat' to a 'ten-room mansion flat'. All flats were wired for telephones and 'piped' radio from a giant receiving set on the roof. Rubbish from the flats was disposed of down a chute and into a railway wagon left on a siding next to platform one.

A main central staircase enabled residents to reach an enlarged restaurant opened on 15th November 1929, which was also accessible from the station and through a marble-lined vestibule from the street. The restaurant itself seated 250 people and had walls of light fumed oak and gilded fibrous plaster decoration with crests on the ceiling representing areas served by the Metropolitan Railway. Metal grilles in the ceiling concealed artificial lighting which could be varied for day or night-time effects. Over a smaller annex there was a balcony for bands. At the west end of the block a shopping arcade opened on 1st July 1930, and beneath the Allsop Place wing there was a ballroom/concert hall.

HUBS OF EMPIRE

By the early 1920s facilities at Piccadilly Circus were becoming inadequate for the rising levels of traffic. At Bank station the subsurface concourse scheme had been found satisfactory, and it was decided to rebuild Piccadilly on similar lines with a ticket hall under the Circus itself to replace the old station and its eight lifts. Consulting architects were Adams, Holden and Pearson, in collaboration with S. A. Heaps, and the consulting engineer Harley Hugh (later Sir Harley) Dalrymple-Hay. A full-size mock-up of the sub-surface ticket hall was erected in an exhibition building at Earl's Court using scaffold poles and sheeting. This was tested and rearranged to get the best positioning of escalators and other equipment. Wooden mock-ups of the street entrances, painted with bold coloured stripes, were placed around the Circus at the intended locations of stairwells.

In 1924 the Shaftesbury Memorial (now generally known as 'Eros') was dismantled to clear the island site for a working shaft; the base was to be stored in an Underground depot and the statue removed to Embankment Gardens for the duration of the work. Construction started in February 1925. From the shaft, headings were driven in various directions and at various depths. Complex tunnelling was required and many sets of plans were produced before approval was gained from the various authorities concerned. The high costs incurred in preparing the site for this public facility prompted the Office of Woods and Forests to transfer the rights in the subsoil of the Circus to the Underground for a nominal ten pounds. The ticket hall was excavated 9ft below the road surface by driving further headings through which steel work for the roof was passed and erected to support the ground above. Concrete was then laid between the frame members. The central portion of the roof rested on four columns, with fifty other columns spaced around the perimeter of the hall in two rows. Five subways connected the elliptical hall to the surface, including one from the old station building on Haymarket. An underground concourse of this size had not previously been possible, and the architects took full advantage of the latest developments in artificial lighting and ventilation to ensure that conditions in the hall were satisfactory.

Walls and stairwells were finished in cream Travertine marble. Coffered fibrous plaster panels formed a false ceiling. The architects realised that by treating the hall as an ambulatory through which travellers and pedestrians alike would pass, it would be of commercial and decorative value, and give additional illumination (without cost to the railway company), to line the hall with showcases (a scheme initially opposed by the London County Council). Columns were clad in maroon scagliola – a colour enhanced by the tungsten lighting then used.

Included in the ticket hall facilities were a travel enquiry office and train interval recorder. This consisted of six dials – one for each Underground line – each carrying a paper chart marked with the twenty-four hours of the day. The dials rotated slowly and as trains passed a given point on the line an inked metal finger struck the paper chart. It was thus possible to gauge by the position and spacing of the marks the frequency of the train service. Another display showed the time at different places around the world. All metalwork was of bronze, this being one of the earliest uses of bronze in place of wood mouldings for Underground finishings.

The artist Mary Adshead had painted a mural to go over the escalator shaft at Bank station in 1926. For Piccadilly Circus her husband Stephen Bone NEAC (1904-58) produced a much larger work with five panels describing in pictures the myriad activities that might be pursued using the Underground for transport. The centre panel was erected in November 1928 and the others followed in March 1929.

The new station was opened by the Mayor of Westminster, Major Vivian B. Rogers DSO, MC, JP on 10th December 1928. As the Mayor threw the switch to start the first escalators a special lamp called the 'Verriers d'Art Light' was illuminated. It may now be seen in the London Transport Museum. The surface station closed on 21st July 1929 except for use as auxiliary entrances on Haymarket, Jermyn Street and Piccadilly Circus. Steen Eiler Rasmussen described Piccadilly Circus station thus: 'in the morning it is like a turbine grinding out human beings on all sides. In the evening it sucks them in again, through the circle and down the escalators to the rushing trains'.[1]

The first fluorescent tube lights on the Underground system came into use on the westbound platform of the Piccadilly line on 2nd October 1945. The booking hall was given a Grade II listing on 7th February 1983.

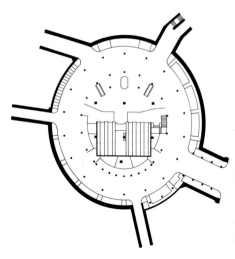

St James's Park opened on 24th December 1868. In 1896 the ticket hall was enlarged, and a new office block with white glazed brick façade and stone-clad bay window designed by Henry L. Florence built in 1898-99. (Florence worked in partnership with the architect Lewis H. Isaacs who was also a Director of the District Railway.) With the construction of the three Underground Group tube railways the facilities were enlarged in 1905, and four years later the District and tube companies' offices were grouped together and the premises named Electric Railway House, with reconstruction carried out by Harry W. Ford. The old overall station roof was removed and steelwork erected to support a new building over the line. This preliminary work was completed when architects Albert Richardson PPRA FSA FRIBA (1880-1964) and Charles Lovett Gill FRIBA (1880-1960) designed a further six-storey block built between 1922 and 1924 to occupy the space directly over the railway station.

By the late 1920s the Underground Group was again outgrowing the existing premises, and wanted a modern and efficient office block. Charles Holden was commissioned to produce designs, and for the first time the Underground gave him complete control over the planning. The building was to occupy a triangular corner site bounded by Broadway, Tothill and Palmer streets to the east of Electric Railway House, and would be named after its postal address: 55 Broadway.

An early plan shows a structure of conventional form with high façades and three internal light wells. In a building of this height the lower floors would require artificial lighting for most of the day – an unsatisfactory arrangement. Holden later described the way in which the final layout of the building was arrived at: "When we began work on the plans for the Underground Office Building, we found it difficult to get up any enthusiasm for the site, which was very shapeless and irregular. Plan after plan was tried and discarded for its dullness, without even attempting to set it up in elevation. It was, I think, a fellow feeling for the office worker in Victoria Street that finally suggested the short cut across the site to St James's Park station, and, at the risk of having the scheme turned down for making a thoroughfare of the building, it was decided to explore the possibilities of the 'short-cut' plan. With the 'short-cut' as the transverse axis, the longitudinal axis followed with no great effort of imagination. I remember the thrill of those two crossed lines on the paper and all that they implied: order out of chaos, a building with few corridors, perfect light and air to the offices, and a plan that could be almost said to design itself externally."[2] Cruciform plans were already used by Adams, Holden & Pearson and other architects in the design of hospitals.

Even when the plan had been decided the façade underwent some further development. Rather than the sheer walls of the finished design, preliminary sketches show a building with many more windows, adorned with stone festoons and balustered parapets, and topped by a domed, pedimented tower. The first two storeys would be clad in rusticated stone blocks.

Construction began in July 1927 with driving of the 700 foundation piles to carry the structural steel frame, using what was then the most powerful plant in the world. In one pile was placed a 'time capsule' inscribed with notes about the building and the Underground Group, and containing photographs of the site, a railway car, and a General bus. Stone blocks were cut to fit around the frame members and backed with a skin of brick and concrete. Foundation stones were laid by the foreman stonemason in charge of the works, and by the Housekeeper to the Underground: these men were selected in recognition of the contribution made by the many ordinary workmen who created the building.

Aerial view of 55 Broadway, in which the cruciform plan is evident. At the time of opening, this was the tallest office building in London. Victoria Street runs across the foreground, and St James's Park is seen top right.

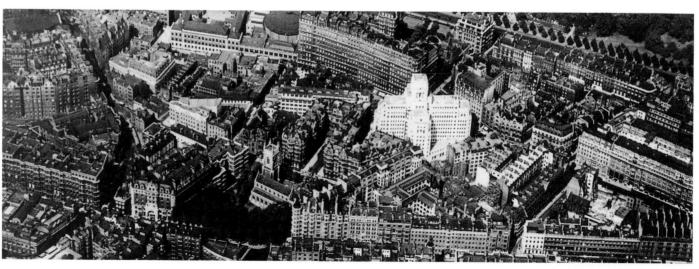

The east wing, with the sculpture 'Day' on the left above the ground floor. By using a cruciform arrangement, the light wells were brought out from the centre of the building to make maximum use of available light, and lifts and services could be placed centrally, with few corridors required. Influenced by American practice, offices were open plan, permitting the spread of light and making their layout easy to alter. In this single building was contained the centralised government and complex secretariat of the Underground empire, controlling almost all of London's buses, coaches, tramways and underground railways from July 1933.

The plinth and columns to the ground floor façades were of blue-grey granite brought from Norway and polished in Aberdeen, with capitals of black Belgian marble. Above the two storey podium the building was carried up for seven storeys, with a clock tower for a further four storeys. Open shafts at the wing intersections carried pipes and fire escape stairs with arches at seventh floor height serving to link the wings visually. Stonework was lightly detailed, and instead of sitting heavily upon the ground, the building gives the impression of soaring upwards. The building was set back above the seventh, ninth and tenth floors in compliance with London Building Act requirements. In a speech given some years later Holden stated that 'Speaking of sculptural architecture I find it useful in designs to visualise the building arising from the plan in some form pertaining to sculpture...In the case of the Underground office building I had in mind a figure astride a horse with panniers, hence the broadening of the tower laterally'. Adams, Holden and Pearson were awarded the London Architecture Medal in 1929 for the building. The tower motif would be used by Adams, Holden and Pearson in the design of St Luke's Hospital, Malta (1929-30) and the University of London Senate House (1931-7), and appears in Holden's designs for the South Bank reconstruction scheme.

Above left **The sculptor Jacob Epstein standing beside 'Night' under its shelter.** Above right **'Day' after some years exposure to the elements.**

Holden had a particular and enduring interest in the use of sculpture on his buildings, and Jacob (later Sir Jacob) Epstein KBE LG (1880-1959) had first worked for him in 1908 when he produced a frieze of figures for the British Medical Association headquarters in the Strand. Epstein's work frequently caused some public concern and Holden was instructed by the Underground management not to use him for 55 Broadway, but after the architect had persuaded Frank Pick to visit Epstein's studio with him, Pick was won over.

Epstein carved two figure groups for 55 Broadway. Huts were erected over the sculpture sites to give protection from the elements and inquisitive onlookers; despite the shelters Epstein had to endure the fierce winter of 1928-29. 'Day' was placed on the south-east front and faced the direction of the rising sun, and 'Night' over the auxiliary entrance in the north-east front to face the setting sun. For many years sculptors had been taught to follow the Greek and Roman styles – European ideals of beauty and proportion – without deviation. Epstein and his contemporaries began to draw from wider sources – Egyptian, Asian, Central American and especially African works – the discoveries made by nineteenth century archaeologists of previously little-known civilisations. The handling of material and form, and the vitality in these primitive works appealed to artists looking for a new expression of their ideas.

'Night' was the first to be revealed. The groups were designed to be viewed from street level, and some distortion would be apparent if viewed from the same height, which was unfortunately how photographs showed them. Epstein said that the figures were conceived with the mass of the building in mind. 'Day' was started when the building had been erected up to parapet level only, whereas Epstein had the advantage of seeing the main part of the building behind his work when he started 'Night'; Holden felt that the latter group was the more successful for this advantage.

Epstein's work again received criticism when it was unveiled to the public and caused some controversy amongst the Underground's management. Much correspondence was reported throughout the world's press and 'Night' was tarred and feathered in the protest. Two holes detected in 'Day' were rumoured to be bullet holes, but the Underground discounted this and said that they were caused by objects which had accidentally been dropped from the building works above. The generous size of the boy's genitalia was criticised as unnatural, and many contemporary press photographs were retouched. Epstein was subsequently required to shorten the member[3]. Holden had great faith in Epstein and, writing in 1940 of the artist's work for 55 Broadway, said that it was: 'well known, great elemental stuff, ugly perhaps, deformed perhaps, unnecessarily so in some respects, but as alive and pulsating as Van Gogh's sunflower and shouting robust delight and adventure in every cut of the chisel'[4].

Six of the eight 'Winds' carved for the walls of 55 Broadway. Top row **North Wind, west side of west wing – A.H. Gerrard; South Wind, west side of north wing – Eric Aumonier;** middle row **East Wind, north side of west wing – Eric Gill; East Wind, south side of west wing – Allan Wyon;** bottom row **West Wind, south side of east wing – Samuel Rabinovitch; West Wind, north side of east wing – Henry Moore.** One critic commented that the sculptures seemed to have been added as an afterthought, and another that the styling of some of them was somewhat ineffectual; they do, however, provide points of interest on an otherwise plain elevation, albeit at high level.

Six other sculptors were commissioned to produce bas-reliefs representing the four winds – a theme suggested by the alignment of the building and the height of the proposed figures, and perhaps inspired by the 'Tower of the Winds' at Athens. Eric Gill ARA RDI Hon ARIBA (1882-1940) carried out three of the reliefs, and the others were executed by Eric Aumonier, A.H.Gerrard, Henry Moore OM CH (1898-1986) – recommended by Epstein, Samuel Rabinovitch and Allan Wyon. Moore and Rabinovitch were already known for their work, but this was their first large public commission. Holden selected the artists to represent the whole or nearly the whole field of contemporary sculpture, and the sculptors were chosen because they all carved straight onto the stone: this was a trend in sculpture from the mid-1920s as some artists sought a more direct expression of their ideas. Once the preliminary sketches had been approved the sculptors were given a free hand. Carving was completed by the sculptors working from suspended cradles after the stones had been hoisted into position. Subsequent rains have washed soot into recesses in the reliefs adding emphasis to the forms.

The intersection of halls on the ground floor formed an entrance foyer with lift lobby to one side. The four lift cars were lined with fluted bronze panelling and mirrors and had grilles of bronze bars which rolled back into the sides of the cars. Adjacent to the main staircase was a letter chute from all floors. All central halls, corridors and floors were finished in travertine marble which has a pitted surface – making it non-slip and therefore suitable for flooring. Joseph Armitage carved six travertine clock panels for the halls. Floors and ceilings were coved at the sides to prevent dust settling. *Building* magazine considered it 'a grand stroke of architectural generosity'[5] that the public halls were decorated to the same standard as those for the staff of the building.

The building was officially opened on 1st December 1929, and was acclaimed for its (then) revolutionary design. Originally the Underground occupied floors one to three and seven, on which level was the chairman's room; floors four to six and eight were leased to tenants, and the London Building Act prevented the ninth floor and tower being occupied. A new St James's Park station was incorporated in the block.

The west wing received a direct bomb hit during World War II and was rebuilt partially without the Portland stone facing. In the mid 1980s Michael Manser Associates were appointed to redesign the ground floor, creating an improved reception area and new shopping mall. Existing shops and offices were cleared and the mall laid out around a reinstated central lobby. The library occupying the east hall had been closed some years previously and the entrance was reopened as the main approach to the shopping mall. Lord Ashfield's memorial plaque was removed to a position in the mall and unveiled by the then London Regional Transport Chairman Sir Neil Shields on 5th December 1988.

Hounslow West – then a terminus of the District Railway – represents the ultimate development of the Morden style, here expressed in a three-dimensional ticket hall tower. By this time granite was being used for the lower walls as it was more durable and did not discolour with wear like Portland stone. St Pauls and Mansion House were rebuilt with new frontages using these materials during 1928-29.

Reconstruction of Ealing Common and Hounslow West stations became necessary with the extension of Piccadilly trains to Hounslow and South Harrow. Work on the designs by Adams, Holden and Pearson with Stanley A. Heaps was started in 1929 and new facilities opened at Ealing on 1st March 1931 and Hounslow on 5th July 1931. Similar in style, these buildings were to be the last of the Portland stone-clad stations. Here the Morden plan was adapted: the vestibule dispensed with and the heptagonal ticket hall (to marry the angles of road and rail approaches) brought forward between the wings in the form of a tower.

Exteriors were faced in Aberdeen grey granite up to door height and Portland stone above: the underlying structure of the buildings was mass brickwork. Walls were built up to the top of the tower windows and then the reinforced concrete roof cast in-situ. A stone parapet was added afterwards, and the edges of the concrete roof concealed behind an enamelled-iron frieze bearing the station name; that at Ealing Common was later removed and the front portion has now been replaced by ceramic tiles. Ealing Common also appears to have been the first Underground station at which a backlit entrance canopy was used to display the station name on an all-glass panel.

Basil Ionides FRIBA (1884-1950), a leading interior designer of the day whose work on the Savoy Theatre (1929) established a new and influential style in theatre design, decorated the ticket halls. At Hounslow West Ionides chose a colour scheme of pink, cream and red for the terrazzo dado and tiled frieze; for Ealing Common the colours were grey, green and cream. The upper walls and ceiling were rendered and painted. The floor at Ealing was inlaid with a black star motif.

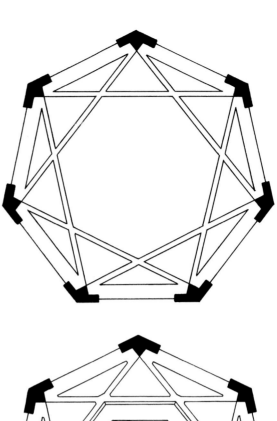

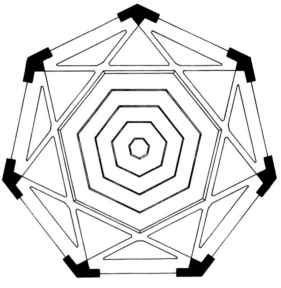

Interior of the ticket hall at Hounslow West, showing the tiled frieze by Basil Ionides and moulded plaster ceiling, echoing the pattern made by the roof's steel frame. The stepped motif is a recurring theme in Holden's work.

Above **Ceiling designs, Ealing Common and Hounslow West.**

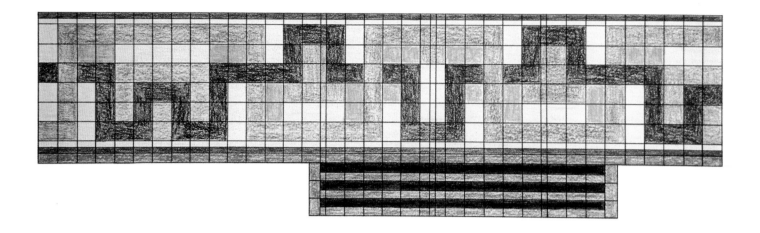

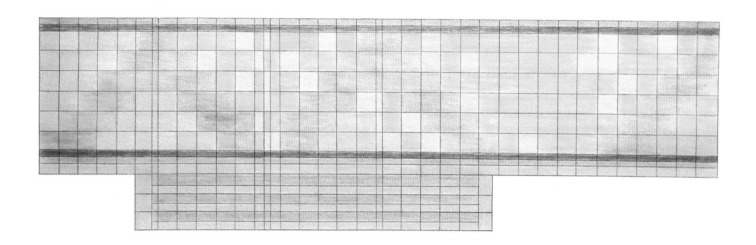

Above **Detail of tile friezes at Ealing Common and Hounslow West.**

Left **A view of the chandelier at Hounslow West.**

Artist's impression of Ealing Common station, completed in a similar style to Hounslow West.

The platforms at Ealing Common included one of Holden's first clerestory platform roofs.

A NEW ARCHITECTURE IN SUBURBIA

Platform cross passage at Southgate with bronze uplighter in lower escalator landing. Holden's step motif is seen here in the wall treatment.

The 1930s would see the emergence of a building type which began a new epoch in the history of British station design.

After completion of 55 Broadway, the Underground Group turned its attention to developments in north and west Middlesex. New and improved railway facilities were required to service the growing industrial and residential areas where existing public transport was becoming increasingly taxed, and also to open up new territory for suburban development by speculative house builders. The 'New Works Programme 1930' was drawn up by the Underground to improve the situation, and this was supplemented after the London Passenger Transport Board (LPTB) was created on 1st July 1933 by the 'New Works Programme 1935/40'.

The 1930 plan included the extension of the London Electric Railway's Piccadilly line from Finsbury Park to Southgate and ultimately Cockfosters to alleviate the traffic situation in north London. Piccadilly services were also to be projected from Hammersmith westward over the existing Hounslow, Harrow and Uxbridge branches to serve the new housing estates and take some of the traffic which was overloading the District. London businesses were moving westward from the City; through-running Piccadilly trains, travelling at express speeds from Acton Town and Northfields to Hammersmith, would provide much improved services for the ever increasing number of commuters to the West End from outlying districts. Completely new stations would be needed on the Cockfosters extension, and the stations in the west would have to be improved by reconstruction. Several central London stations were also to be rebuilt with escalators.

A trip to Europe

The development of modern architecture is generally dated back to the technological advances in cast-iron building construction made by the great engineers of the nineteenth century: the railway termini, suspension bridges and structures such as the Crystal Palace – built to house the Great Exhibition of 1851 and constructed entirely from prefabricated iron and glass parts. The use of a structural steel frame in buildings was perfected by architects designing skyscrapers in America beginning with the 'Chicago School' towards the end of the nineteenth century. Industry was becoming increasingly mechanised, and like the Railway Age before it, this 'Age of Machines' placed new demands on architecture.

The work of Frank Lloyd Wright (1887-1959) in America – with his use of cubic forms, overhanging roofs and free handling of ground plans – had caught the attention of European architects such as Le Corbusier (1887-1965) in France, and H.P.Berlage (1856-1934) in Holland who himself influenced the Amsterdam School and De Stijl groups. (The work of Wright may have been familiar to Holden from his time in the office of C.R.Ashbee, who knew the American architect.) W.M. Dudok (1884-1974) found for himself an individual style, whilst absorbing elements from the Amsterdam School and De Stijl, and was to be a prominent European architect throughout the 1930s, features of his work being taken up by architects in England. In Holland and Germany many state-subsidised post-war rebuilding programmes were under way, and the municipal authorities employed architects working in the new style to design housing estates and public buildings.

The Underground Group had for some years maintained a policy of sending its officers on study visits to the Continent, and prompted by accounts of European developments, Frank Pick and Charles Holden, accompanied by Lord Ashfield's secretary W.P.N.Edwards, went on a trip to Sweden, Denmark, Holland and Northern Germany between 20th June and 7th July 1930. After the tour a report was written by Edwards from his notes made on the journey, outlining some of the observations and views expressed by Pick and Holden, and including photographs of the buildings they found interesting.

During the trip they saw the emergence of a new theme in architecture referred to as 'functionalism': one of the principles which some architects were advancing and which had been gathering momentum throughout the 1920s. Like the Arts and Crafts architects before them, the functionalists rejected the unnecessary decoration of buildings and sought an honesty in design. They believed that good architecture was the fulfilment of the required function and that the beauty of the building was a product of the efficiency of the design. The prime considerations were the most efficient utilisation of internal space and freedom of movement. Scale and proportion, and the arrangement of forms came to the fore; cubic and cylindrical shapes – the basic classical forms – with clean planes and sweeping curves, were adopted by the movement as expressions of the 'machine' aesthetic. Such decorative ornament as was of service in repeating or signifying the function of the building was permitted. Omission of other ornament brought cost savings.

New materials

The emerging architecture coincided with changing construction technology and new materials – steel, reinforced concrete and plate glass – realised by rapid advances in science and industry which liberated architects from many former restrictions. Buildings had traditionally been constructed with brick walls which served as continuous supports to the structure, limiting the size and placing of windows. With the superior strength of steel and reinforced concrete it was possible to return to frame construction, allowing a much freer, open plan and giving a sense of lightness to the structure. The frame would consist mainly of right-angles, and straight walls and flat roofs became logical features. The heavy horizontal girders of a framed building and the increasing size of structures caused architects to place a new emphasis on the horizontal line in their designs. Cantilevering enabled canopies to be projected out from walls without additional vertical support.

The possibilities of building with reinforced concrete had early been realised by architects on the Continent, but the material was slow to be exploited in England because of restrictive building regulations. After the First World War there was a shortage of both bricks and bricklayers, and rising building costs and wages made the faster reinforced concrete construction more economical than traditional methods. Charles Holden supervised experiments with concrete mixes and the use of shuttering to achieve the best results. For the Underground stations a thin outer skin of Portland cement with Portland stone aggregate was cast with the concrete and polished after setting to give an attractive surface finish. Unfortunately much of the early concrete work has subsequently failed due to its composition and the effects of weathering.

Tower and finial of the 'Telegraaf' building, Voorburgwal, Amsterdam by J. F. Staal and G. J. Langhout 1927-30 (sculpture by Hildo Krop) seen on the European Tour, and a possible model for the lighting beacon at Osterley (see page 111).

New materials were compatible with the emergence of functionalist architecture, which required a change from traditional building materials to realise its demand for efficiency and sparing use of decoration. In turn, to some extent the materials themselves demanded a revised approach to building design and form.

The Dutch pioneered a revival of brick in the early twentieth century when architects such as H.P.Berlage, Michael De Klerk (1884-1923) and W.M.Dudok employed it to great effect in modern buildings; brick was also used extensively in northern Germany and Scandinavia. In response to competition from the manufacturers of cement products in the first decade of this century the brickmakers developed new brick types, particularly the multi-coloured facing variety. Freed from structural constraints, brick could be used as an infilling or external skin to the concrete frame – architects were still experimenting with the surface treatment of concrete at this time.

Developments in science suggesting that sunlight was beneficial to health created a demand for more light and space within buildings. Large windows were employed to take maximum advantage of available sunlight – a necessary consideration given the climate of northern Europe.

Early in 1930 the Underground Architect's office made plans for rebuilding Sudbury Town in brick with an octagonal tower similar to the structures at Ealing Common and Hounslow West which were just being completed. This seems to have been intended by Stanley Heaps as an arrangement to be generally adopted where possible, as the use of the polygonal tower was also employed in initial designs for Arnos Grove, Oakwood and Cockfosters. In form and material this represents a transition between styles of Underground station at this time. The main-line Southern Railway's Bishopstone, Sussex, station of 1938 comprised a like grouping of forms.

Towards a design policy

Pick and Holden saw a great variety of buildings on their tour, but rather than simply follow the work of others they set about defining the criteria they considered requisites of modern station design. Holden was committed to finding an architecture which was simple, honest, and suited to its application. In a speech of thanks given by Holden when he was presented with the 1929 London Architecture Medal for 55 Broadway he said: 'I have visions of architecture as pure and as true as a Bach fugue; an architecture as telling of joy in plan, structure and material; joy, too, in all the human and even the mechanical activities which make up architecture today – and without the use of adventitious aids to emotion.'[1]

Holden was most impressed by those European works which succeeded in combining modern materials and methods of construction with traditional elements to produce a building suited to the conditions of the day. Like the Arts and Crafts architects who believed in using the best of past styles where appropriate, he saw through the superficial appearance of functionalism to the underlying concepts which had been present in all great architectural movements: 'a greater reliance on the more permanent basic factors of architecture: namely the plan of service and the planes and massing arising out of that plan...'[2]

Continental and American stations of the day had a circulating area or concourse as the nucleus of the station plan, with accommodation for the public – shops and the essential services – grouped around in a logical sequence. This principle had generally not been applied to the design of English stations, but it was adopted for the new Underground facilities where the ticket hall became the dominant element of the building. To deal with the expected increases in passenger levels it was seen as inevitable that the new stations be devised for the uninterrupted flow of traffic using the most efficient plan. The building was to be so designed that logical sense of movement was suggested. When describing in 1944 how the design of Sudbury Town was arrived at Holden stated that: 'The first stage was to prepare a graph of the passengers' movements. . .The ultimate plan was produced by enclosing the graph by walls.'[3]

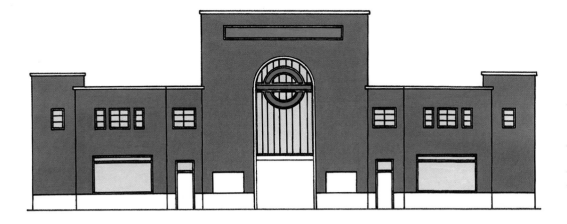

Located in built-up areas, the Morden line stations were really only façades behind which lay ticket halls and escalator approaches designed by the railway engineers, but the new buildings in Middlesex were entrusted completely to Holden, and would be designed 'in the round', with equal attention to all aspects and not just to the main frontage. Careful consideration was given to the surroundings so that the building was in keeping with the scale and character of its neighbours, although in retrospect the new stations must have appeared somewhat unusual alongside the mock-tudor semi-detached houses then so popular with the speculative developers. The planners could not always be sure of future traffic levels, and some of the stations were later criticised as being too big.

The architects' role was seen as being to rationalise the design, providing a well-proportioned structure of straightforward shape and expressive of its purpose. Holden wrote in 1944: 'ruthlessly analyse your motives, eliminate everything which does not fulfil a definite and necessary function.'[4] With the subtraction of superfluous features and obsolete details even greater sensitivity of handling was called for; the simplicity of forms demanded that attention be paid to refining the remaining design: 'form which is purposeful in all its parts arising from the play of the imagination on hard facts and natural forces rather than from free and uncontrolled fantasy.'[5] The use of clear simple forms also imparts to the stations an air of authority, and makes them easily recognisable.

Throughout middle Europe, railway companies had adopted the German tradition of placing the station in a spacious setting; the station would become a focal point in the locality. Arrangements for the interchange of trains, buses, cars and pedestrians needed to be made, and designed into the layout of the station with consideration of the traffic approaches to the site. This type of comprehensive planning was a significant advance in the field of station design, and was something which British architects were still getting to grips with in the 1960s.

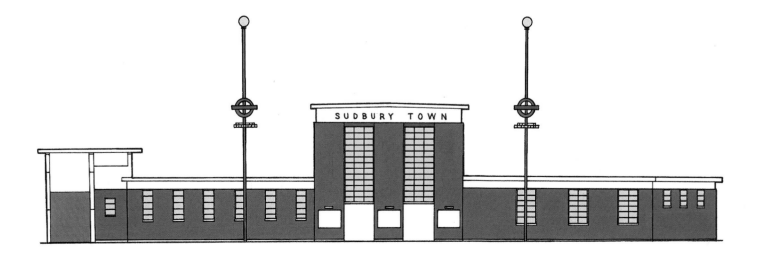

Sudbury Town after opening. To the left of the ticket hall is the footbridge stairway and ramp, and on the right is the buffet.

Charles Holden chose to leave his brickwork exposed both to the interior and exterior as this was considered appropriate in the suburban countryside of north and west Middlesex, and it was a statement of the building's functional nature; exposed brick walls also imparted a feeling of warmth to ticket hall interiors. Brick was the traditional English building material and it was cheaper than stone. Speaking about his brick stations of the 1930s, Holden said: 'On these stations we took infinite trouble in the choices of suitable bricks for colour and weathering qualities and for good appearance over a number of years. The bond, the mortar and method of striking the joints were also carefully considered.'[6] The bricks at Holden stations were mostly laid in variants of English bond, but in buildings by other architects the bond varied. Holden would do small diagrams on his drawings to specify the brick bond to be used in each part of a structure. When used with a contrasting colour of mortar, English bond was especially useful for emphasising the horizontal line. The type of brick used was varied from station to station and within a station to give individual character, but a general similarity of materials ensured that there was a continuity to the design.

The practice in contemporary Continental stations was to create a general diffused lighting. Large clerestory windows were used to provide good natural light by day, and at night uplighters – lamps on pylons with their shades directed upwards – provided illumination from a concealed source which reflected off the walls and ceiling without glare or shadow. The large windows also enhanced the exterior of the station at night. Holden made use of machine-made plate glass and mass-produced steel frames, with the glass mounted flush inside the frame and the putty behind it. Glazing bars were employed in the windows of the earlier stations, emphasising the horizontal line – a recurring theme in much early Modernist architecture – but these fell out of use from the middle of the decade as the waste of cutting large sheets of glass into smaller pieces, only to be rejoined with glazing bars, became apparent. It was also considered that the glazing bars impaired the full passage of light.

The tiling used for station interiors was varied between locations, the predominant colour

being 'biscuit-cream', so-called because of the tiny brown speckles in the cream glaze. Ceramics of this colour had been used at Clapham South in 1926 and were also to be found on the Berlin U-Bahn system. The glaze was semi-matt, combining with the colour to reflect a soft glow of light. Glazes in bright colours were being developed for architectural applications and, for decorative relief, coloured bands were used to pick out details; bright colours were the only ones which retained their hue in the glow of the tungsten lamps then used. Brown, grey and light blue appeared later. Enamelled bricks, which were both easy to clean and had reflective properties, or quarry tiles were used for ticket hall walls, and towards the middle of the 1930s faience slabs were used in subsurface passages and halls.

White pressed cement tiles treated with carborundum to make them hard-wearing and non-slip would be used for floor covering, as also would be terrazzo. Rubber flooring was laid at escalator approaches. Bronze and similar alloys were adopted for the metal work on passimeters, stalls, poster frames and handrails, replacing the wooden mouldings that had been almost universal until this time. Handrails were welded and jointless, making them more comfortable to hold.

Signs and notices would have a logical colour scheme and be integrated into the overall design. It was felt that, if properly placed, posters could form an attractive 'mural' effect: the location and grouping of advertising and publicity poster displays was therefore given consideration. Muted colour schemes and careful lighting ensured that posters were the main point of decoration and displayed with maximum advantage. This increased the commercial value of the advertising spaces and made them more attractive to potential clients. Provision for the accommodation of vending machines and other equipment would be made when the building was designed: they would not be installed as an afterthought. To add a touch of humanity and interest to the efficiency of buildings, Holden would always include little details and enrichments here and there – be they decorated vent grilles, telephone directory lecterns, or perhaps just a fluted bronze strip.

Holden was made fully responsible for the design of Sudbury Town, Chiswick Park, Acton Town, Boston Manor, Eastcote, Ruislip Manor, Green Park, Hyde Park Corner, Highgate, and all the stations on the Cockfosters extension. Additional work was taken over from the Underground Architects' office at Frank Pick's request in 1931 'so that it could be carried out more quickly'. Holden would produce the initial sketches, at times perhaps only doodles, but embodying the essence of the building nonetheless, and pass them to his assistants who would work out the designs in detail. These would then be shown to Holden, who might suggest amendments. Pick would approve the designs at this stage and then the working drawings would be started and passed to the builders as the job progressed.

Further stations – Alperton, Sudbury Hill, Northfields, Hammersmith, Osterley, South Harrow, Warren Street, Leicester Square, Knightsbridge and Archway – were designed and detailed by Adams, Holden & Pearson and the working drawings done in the office of the Underground Chief Architect Stanley Heaps, which then arranged the building contract and carried out the work. The design and finish of platforms, tunnels and escalator shafts was the responsibility of Heaps with Adams, Holden and Pearson acting as consultants; many of the standard designs were originated by Holden and adapted by subsequent architects. The effects of the industrial depression caused busy architects to share work that otherwise might have been undertaken by one practice. Other architects collaborated on certain stations, with Holden and his assistants again preparing the original sketches, after which the architects did the working drawings and carried out the work under Holden's overall control; these stations are mentioned in the main text. Pick objected to Holden's use of other architects as it was contrary to their original agreement, but Holden persuaded Pick that the arrangement was necessary because of his heavy workload. Other buildings such as electrical substations and signal cabins were designed in harmony with the stations, usually by Heaps and his assistants.

The style of architecture which was introduced to the Underground with the new Sudbury Town station of 1931 was virtually unprecedented in this country. The traditional format of the roadside station – originally modelled on the domestic dwelling – was abandoned in favour of a purpose-designed structure suited for its function in both layout and appearance. This practice was to be adopted to some extent by the Southern Railway and other main-line companies during this period, particularly as the spread of electrification prompted a new architectural expression to attract custom.

Good design was good for business. Design improvements would produce an environment for passengers that was pleasant, orderly and clean, with light and airy ticket halls and convenient newspaper, confectionery and flower kiosks. By the good example it set, the Underground was gradually able to change the travelling public's attitude to railway stations which had in the past often been shabby and uncomfortable places. It was seen that by giving the same consideration to the staff areas, better working conditions would result in a sense of pride and an improved attitude amongst the employees.

Holden approached each station as an individual problem requiring its own solution, rejecting the idea of 'design by formula', and saying that every station was 'a new adventure in design.'[7] Through his skill in finding a building type which would be suitable for many locations and purposes, and through the use of similar materials, the homogeneous appearance of different buildings was achieved. Holden developed standardised basic elements bearing in mind that they could be taken up by other designers working on buildings for different sites without losing the overall style.

The Underground system would have been much less hospitable had expense been spared in the provision of spacious facilities of a high standard, infused with a character and humanity. It is due to the good design of these stations, with the attention to detail, and the thought given to both the needs of the day and future requirements, that many stations remain virtually unchanged and still function properly after more than half a century.

With the creation of the LPTB in 1933, the expanding transport empire required a considerable amount of new building work in the form of bus and coach stations and garages, booking halls and waiting rooms. This was carried out through a multitude of structures of vast variety but all in the same spirit and showing a common approach, using the basic features established by Holden.

Charles Holden brought the Underground railway station to the forefront of modern architecture; this coherence in design has arguably never been equalled by another English railway company on such a scale before or since. It was made possible by the unusual one-to-one relationship enjoyed by Pick as the client and Holden the architect which permitted the works to be carried out within a relatively short space of time without the interference of

Clock and Barometer in booking hall at Sudbury Town.

committees. Pick saw the chaos that would ensue if the effects of the modern world were to go uncontrolled, and he was aware of his responsibility to manage the changes within his sphere of influence. Sir Nikolaus Pevsner has said that Pick saw in every detail a 'visual propaganda', and he used this not only to promote the Underground, but also to improve surroundings for the public as a whole.

Comparisons have been drawn between Holden's stations of the 1930s and contemporary Dutch and German architecture. It should be remembered that at the time of the Continental tour Holden was in his fifties, with many years experience of different building types and materials. New European works were receiving widespread coverage in the architectural press at this time, but whilst Holden may have borrowed stylistic details from German and Dutch architects, his stations possess a sensitivity of handling which many Continental buildings constructed for similar purposes lacked. Although the functionalists claimed that their buildings were the product of an efficient design, they still followed a general trend in the use of material and treatment of detail. Architects have to design buildings which satisfy their clients, and the clients often use contemporary building practice as a guide to their own requirements. Holden had the advantage that, within precise limits, Frank Pick allowed him a much freer hand than many other clients would have done. The important point is that the stations achieve the aim of the architect in serving the public. If Holden's station work were to be compared to a particular movement it might best be 'Rationalism', a wider interpretation of functional building design whose protagonists believed in economy of plan, method, material and the omission of decoration; and ultimately sought a better society through the advancement of architecture, industrial design and town planning.

After the trip to Europe, Sudbury Town was chosen as the site for a new station of experimental design to replace the primitive corrugated-iron hut built for the opening of the line in 1903. Adams, Holden & Pearson, worked on various designs as late as November 1930. Construction was started on 13th December 1930 and the station was opened on 19th July 1931.

The new facility was designed around the principles and features that Pick and Holden saw as being important in the modern station, and marked a turning point in architectural style. A link with the foregoing architecture was that no supporting frame was used for the building; the mass brick walls were load-bearing and the concrete cap to the booking hall was cast in-situ. This was found to be unsatisfactory because the presence of the walls made it difficult to construct full formwork for the concreting, and leakages of cement slurry stained the walls. Washing-down was not effective, and after the difficulties at Sudbury Town the method of construction was changed so that the brickwork was added after the steel frame and concreting had been completed. The low-level buildings were of reinforced concrete finished in white cement.

Internal illumination also served to advertise the station at night. *The Railway Gazette* described this effect as "like a house inviting guests to a Christmas party". The neon sign can be clearly seen.

Above **The round end to the waiting room was a feature of the 'streamlining' applied to buildings which became popular in the 1920s. The vertical supports break up the window area and in subsequent designs were superseded by columns behind the glazing. Reinforced concrete beams were continued out through the wall as cantilever supports to the canopy.**

Opposite **Flared uplighters were at first incorporated into the poster display stands, but these were replaced after criticism from Frank Pick with lighting pylons painted in yellow fading to white with green bands. A clock and barometer were mounted high on the end walls and the coffered ceiling painted grey with saxe blue beams. A refreshment room was furnished with green cane tables and chairs.**

Right **Unusual seriffed version of Johnston lettering on signs at Sudbury Town.**

The main facilities were located on the north side of the tracks, overlooking a forecourt and bus terminus. The dominating feature of the structure was the ticket hall itself – a brick box 54ft-long and 27ft-high. The double-height hall gave a sense of spaciousness and lightness to the interior, and this feature was subsequently employed in the design of many stations. With a north-west/south-east alignment the ticket hall was well lit by a north light through the four long vertical windows in the front wall. Window frames were painted blue to blend in with the reflection of the sky on the glass when viewed from outside, and were only painted white in later years. On the cornice of the ticket hall roof were mounted 'Claudegen' neon signs in two colours – the first and only neon signs to be used on a London Underground station (see notes on Chiswick Park). The station name is believed to have been shown in red, and the border with its large 'U' and 'D' letters in blue. The soffit of the cornices to ticket hall and buffet roofs were moulded with three shallow steps, a feature Holden introduced to break up the plain concrete surface by the play of light and shadow.

To the side of the ticket hall an extension enclosed stairs leading to the footbridge which also functioned as a public crossing place, with gentle ramps at each end for prams. The bridge was unglazed and the concrete left with the shuttering marks exposed. On the westbound platform was an auxiliary booking office and partially screened waiting area.

The form of the building was derived from a plan of the traffic flow, and most areas within the station were accessible from the ticket hall. A passimeter and ticket machines were placed in the path of the passenger who could wait in shelter after purchasing a ticket without having to step out onto the platform.

On 19th February 1971 the station gained a Grade II listing as being of special architectural and historical interest. When the Underground Ticketing system was introduced in 1986-7 a new wall-type booking office was built and the passimeter closed; the station has otherwise been maintained in near-original condition.

SUDBURY TOWN

Early plans by the Underground Architect proposed that the building for Arnos Grove be based on the Hounslow West type with a polygonal ticket hall behind a curved colonnade. Adams, Holden & Pearson adapted the Sudbury Town theme (shown in a preliminary sketch for Arnos Grove as a wide rectangular tower similar to Enfield West) to produce a cylindrical ticket hall tower 30ft-high and 57ft in diameter, rising from a square lower range of buildings. The absence of any development in the area gave the designers a completely free hand and the circular ticket hall seemed the ideal basis for the plan – traffic flow was the prime consideration and the roundabout is one of the best ways of regulating this. Charles Holden later wrote that the tower was 'felt to be the most suitable form externally to counter the big fall in the roadway', and the 'strong horizontal baseline was influenced by the parapet wall of the bridge.'[8]

Arnos Grove was designed immediately following Sudbury Town and it was intended that the use of load-bearing walls be continued, but the problems with leaking shuttering at Sudbury Town led to the adoption of a steel frame so that the concreting could be carried out before the brickwork was started. The initial design of Arnos Grove had to be reworked by Holden's assistant Charles Hutton to accommodate the structural frame, and the entrances were repositioned to suit the sixteen vertical stanchions grouped around the tower wall in pairs between the windows. Hutton also lowered the gallery behind the bridge parapet and altered the proportions of the building.

Brindled Staffordshire bricks were used for the lower buildings to match the parapets of the adjacent road bridge. Window frames were painted emerald green. Beneath the ground floor windows was placed a sill of artificial stone integral with the capping of low walls enclosing L-shaped flower beds on three corners of the building to be planted with euonymus, a low flowering shrub with variegated leaves. The ground floor roof was cantilevered out from the main frame so that it could be concreted before the brick walls were built; this meant that deep cantilever beams were required with the consequence of a deep cornice. The designers felt that the cornice might appear unnecessarily heavy, so the idea of relieving the plain concrete with a band of bright blue faience tiles was introduced. This also formed a good background for the station name which was set in an illuminated panel above the entrances. Cavities containing lamps behind the station name had opal glass set beneath them so that light was cast down onto the entrances at night.

Arnos Grove was the temporary terminus of the four-mile Piccadilly line extension towards Cockfosters which opened on Monday 19th September 1932. The station was built from start to finish in some six months. After completion Frederick Towndrow writing in *The Observer* described it as an 'architectural gem of unusual purity,'[9] and *The Architect and Building News* commented that it 'may be regarded as a model station, which in design and planning could hardly be improved.'[10] Charles Hutton recalls Holden telling him that it was his own favourite station. The building was listed on 19th February 1971 and the passimeter has been preserved in situ although following the introduction of the Underground Ticketing System in 1987 is no longer in use. It was restored to near original condition in 1990 and used for the display of a small exhibition detailing the history of Charles Holden's work for the Underground Group and London Transport.

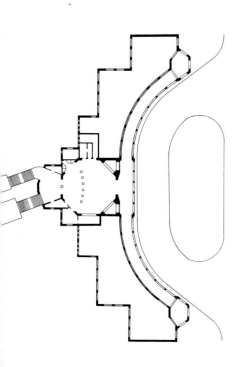

The roof of the ticket hall was supported centrally by a single 16-sided concrete column with a circular passimeter at its base. All the facilities were arranged around the perimeter of the hall, with a fruit stall and newspaper and tobacco kiosks to the front of the building, and staff accommodation to the rear. (Fruit and confectionery stalls were introduced to many stations for the first time during this period.) The lower part of the hall was faced with brindled Staffordshire engineering bricks up to the deep concrete ring beam which contained ducting for all the services. Above the ring beam Buckinghamshire multi-coloured facings were used, with brick pilasters on each side of the windows. The bricks were laid in stretcher bond except for the set-back portions at the side of each window which were laid in English bond. Rainwater pipes were set into a recess in the pilaster at one side of alternate windows. Doors were finished in teak and nameplates were of bronze with engraved lettering painted white. Floodlights on the passimeter roof served to illuminate the interior by night.

The brick drum was capped by a reinforced concrete roof cast in-situ with an aggregate of Portland stone. Originally the cornice was to have a stepped soffit like those on the square towers, but the difficulty of making long, curved shuttering boards to form concentric rings prompted the idea of rectangular coffers which could be made up using short lengths of board. Meticulous formwork was still required. Below Detail of tower cornice soffit.

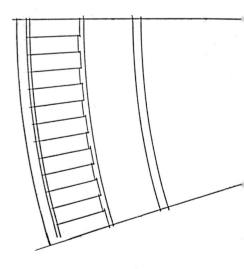

Right and centre **Stairs connected with a glazed concrete gallery leading to the platforms, with seated waiting areas beneath the stairs. A painted dado, characteristic of these early 1930s stations, reduced the scuffing of the concrete. The ordered arrangement of signage, notices, train indicator and signal lamps is evident here. Platform canopies were designed by Stanley Heaps.**

Below **Chiswick Park ticket hall with early pattern of passimeter by Charles Holden. Blue-black enamelled bricks were carried up to the ring beam as a durable wall lining (also used at Northfields, Oakwood, Rayners Lane and Eastcote), and the hung plaster ceiling featured a decorative moulding of fluted panels.**
Below right **The cantilevered platform canopy (westbound side), an unusual design found also at Stamford Brook, and similar to canopies at stations on the Southern Railway's Chessington branch.**

During the same period that Arnos Grove was designed, plans were made for the reconstruction of Chiswick Park. The first station had opened here as Acton Green on 1st July 1879 when the District Railway extension to Ealing Broadway, from a junction with the London & South Western Railway's Kensington & Richmond line at Turnham Green, came into operation. It was renamed Chiswick Park & Acton Green in March 1887, and Chiswick Park on 1st March 1910.

The quadrupling of tracks for the projection of Piccadilly line services required that the station be rebuilt and platforms resited to make room for the additional lines. A temporary booking office opened on 5th July 1931, and the old station was demolished later in the year. Most of the new structure was completed by April 1932. By August the building was in use and work was finally completed in 1933. A new eastbound platform opened 20th September 1931, and the replacement westbound platform had come into use by June of 1932. Platforms serve the District line only.

The principal feature of the building is the semi-circular ticket hall with its great expanse of windows. To one side of the hall was built a tower to advertise the presence of the station, bearing a bullseye sign and the station name on blue enamel plates over a cast-stone band. A preliminary design sketch dated 24th December 1930 had placed this tower on the other side of the ticket hall and surmounted by a bullseye symbol of braced neon tubing. A frieze of blue tiles ran along the front edge of the lower range of buildings below the concrete canopy. Hand-made sandfaced multi-red bricks laid in English bond were used for the exterior facing. On the upper frieze the station name was shown in bronze letters.

The platform shelters, with their curved, cantilevered canopies were constructed from reinforced concrete left with the board marks from the shuttering. A notable feature of the platform walls was the biscuit-cream and black tile work forming surrounds to the bullseye station nameboards and incorporating poster display spaces. Fluorescent lighting was introduced in 1981 but the original lamp standards were retained. The ticket hall underwent some rebuilding in 1988-89 when a new booking office was constructed, detracting from the spacious hall.

Above **Chiswick Park was considered by the Underground's management to be one of the less successful designs, but occupied an awkward site.**

Below **Preliminary scheme for Chiswick Park with neon tube Underground symbol on the tower.**

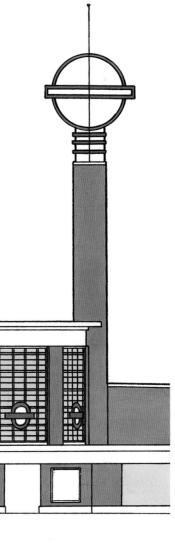

For Northfields, glazed bricks were used to face most of the ground floor exterior, and a stained glass bullseye introduced for the single front window.

Northfield (Ealing) Halt – on the District Railway's Hounslow branch – was opened on 16th April 1908, on the western side of the Northfield Avenue overbridge. To accommodate traffic growth, it was rebuilt to a full size station in 1911 to a design by Harry W. Ford and renamed Northfields and Little Ealing from 11th December that year.

A new facility with two island platforms was to be constructed on the eastern side of the overbridge in preparation for the Piccadilly line extension. Work commenced in late 1930 and a temporary station called Northfields opened 19th May 1932 to enable the old buildings to be cleared away.

The permanent station was opened on 18th December 1932. The nature of the site required that the building be set back from the roadway behind a forecourt. Although based on the Sudbury Town 'box' design, the ticket hall tower was elongated from front to rear with large windows set in all four walls. The wide lower range of buildings fronting the road had a canopy of concrete with Portland stone aggregate and blue faience tiles on the cornice. All bricks were laid in Flemish bond, with the central portion of the ground floor exterior faced in blue-black enamelled bricks. The skirting was of concrete containing an aggregate of Portland stone and Kentish Rag stone. The windows featured bullseye symbols in red and blue stained glass. Unlike Sudbury Town the roof was of precast concrete slabs supported by four deep transverse beams. Precast slabs were stronger and lighter than a solid roof and had the added benefit of giving a decorative coffered effect to the ceiling.

A single storey colonnade, which also formed a loggia at the front and a gallery at the rear flanked the ticket hall itself. The vertical frame stanchions were enclosed as piers which connected above the ring beam with brick pilasters. Lower walls and piers were faced in blue-black enamelled bricks. Pavement lights were set into the roof on each side of the tower. The enclosed gallery at the rear of the building gave access to the two island platforms, with a cycle store at its south end from which a gangway led to the 71-lever signal cabin. The gallery and cantilevered platform canopies were all of exposed concrete which has since been painted over. A full service of Piccadilly line trains called at the new station from 9th January 1933 and was extended to Hounslow West just over two months later on 13th March. In the late 1980s a new booking office was built within the ticket hall occupying part of the original colonnade on the south side. The signal cabin is now the office of the station manager.

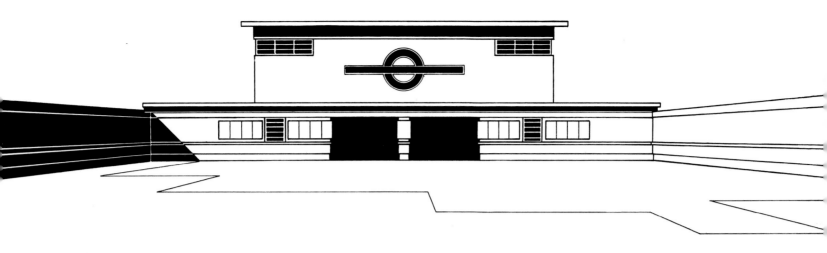

Above **Proposed design for Northfields of July 1931,** rejected soon after its submission. There is a heavy emphasis on the horizontal plane, and the tower is wider and lower than in the finished version. High corner windows were a popular motif of the time, but would have severely restricted the admission of daylight to the ticket hall; Holden did frequently use them in his signal cabins. The station name would have been placed on the elongated bar of the bullseye symbol.

Left **The interior at Northfields with automatic ticket machines in the foreground.**

Westbound platform with seating in niches between platform canopy supports. The footbridge at the far end led to a raised walkway (nicknamed 'Southend Pier' by local residents) and auxiliary entrance on Weymouth Avenue (closed 1942).

The first station on the northern extension of the Piccadilly line beyond Finsbury Park, which opened on 19th September 1932, was located close to the Manor House public house and excavated below the intersection of Seven Sisters Road and Green Lanes, on which widening work began in 1930. Access to the subsurface ticket hall was via nine stairways located at various points around the road junction, and the only ground-level structures were a waiting shelter on Green Lanes and a tram station in Seven Sisters Road by which interchange between road and Underground services could be made completely under cover.

Two tram shelters on loading islands 80ft-long were of reinforced concrete with an aggregate of Portland stone; the skirting was of black 'Biancola' terrazzo, and the subway walls lined with 'Unicola' terrazzo. A similar facility was provided at Turnpike Lane, and a further one had been planned for Wood Green; engineering difficulties caused by the sloping site prevented the latter work being carried out. An unusual direction sign built around a traction standard for the tram overhead was erected in the middle of the road junction. The lower part of the sign was faced in black Belgian marble mosaic, and the upper part formed of precast concrete blocks. Sign boxes of black-enamelled iron were illuminated at night so that the lettering glowed orange. The tram span pole was surmounted by a bronze finial based on the letters 'U' and 'D'. The tram shelters became disused in 1939 after trolleybuses were introduced and they were removed in 1951.

The subsurface ticket hall was designed around the most efficient flow of traffic, which resulted in an asymmetrical plan with no wasted corners or spaces; any 'dead' areas were utilised for the installation of kiosks or other facilities. The ceiling was decorated with a pattern of circular mouldings which fitted the awkward shape.

Tram overhead wires dominating the sky give this post-1935 view of Turnpike Lane a marked European feel. With a bus yard adjoining the station and the tram loading islands in the road opposite, Turnpike Lane formed a comprehensive transport interchange. A shopping block beyond the station was also by Adams, Holden & Pearson. Below **A balanced arrangement of passimeter, ticket machines and lighting was carefully worked out for**

Turnpike Lane station was built as part of a shopping centre and transport interchange between train, bus and tram. The siting of the entrance was deceptive: the ticket hall floor was sunk some feet below ground to give level access from the subway leading to tram loading islands. Here, the ventilation tower serves also to draw attention to the station. Behind the tower was a staff canteen over the escalator hall, but other facilities were accommodated beneath the pavement.

Beyond Turnpike Lane lay the established residential and shopping area of Wood Green. The surface building was to fit a corner site in a parade of shops, and the street frontage, with its large area of brickwork and narrow band of windows, was considered a suitable treatment for the difficult curved and sloping site. Ventilation towers were placed at each end of the roof; these were built the same height, but the left-hand one has subsequently been extended. Slabs of Cornish granite were used to face the ground floor exterior and interior walls. Low railings beneath the canopy were decorated with a motif of diamonds and discs in the uprights (a pattern also seen in railings around Holden's University of London buildings).

The ticket hall was laid out to an elliptical plan, with an exhibition space at the rear (which saw little use). The vertical face of the ring beam was cast with a stepped pattern. The central portion of the rear wall was set back to mirror the position of the main window: quoins and jambs of the window and the set-back were faced in orange-red sandfaced bricks, with brown-grey bricks for the rest of the walls. Roof beams divided the central portion of the ceiling into three bays and formed a clerestory. The floors of the escalator landings were at first flagged in a yellow rubber material so as to be non-slip; this material soon showed the dirt and was later replaced at some stations by a darker coloured rubber. Escalator treads were originally painted alternately black and white for safety. The side panels were of polished teak-faced plywood backed with galvanised steel. Above the escalators, visible to passengers coming up from the platforms, was a sign indicating when a tram was waiting to pick-up in Lordship Lane.

In 1988 a new booking office was constructed against the back wall of the ticket hall.

A staff canteen was provided on the first floor of the block seen here on the left of Wood Green ticket hall.

A raised clerestory roof was concealed behind the parapet wall. Artificial lighting was provided by banks of pressed glass shades on the walls.

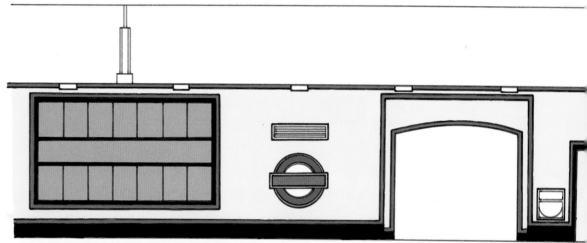

Platforms at Manor House, Turnpike Lane and Wood Green were wider than the other extension stations to cope with the expected heavier traffic.

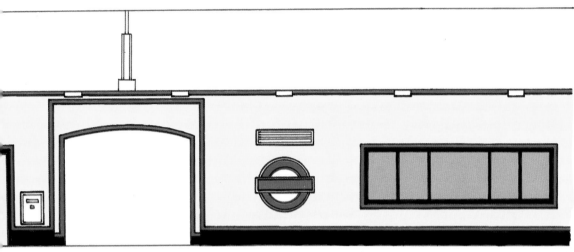

Tunnels at Manor House, Turnpike Lane and Wood Green were lined to give an elliptical profile enabling furniture and equipment to be recessed without disturbing the general line and also lessening the distortion of posters on the walls. Wall surfaces were finished with biscuit-cream tiles, relieved by narrow bands of coloured tiles around the archways, tunnel mouth and recesses, and with further bands along the platform and trackside. Platforms had variously coloured bands of tiles, those at Manor House being bright blue, those at Turnpike Lane chrome yellow and those at Wood Green being green and cream. Ceilings were separated from the walls by a cornice over the poster panels onto which lighting units were fixed at 7ft intervals. For the first time bullseye nameboards were mounted on both platform and trackside walls for easier station recognition. Signal lamps, tunnel lighting switches, telephones and headway clocks were set in bronze panels in the false headwalls. A pit was dug between the running rails to deter suicides and to give access for rescue workers, and lighted spaces under the platforms gave better access to the tracks in the event of attention being required to a train for any reason.

Pressure fans supplied fresh air to the platforms and staff accommodation at platform level. Ventilation ducts connected to the surface were built into the platform walls at a height of 7ft to allow the station to 'breathe' and reduce the draught caused by trains entering and leaving the station. The ducts were concealed by decorative alloy grilles 18ins high by 54ins wide designed by Harold Stabler.[11]

Alloy ventilation grilles by Harold Stabler for Manor House (top), Turnpike Lane (middle) and Wood Green (lower) represent somewhat idealised visions evoked by the names of the localities served. Stylistically the grilles recall the work of sculptor Edgar Brandt.

Above **The compact ticket hall box at Bounds Green, with single-storey escalator hall alongside. The octagonal form is unique on the Underground system. Bullseye signs are fixed to artificial stone panels - a feature abandoned after the Cockfosters line was completed.**

The extension continued north-west under Bounds Green Road to reach Bounds Green. Charles Holden had worked with C.H. James when they designed the Empire Marketing Board stand for an exhibition at Olympia in 1931, and he asked James to carry out the design of this station. An Adams, Holden & Pearson drawing from January 1931 shows a double height building with ticket hall of half-octagon plan. James developed this arrangement so that the ticket hall tower was based on a full octagon – the chamfered box form was a product of the restricted corner site. A prominent feature of this station was the louvred ventilation tower which also served to advertise the presence of the station. The walls of the lower range of buildings were twice set back to form steps – a feature repeated at Enfield West (now Oakwood, also by James with Holden). The canopy was of plain concrete with a stepped moulding on the soffit, the illuminated station name panel forming a frieze below the canopy. Window frames were painted light green, and for ventilation the top sections of glass in the ticket hall tower were omitted; metal hoods were later placed over these voids.

In contrast to the exposed brick of other Cockfosters line stations, C.H. James selected grey, black and flame red tiling and black terrazzo for the ticket hall interior.

A further extension of the Piccadilly line was made on 13th March 1933 from Arnos Grove to Enfield West with an intermediate station at Southgate. Railways had previously avoided this settlement on high ground because of the expensive earthworks which would be involved. To maintain a reasonable gradient the Piccadilly platforms had to be constructed in a short length of tunnel.

Before the layout was finalised there had been various design proposals taking advantage of the difficult corner location by creating an elliptical island with bus pull-in behind. The first scheme was to erect shops around the island following the elliptical plan; a curved parade and the station ticket hall would be built on the perimeter of the pull-in. A second scheme placed the station on the island with the bus pull-in under a glazed overall roof. The final design for a circular structure dates from early 1931. The building was listed as being of architectural and historical interest on 19th February 1971. New escalators were installed in 1991 and the original lighting reinstated but adapted to meet modern illumination standards.

Inside the building thirteen pilasters faced with black tiles enclosed stanchions to the roof-supporting columns, and the deep ring beam had an inset of biscuit-cream tiles edged in black. A fluted bronze fascia strip ran around the wall beneath the beam. Above each of the three entrances to the hall the suspended plaster ceiling was twice stepped up in height and lamps set into each step. The shop fronts were finished in bronze with stallboards of similar painted cast-iron panels to those used on the exterior. Around the top of the central column the rubbed concrete ceiling was finished with a moulding of four concentric rings.

Platform tunnels and the lower landing were lined in biscuit-cream and chrome yellow tiles, and the air vents were covered by plain mesh grilles.

On either side of the station building stood a combined lighting mast and shelter of reinforced concrete carrying an illuminated bullseye sign. These shelters were similar to those at Oakwood, but in this case were designed by S.A. Heaps. In the quadrant formed by High Street and Chase Side was constructed a curved bus pull-in to facilitate the easy transfer of passengers between bus and train. A parade of shops was built behind the pull-in, the first of four such developments planned for stations on the extension. (Others were projected for Turnpike Lane, Enfield West and Cockfosters; only the Turnpike Lane development was completed.) The concrete-framed building had two storeys, but was designed to take a third if required, and indeed one was considered in 1954. Between the end wings the shop fronts were set back behind a colonnade of piers faced with mosaic of black Belgian marble.

Station and shopping parade at Southgate, one of the most complete and integrated schemes designed by Charles Holden for the Underground. Signalling apparatus ensured that buses were held for passengers when a train was approaching.

The building at Southgate comprised two stages, with ticket hall roof taken up above a continuous clerestory window. Half of the building contained the station offices and the other half was given over to shops. A steel column supported the roof at its centre, and slender steel columns were placed behind the windows on its perimeter. Below a wide canopy of polished concrete with Portland stone aggregate was a lighting box of blue enamelled steel with the station name stencilled into it. The box was glazed top and bottom, casting light onto the soffit of the canopy and down over the shop fronts and entrances. Beneath the box was a fascia of fluted bronze backed with hardwood. Office windows were glazed with reeded glass above a dado of decorative cast iron panels. Multi-coloured bricks were laid in stretcher bond, with English bond for the entrance side walls, all on a plinth of grey Cornish granite. Two relief vents from the platform were concealed in the outside wall. Window frames were painted a dull red. The design of the lantern suggested a motif for electricity and served to make the station prominent at night. It was constructed from cast stone rings, and between the rings sliding panels of opal glass gave access to the lamp units. The whole assembly was topped by a spun copper ball. Finials such as these were to be found on several European buildings, including the tram station at Le Havre of 1932-33 by Henri Paçon.

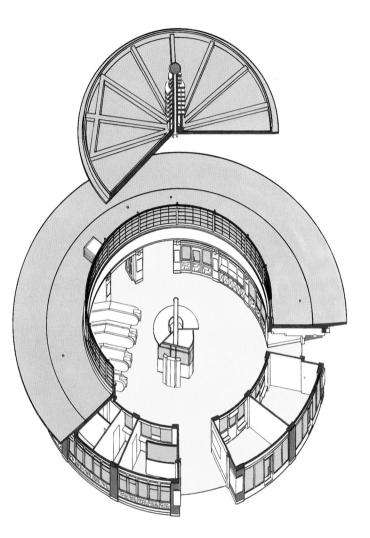

Opposite page bottom **A shop of circular plan completed the south wing; around the central supporting column within this shop was a combined lantern and skylight of frosted glass. The large clock had a face of artificial stone and gilded details; a thin band of green and white marble cubes linked each hour stud.**

Above left **Axonometric showing the structure of the station.** Above right **The ticket hall by day and night, with floodlighting from the passimeter roof. Left Detail of the lighting beacon.**

The designers provided Enfield West with a generously sized station building and forecourt for buses, anticipating a high volume of traffic from the new residential developments. Around the forecourt a low brick wall carries railings whose supports are fashioned with the recurring Holden motif of a stepped, plant-like form – also found in the decoration at 55 Broadway and the University of London. Combined shelters and lighting standards stood at each end of the forecourt.

Initially referred to as 'East Barnet', the name Enfield West was chosen for the station now known as Oakwood as it was expected that Enfield would be the main source of traffic, although it was some distance from the station.[12]

C.H. James carried out the design with Adams, Holden & Pearson as consulting architects. The ticket hall tower was of considerable size, the dimensions and position of the hall dictated by the spacing and span of the beams carrying the building over the railway. The external brickwork was of 'No. 2 light brown' Welsh pressed bricks set back at the seventh course above a plinth of polished grey granite, and the tower was finished in Buckinghamshire multi-coloured facings. Around the cornice of the lower buildings was a band of green tiles. Beneath the canopy a bell was fixed which rang to notify bus conductors to await passengers from an approaching northbound train.

Inside the canopied area was an enclosed waiting space with a bench at each end. Swing doors were fitted to the main entrance and exit points to reduce the draughts which had been found to cause problems in some of Holden's earlier buildings for the Underground, and these doors were used wherever possible in future stations. Black glazed bricks with white pointing lined the hall up to a height of 7ft 9ins, and above the ring beam walls were of light brown brick. Shopfronts were of bronze and light green painted wood. At the rear of the hall was a gallery with steps down to the single island platform. The ends of the gallery have since been closed off and converted into offices. The station is located some 300ft above sea level and a plaque announcing this claim – 'the highest point in Europe in a direct line west of the Ural Mountains of Russia' – was originally fixed in the ticket hall.

The vestibule and waiting area inside the station entrance.

Designed by Stanley Heaps, the concrete platform canopy was cantilevered from a single row of piers. Seats built between the piers were fitted with glass screens as windbreaks. The piers, staircase and nameboard plinths were painted in three colours: black skirting, elephant grey dado and green waistband. The colour scheme for the canopies also included yellow and pale primrose. On the outer sides of the tracks stood concrete poster hoardings with the poster spaces picked out in light green tiles. The signal cabin a short distance from the station was designed by Harold G. Cherry.[13]

Plans for a London General Omnibus Company garage and stand next to the station were deposited before Southgate Council in March 1933 and gained approval, but the project did not come to fruition. The station became a Grade II listed building in 1971.

Top **Enfield West platform.**
Above **Coat of arms of Southgate Urban District Council, granted to the borough in July 1933 and fixed to platform canopy supports at Enfield West.** Left **Ticket hall at night, with coffered pattern of roof slabs clearly discernible.**

Above left **The modest road entrance, enclosing stairs and waiting area for bus passengers.**

Above right **Concourse seating area.**

Cockfosters became the ultimate northern terminus of the Piccadilly line when the final extension was opened on 31st July 1933 under the auspices of the newly-created London Passenger Transport Board. This part of north Middlesex was still rural until after the railway arrived and Cockfosters little more than a hamlet.

There had been various proposals for the station to form the focal point of a new suburb, but although some development eventually took place to the south and west, the area to the north and east was subsequently protected as part of the London Green Belt. One early sketch shows a building with hexagonal ticket hall and flanking shops, similar in plan to the station at Hounslow West, facing north-west onto a corner site formed by a bus pull-in and triangular green. A second scheme was for a surface ticket hall on the south side of the station fronting onto a bus stand and car park with control tower and access to the stand from a circus laid out in the main road. A drawing dated October 1932 shows an entrance building with shops either side and a similar structure on the opposite side of the road. By November a tower had been added at each end of the shops, but after the shops had been set aside for a later stage of the development (never to be executed) the towers were moved in to the ends of the entrance structure – thus resulting in the final design.

The majority of the station is situated in a shallow cutting at an angle to the main road. At street level a low building of multi-coloured facing bricks forms a waiting shelter and entrance with double stairways down to the sub-surface concourse. Beneath the canopy a light box displayed the station name in white letters on a grey ground. There is a small entrance from the car park north of the station, and a third entrance intended to serve the future bus yard was built on the south side; this is now out of use. On the west side of Cockfosters Road behind a bus pull-in a (temporary) wood and glass shelter encloses two double staircases down to a subway for the ticket hall.

There were plans to develop the station site further. In 1934 the main entrance at road level was to have a second storey added and be flanked on either side by shops. One sketch shows the shops set back behind colonnades with a large cinema and flats over the subway entrance on the other side of Cockfosters Road.

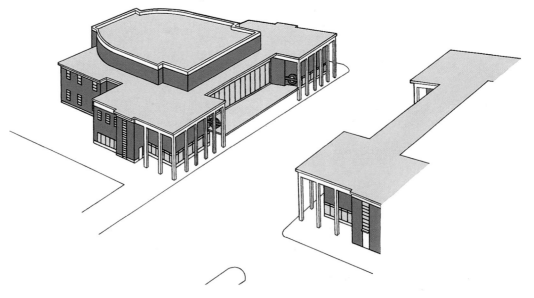

The alignment of road and rail approaches was developed to produce a ticket hall concourse of pentagonal plan. Reinforced concrete was used for the entire concourse and trainshed, and the board-marks left exposed; the presentation of concrete in such a frank manner was a new departure in this country at the time. Siting of the station in partial cutting required that most daylight enter the building from above, and so the roof was built in two levels with an arrangement of inclined clerestory windows running its full 230ft length and terminating in an apex above the concourse. Pavement lights were set into the lower roof above the perimeter of the concourse and the outer platform faces.

Concourse, subway and trainshed were decorated in yellow, grey, dark green and black against the natural colour of the concrete and plaster. *The Architect & Building News* noted that 'this grey, yellow and black combination was effectively used by Mr Holden more than twenty years ago at Belgrave Children's Hospital'[14]. All facilities were grouped around the concourse, including offices for the station master and carriage examiner, a first aid room, a tobacconist and a newsagent.

Above left **Ticket hall concourse.**

Above right **The trainshed reinterpreted in concrete. This was to have been three bays longer than built, with a second entrance from the bus yard to a ticket hall over the platforms at the south-east end. The work was never carried out, but projecting concrete beams ready to meet the unbuilt section remain as evidence of the planned extension.**

A feature of the circulating area was the combined clock and train departure indicator suspended from the roof. Three tracks served four platform faces. Concrete piers forming the legs of roof trusses were spaced in pairs along the two platforms and on the far side of the outer tracks in eight independent units 25ft long, this dimension being determined by the spacing of bullseye signs, which were mounted between the piers and needed to be at intervals equal to the length of one carriage. Suspended teak seats and concrete plinths for the bullseyes were mounted alternately between the twin piers. The nameboards were of uncommon design in that they did not have the white semicircles within the ring of the symbol, the natural colour of the plinth being used instead. The plinths were originally painted dark green around the signs and the full colour scheme has recently been restored.

At other locations the box form of the ticket hall tower was adapted to suit the exigencies of the site. A footbridge adjoins Sudbury Hill ticket hall, giving access to the platforms in cutting below; the reverse arrangement applies at Alperton, where the platform shelters are on an embankment, with stairs up from the ticket hall (a single 'up' escalator, now removed, was later installed on the eastbound side). In both cases the platform buildings are integrated into the overall design. Both stations were completed in 1932 and were followed in the next year by a similar structure at Acton Town.

The extensions and improvements to the Underground were widely reported in the architectural press. The Prince of Wales (afterwards Edward VIII) visited the works on 14th March 1933, riding from Piccadilly Circus to Manor House, and driving the train from there to Wood Green. Banners and bunting were draped over the exteriors of station buildings on the opening days. The Design and Industries Association looked over the Piccadilly extension on 20th June 1933, and the Royal Institute of British Architects made a visit on 9th October, conducted around the new works by Charles Holden and C.H. James. In a report on the visit, the writer noted 'the consummate skill that has been shown in the solution of every problem... That the directors of the Underground Railway should have so correlated every part of their organisation that everything from a poster or a doorknob to a complete station should so clearly express *Underground* [their italics] is an achievement of which they have good reason to be proud.'[15]

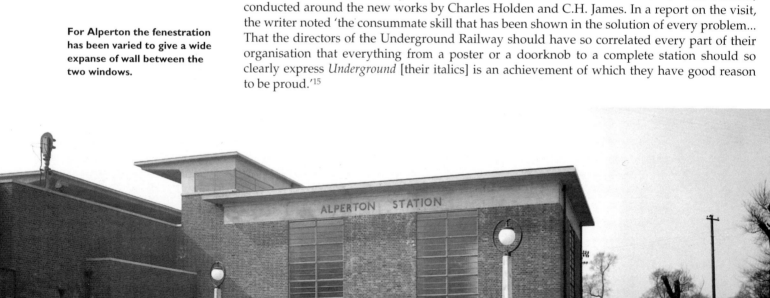

During this period of Underground extensions the Metropolitan Railway built what was to be its last new line before being taken over by the London Passenger Transport Board: a four-mile branch opened to the public on 10th December 1932 from Wembley Park to Stanmore with intermediate stations at Kingsbury and Canons Park (Queensbury opened in 1934).

When it came to providing stations for the Stanmore branch the Metropolitan Railway's architect Charles W. Clark chose to keep with a traditional building type he had used at Croxley and Watford. For Kingsbury and Stanmore he produced similar stations in red sandfaced brick with pitched roofs of multi-coloured tiles and dormer windows either side of a central gable enclosing the vaulted ticket hall ceiling. The style was to be used in simplified form for Northwood Hills (1933), his last work before being retired by the LPTB after it took over. Kingsbury and Stanmore booking offices (with 'hole-in-the-wall' ticket windows) were lined in cream and dark turquoise tiles, with oak joinery and red and beige linoleum.

At Acton Town the lower buildings were extended to provide an entrance from Bollo Lane. The ticket hall was lined with quarry tiles, and a system of footbridges and gangways separated passenger flows.

A domestic style was still appropriate for the comparatively rural areas served by the Stanmore branch.

The exterior of the rebuilt Highgate (now Archway) evolved through several striking prototypes to emerge as a variant of the Hammersmith (Queen Caroline Street) design, one in render, the other in stone. Both examples have now been demolished, the former in 1977, the latter in 1988/89.

The extension of the Piccadilly line beyond Hammersmith in 1932 necessitated considerable alterations to the former terminus and adjacent District station. Reconstruction work – to designs by Stanley A. Heaps – was started in December 1930 and substantially completed in June 1932. The dead-end tracks and platforms of the Piccadilly line were removed and replaced by temporary wooden platforms. A new covered way was dug under Hammersmith Broadway and Beadon Road and a major task included in the excavation works was the diversion of the Brook Green sewer.

Commissioned on 29th May 1931 the first new structure was a 43-lever signal cabin high up on the embankment above the westbound platforms. The cabin had a distinctive v-shaped oriel window and corner windows – popular Modernist details of the period. In the upper walls every fifth course of bricks was set-out to give a ribbed effect.

Platforms and footbridges were rebuilt using a steel frame encased in concrete with a dark grey aggregate of St Austell Granite grit, exposed by polishing. Precast concrete beams were used for the roofing.

Access from Queen Caroline Street was facilitated by the provision of an entrance with Portland stone façade completed in 1934. Behind the tall window with its stained glass bullseye a narrow void was floodlit at night to give the effect of a double-height ticket hall.

The main Broadway entrance was to have been reconstructed in similar style to the Queen Caroline Street frontage, with a wide loggia connected by a shop-lined passage to a

Upper left **Ticket hall and unglazed stairway at Hammersmith looking towards Ravenscourt Park.** Lower left **Ordered arrangement of signage and information integrated with structure and furniture (see note 16 in appendix). Miniature bullseye nameboards were fixed to other piers, mounted at different heights to be visible from within District and Piccadilly cars.** Upper right **Work on replacing the 1906 station and lifts at Knightsbridge began in 1930, and a new sub-surface ticket hall opened on 18th February 1934 with escalators to the old platforms. A second entrance opposite Harrods store came into use on 30th July the same year, with its own ticket hall, escalators and a long, shop-lined arcade. Note the decorative grille to reduce draughts through the entrance.** Lower right **Black bands in the platform tiling were set against a glaze called 'new biscuit cream' – more of a custard yellow, introduced in 1934 and used at a limited number of sites including Chancery Lane and St Pauls.**

rectangular ticket hall. Plans were changed, and instead of the loggia the corridor was made shorter to provide additional space in the ticket hall, and the 1906 frontage retained. This stage of the reconstruction was completed during 1933-34. Walls, columns, and the ceiling of the new ticket hall roof were of exposed concrete, with grey paint up to door height.

Positioning of the District and Piccadilly tracks each side of new island platforms made possible direct interchange between trains. Half way along each platform, exit stairs and a footbridge linked with a gallery running along the southern side of the station back to the ticket hall. Further stairs and a covered way served the Talgarth Road entrance and the exit to Butterwick bus and trolleybus station added in 1958.

On the front of Boston Manor's tower a casement of steel and reeded glass panels formed a sky sign to identify the location of the railway by night. Almost immediately the station opened, opal glass was fitted instead as it gave more concentrated light. The upper portion of the tower was faced with frost proof biscuit-cream faience. Below the entrance canopy an illuminated frieze displayed the station name in grey on a white ground. In line with changing trends, windows in this building had fewer glazing bars than foregoing Underground stations.

Right **The former de Volharding department store, The Hague, Netherlands.**

Far right **Erich Richter's 1928 design for a tramway waiting hall and cafe at Berlin Tempelhof Airport (from *Bauwelt* magazine).**

In late 1932 work started on demolition of the old street-level buildings at Boston Manor to make space for rail access to the new Northfields rolling stock depot. The rebuilt station came into use on Sunday 25th March 1934. The depot approach reduced the width of the site, so the station was extended on girders over the tracks. The arrangement of prominent tower and low level buildings was a departure from the established 'box' form, and was chosen to harmonise with the surrounding housing whilst still being clearly visible from a distance. The tower as an advertising feature had been particularly popular with Dutch and German architects: a similar lighting tower had been used in 1928 on the de Volharding co-operative store at the Hague, Holland (by J.W.E. Buys with J.B. Lursen), and an unexecuted design also of 1928 for a tramway waiting hall by Erich Richter bears some formal similarities to Boston Manor[17]. To save space, staff rooms were at platform level under the stairs. There was little change to the platform structures, where the District Railway valanced wooden canopies and now-disused signalbox remain to this day.

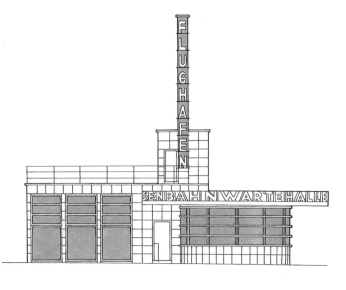

The Osterley exterior was of grey-brown Buckinghamshire facings laid in monk bond. Tubular steel columns carried the clerestory, kiosk and footbridge roofs to give almost uninterrupted glazing. On top of the 70ft-high tower was placed a lighting beacon of concrete with pressed glass lenses set into it. This has been compared to Hildo Krop's sculpture for the former 'de Telegraaf' newspaper offices in Amsterdam (see illustration on page 77), although Charles Hutton, who worked on the design, has said that it was merely a structure to carry the lamp units, inspired by a natural form such as a cactus.

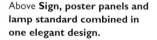

Above **Sign, poster panels and lamp standard combined in one elegant design.**

Left **Footbridge and eastbound platform, with clerestory sections to the canopy.**

As early as June 1931 it had been decided to relocate Osterley station further west at the side of the Great West Road, where housing and industrial developments were progressing rapidly. The road was then the busiest arterial route in London and a good potential source of traffic. A preliminary plan for the station – then identified as 'Osterley Park' – comprised a ticket hall tower of the 'box' type, but the final scheme by S.A. Heaps was devised on similar lines to Boston Manor to suit the housing of the area and yet be easily found by travellers. The rebuilt facility opened the same day as the new Boston Manor. Part of the shelter on the eastbound platform has since been enclosed as a waiting room. The passimeter was replaced by a new booking office in 1989. The station is a listed building. Awnings and retaining walls at the old station were demolished in 1957 but the road-level building still remains.

Top **In contrast to the domestic style for the other stations on the Stanmore branch of 1932, Charles Clark introduced modernistic forms and detailing at Canons Park. The ticket hall** above left **was located within the bridge abutment between the canopied entrances.** Above right **Another break from the traditional style was the 1931 rebuilding at the rather cramped Northwick Park site.** Right **Clark's last work for the Metropolitan Railway, carried out before he was retired by the London Passenger Transport Board, who had taken over his formerly independent employer and wished to pursue a different direction in design with their own architects.**

Arsenal (known as Gillespie Road until 31st October 1932) and Warren Street were both reconstructions of Leslie Green stations completed as part of the Underground's improvements of the early 1930s. Arsenal was rebuilt and enlarged around the existing structure with a rendered frontage to which a large mosaic bullseye was applied (compare this with the view on page 27). Inclined footways led to the platforms. The width of the façade was doubled by the acquisition and demolishing of an adjoining house.

Warren Street was relocated to the corner of Tottenham Court Road and Euston Road, with escalators replacing the lifts and a stone façade designed by Adams, Holden & Pearson carried out by Stanley Heaps, after a brick and stone design with a ticket hall drum similar to that at Chiswick Park, but with fourteen windows, had been rejected.

Attention to station lighting made the new stations of the 1920s and 1930s stand out not only during the day but also at night.

South Wimbledon station shortly after completion. Some of the stations on this line had searchlights mounted on the roof for additional publicity.

Before the advent of the electric light there was little to attract people into the centre of towns at night. When government building restrictions were lifted after World War One large cinemas began to appear in many towns and the proprietors of these picture houses realised that the buildings themselves could be used as advertisements to attract custom after dark; the idea was developed to a great extent in Germany. Powerful floodlighting equipment became available in the 1920s, and the completion of the National Grid in the early 1930s brought cheap electricity to many areas. The stations of the Underground Group's Morden extension and its 55 Broadway headquarters building were some of the first new structures to feature floodlighting.

During the Faraday Centenary celebrations of 1931 many noted buildings in London were floodlit for the first time and architects began to see the potential of designing façades with the effects of night-time illumination in mind. The contrast of bright areas and shadows with varying surface textures could be manipulated to give striking and dramatic effects. Stone or faience exteriors with reflective surfaces, smooth planes and clean lines were found to benefit best from floodlighting. Charles Holden designed his stations to be attractive by day and night, with illuminated signs or other features where they would assist the advertisement of the railway.

An understanding of light's psychological effects came to be appreciated: a yellowish glow was welcoming, imparting a sense of warmth and comfort. At Wood Green it was found that the brick walls reflected too much of the harsh white light, so red filters were fitted to the lamps.

WOOD GREEN STATION

Wood Green – a later variant on the curved façade.

By carefully selecting the interior finishes for a building and the lighting units to be fitted, a pleasing and attractive environment could be created. Ceilings of Underground stations were finished in muted colours, and walls similarly treated or faced in reflective materials such as faience and glazed brick. The use of large windows enabled interior lighting to become part of the façade at night, thereby providing an alternative to floodlighting. In the 1930s the Underground was a pioneer in the use of tungsten lighting for railway stations when the mainline companies still lit their stations with oil and gas. The designers worked closely with the General Electric Company to develop improved lighting; the power of the individual units was increased, but the real gain in illumination was made by using many more units together than was usual. At Hyde Park Corner and Marble Arch for example, continuous beams of lamps were mounted around the ticket hall ceilings.

Special opal glass shades were designed to suit particular applications, all based on the primary forms of cube, rectangle, sphere and cylinder. The German Bauhaus had used spherical lamp fittings from the early 1920s and they became common in England towards the end of the decade. Opal glass was a comparatively new innovation for the period, giving a good diffuse light without reducing the efficiency of the tungsten bulb. The shades were given names such as 'Equiluxo' – an 18in x 12in fitting used in the lighting beacon at Osterley and elsewhere; 'Doric' – with fluted sides; and 'Britalux' – a cylindrical shade often used under platform canopies. Smaller cubic and globe fittings were made for various applications. Spherical pendant lamps found greater use from the middle of the 1930s for ticket halls, trainsheds and stairwells.

Enfield West, since renamed Oakwood.

Holden also designed bronze column uplighters with plaster reflector shades that threw light upward and outward onto the walls and ceiling, giving a bright and evenly lit interior without glare (see page 76). Smaller uplighters with glass lenses were fitted to escalator balustrades. Later generations of lighting engineers considered the escalator uplighters inefficient – they did not give the intensity of illumination now required for public buildings – and prone to the accumulation of dirt; most of them have been removed and scrapped.

The standard mast-mounted lamp designed by Holden for the new stations was termed the 'parrot-ring' because of the way the opal 'Superlux' globe was suspended in a wrought-iron frame. A similar design was used by Holden for lights within the grounds of his University of London buildings.

Experimental fluorescent tubes were first introduced at Piccadilly Circus on 2nd October 1945. Subsequently they were fitted from the start in new buildings, and a major replacement programme continued throughout the 1960s and 1970s. Tubes were mounted without covers for maximum efficiency. In new works of the 1950s and 1960s the fluorescent tubes were recessed behind 'egg-crate' grilles, and in latter years polycarbonate covers have been used.

The carefully planned lighting of the pre-war and immediately post-war periods was integrated within the general design, but the subsequent installation of fluorescent strip lighting and associated trunking has spoilt many interiors by its insensitive application. Modern illumination equipment cannot give an impression of the night atmosphere present in the 1930s and 1940s Underground stations when first opened.

Top **Southgate**
Above **Boston Manor**

BUILDING FOR THE BOARD

Enlargement of Leicester Square station was in progress when the London Passenger Transport Board became the controlling authority for London's public transport in July 1933. The photographs show the Cranbourn Street and Little Newport Street entrances at Leicester Square, the latter now closed. The facing of pillars with granite and cream tile fillets would be used again by Holden for Uxbridge in 1938.

Facing page **The old station and lifts (see page 30) were closed on 29th April 1935, to be cleared and two new stairways built which came into use on 8th June 1936. These were decorated with brightly coloured tile bands and bullseye signs bearing the legend TRAINS. The escalators are seen with their original cast bronze pedestal uplighters, since removed. The ticket hall was based on the Piccadilly Circus layout.**

Rebuilding of Leicester Square station was first proposed in 1923, and high speed lifts were installed in 1926. Increasing traffic levels taxed the existing facilities, so an improvement programme was begun in May 1932 to enlarge the station with a concourse ticket hall beneath Charing Cross Road and Cranbourn Street. The 1906 building, the Crown Hotel and Hippodrome theatre were underpinned whilst the steel 'spider's web' frame of the ticket hall roof was assembled. New entrances were opened on the south-east corner of Cranbourn Street, beneath the Hippodrome, and on the north corner of Little Newport Street. Much use was made of polished Creetown granite and ultramarine blue tiling in the exterior finishings.

On the south corner of Cranbourn Street was constructed a building designed by Charles Holden, considered by critics to be one of his less successful works. A preliminary sketch shows sculptured figures mounted on the corners of the building at first and second floor levels. It was occupied by the 'Scotch Stores' public house with bars, dining room and accommodation for the publican. Architects William Petch and Edmund Auguste Fermaud handled the interior design.

All stairwells and the hall itself were faced in 18in x 12in biscuit-cream faience slabs. The perimeter of the painted plaster ceiling was stepped up and finished with wide, shallow coffers. Illuminated box signs were mounted on the ceiling of the hall and set into the architrave over escalators.

Concourse walls were lined with showcases and kiosks. A large W.H. Smith bookstall had its roller shutters decorated by Margaret Blundell with motifs depicting the various activities of the company[1]. On early plans a circular booking office was shown in the middle of the hall, but two conventional passimeters – one for each line – were installed and the central space used for showcases. This space is now occupied by the station control room.

A triple bank of escalators under Charing Cross Road descended 58ft to a circulating area above the Northern line platforms. A further three escalators under Cranbourn Street served the Piccadilly line. These were at the time the longest escalators on the system, with a rise of 80ft in a shaft 161ft long. From the lower landings there were passageways to the platforms. All low-level areas were finished in 'new biscuit-cream' tiles with ultramarine blue banding.

The new station was opened partially and temporarily for Cup Final traffic on 27th April 1935, and permanently on 4th May so that it could be used by the enormous crowds attending the Silver Jubilee celebrations for King George V.

Above **Panorama at South Harrow when new with site of the proposed shops in foreground, and an entrance (now closed) from the bus lay-by.**

Opposite top **Detail of north entrance and kiosk with bullseye showing that the station was constructed under new ownership.**

Opposite below **the platform canopies featured the innovation of tiling to the support piers. In place of clerestory panels pavement lights were set into the roofs.**

With the western extension of Piccadilly services over the District line, South Harrow station was rebuilt in a more central position adjacent to the bridge over Northolt Road, on a site formerly occupied by a small London General Omnibus Company garage. Reconstruction work was completed on 5th July 1935.

As the tracks at this point were on an embankment the station was built on two levels. The first surviving scheme designed by Adams, Holden and Pearson was for a ticket hall tower of the Sudbury Town pattern with adjoining double-height buildings. The final design dates from February 1933, with the round-fronted shop added a little later. A separate block with cafe and three shop units was to have been sited on the corner island.

The ticket hall within the bridge abutments was accessed from three points: a double entrance direct from the street on either side of the railway and one from the bus waiting room to the north. Lower walls were faced in 'No.3 dark purple' Welsh pressed bricks and the upper walls in Essex handmade red bricks laid in Sussex bond. Many of the header bricks were burnt to a dark blue-grey colour – an effect which had been popular with eighteenth century builders working in Flemish bond.

Biscuit-cream faience slabs with ultramarine blue banding lined the ticket hall, and fluted biscuit-cream tiles edged in blue were set into the ring beam. Clerestory windows lit the ends of the ticket hall and pavement lights were set into the roof over the central area.

From each end of the booking hall stairs led up to the platforms. It had been found that the lower surfaces of concrete structures became discoloured by grease and scuff marks from passengers' clothing and shoes; the concrete was almost impossible to clean because of its porous nature, so the solution was found of applying a hard-wearing tile facing. At South Harrow the canopy supporting piers were encased with small brown-black quarry tiles set in a white mortar. This treatment had already been used for the ticket halls at Acton Town and Queensbury and would be repeated at other stations with concrete canopy supports such as Rayners Lane, Harrow-on-the-Hill and Highgate. (At stations reconstructed towards the end of the decade the uprights only were clad in concrete or terrazzo to improve their appearance; after the war the stanchions were merely painted).

South Harrow Market occupies eight arches of the railway viaduct west of the station and at the time of rebuilding the market entrances were given canopies similar to those of the station opposite.

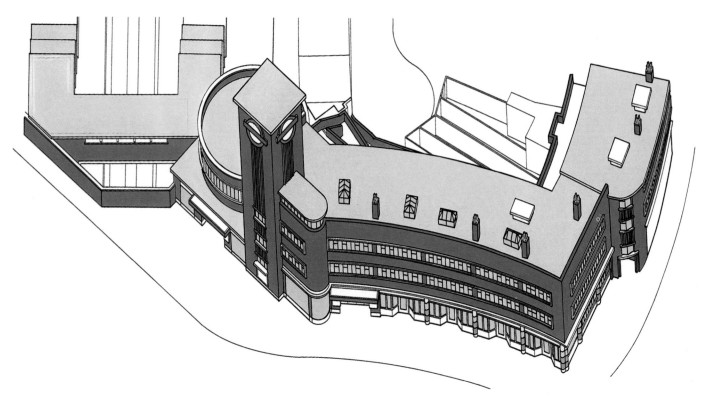

Axonometric of Park Royal showing proposed part-additional floor against tower and parapet to ticket hall drum as suggested by the Underground Architect.

Opposite page top **The high tower dominates the Western Avenue for some distance in either direction, leaving no doubt as to the presence of the station. Flats occupy the two floors above the shops, seen here before letting.**

Opposite page bottom left **Rendering of the new station by Felix Lander.** Opposite page bottom right **View of the ticket hall with distinctive cantilever supports which differ from the standard approach established by Holden for these suburban stations. The passimeter booking booth has been preserved.**

The building company Haymills had begun a speculative housing development known as the Hanger Hill Estate (after a nearby park and house) between north Ealing and Western Avenue in 1928. Architects for the estate were Herbert A. Welch (1889-1953) and Felix J. Lander, associated in the early stages with N.F. Cachemaille-Day (1896-1976) who left the partnership before the project was completed. Welch had worked on various housing estates in north London which established a pattern for suburban domestic architecture during the 1930s. It was in the interests of the developers that a railway station be located nearby – many people at this time did not have private cars – and they offered London Transport free land for the purpose on the condition that the station be designed by the same architects to harmonise the buildings with the rest of the development. New platforms were built in the railway cutting south of the Western Avenue overbridge and a temporary Park Royal station opened 6th July 1931, the 1903 Park Royal and Twyford Abbey station closing the previous evening.

The permanent station and its associated buildings designed by Felix Lander came into use on 1st March 1936. The structure was in the general character of contemporary Underground design, and the architects had the advantage that Felix Lander had worked for a time in Charles Holden's office. The principal feature of the building was the 67ft-high tower with a vertical band of ribbed brick work and illuminated bullseye signs on its four faces. Concrete sills and canopy edges were fluted and the cornices to tower and ticket hall roofs were edged with bright blue tiles. Biscuit-cream faience slabs formed a skirting around the exterior.

Eight precast reinforced concrete cantilevers supported the domed roof of the 40ft-diameter ticket hall, and the ribbing motif was again applied here on the front face of the cantilevers.

The station served as the main entry point to the estate from Western Avenue, and a curved parade of shops was built fronting on to a bus pull-in and lawn area called Hanger Green. Pillars between each shop front were cased in ceramic tiles in four shades of brown, graduating from dark brown at the base to buff at the top. Along the side road – Corringway – a block of flats adjoined the shops. Opposite the shops a second series of buildings by the same architects consisted of a service station with offices over and the Park Royal Hotel. The first floor front had large windows separated by piers of spirally laid bricks, the pattern of which was picked up in the tile cladding of the piers to the service station.

Along the front of the ground floor wall certain brick courses were set-out: this was a feature frequently employed by Herbert Welch and it may be seen repeated in many of the individual houses along Corringway, also by the architects. Behind the triangular green forming the centre of the estate was Hanger Court – the main block of thirty flats, built in a distinctive style with outside stairways up to the first floor entrances.

Aerial view of Earl's Court looking north-east from Warwick Road toward the trainshed of 1878, with the new ticket hall in the right foreground, and gallery leading back to the exhibition ticket hall on the right of the footbridge.

Opposite page **Warwick Road ticket hall with custom-built passimeter. The tile frieze would be used again by Heaps at St John's Wood. At the end of the gallery can be seen the passimeters provided in the rush hall opened on exhibition days to handle the extra traffic.**

An 11.25 acre triangular site between the railway lines west of Earl's Court station and Warwick Road had been used for public displays of various kinds since 1887 and in the early 1930s it was selected as the location for a new purpose-built exhibition hall designed by C. Howard Crane.

Improvement of the dilapidated accommodation at the Warwick Road end of Earl's Court station had been under consideration since at least 1932, and with the exhibition hall development an enlarged modern facility was required. Stanley Heaps designed a circular ticket hall with a round passimeter booth, and inside the building beneath the clerestory window the ring beam was inset with a frieze of ultramarine blue, grey, black and biscuit-cream tiles.

The old covered way was replaced by an unglazed gallery immediately to the north. At the platform end of the gallery an auxiliary ticket hall with three passimeters was provided to deal with the large crowds during exhibition periods.

The footbridge connecting the former gallery and platforms was replaced by a steel and brick glazed structure which also gave access to the gallery along the north side of the station to the Earl's Court Road ticket hall. Dark red Welsh pressed facing bricks were used throughout the reconstruction.

Other new works made for more direct links between the station and new exhibition hall. A circulating area under the platform 1 and 2 island at the head of the Piccadilly line escalators was linked by a subway to platforms 3 and 4 and an additional subway at the west end of the station. A new subway from this circulating area was driven beneath the eastbound tracks to the north side, passing under Warwick Road to two escalators which rose directly into a ticket hall adjoining the concourse in the basement of the exhibition building. Stairwells, subways and halls were finished in biscuit-cream faience slabs with banding of bright blue tiles. The ticket halls, subways and other new works opened on 14th October 1937.

The umbrella roof over the west end of the station was replaced by two new canopies with uprights encased in concrete containing a black grit aggregate.

In the mid-1960s a superstructure was added over the Warwick Road entrance for a new signal and electrical control room. The passimeters were removed and the second ticket hall rebuilt to contain offices. The exhibition hall escalator shaft of 1937 retains its original bronze uplighters.

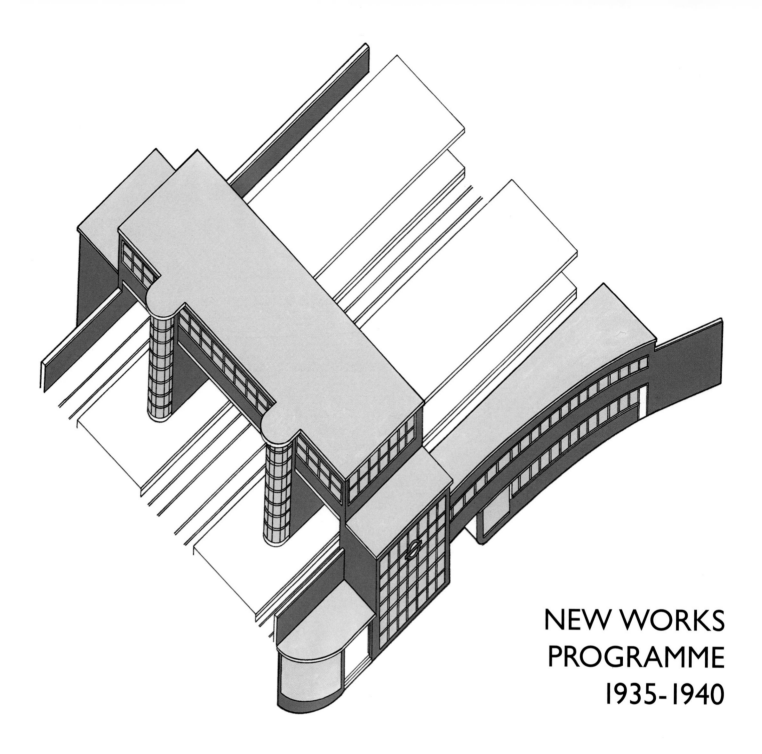

NEW WORKS
PROGRAMME
1935-1940

An early proposal for the new station at East Finchley, with a large area of glass in the main façade. This feature was also included in schemes for Eastcote, Hillingdon, Ruislip Manor and Redbridge – all designed circa 1937-8.

The New Works Programme – estimated to cost some £40 million underwritten by Treasury guarantee – was published on 5th June 1935 and outlined a series of improvements and extensions to the London Transport system. Included in the scheme was the projection of Northern line services over electrified branches formerly operated as part of the London & North Eastern Railway (LNER) suburban network – the same steam-operated branches that had precipitated the extension of the Piccadilly line earlier in the decade. From Archway new tubes would be excavated through Highgate to East Finchley for Northern line trains to run on to High Barnet and via Edgware to a new ultimate terminus at Bushey Heath. Northern City line trains were to be extended from Drayton Park to Alexandra Palace through the existing LNER high-level station at Highgate, where interchange with the Northern line tube would be possible. Bakerloo services would be extended in new tube to Finchley Road and thence over existing tracks to Stanmore. Facilities on the Uxbridge branch of the Metropolitan line would be modernised or reconstructed, and various other stations rebuilt. Central line extensions were also part of the programme but none opened until after the war and these are discussed in the next chapter.

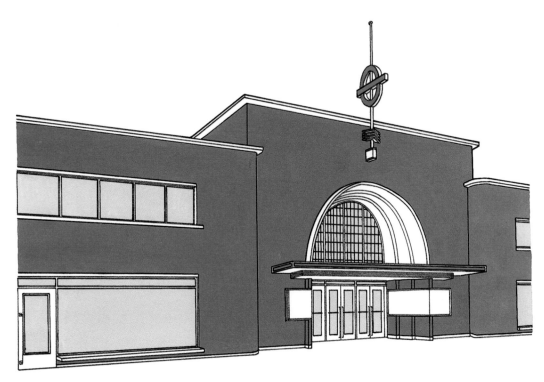

Above and below **Early schemes by the Underground Architect for Rayners Lane, one with an interesting treatment to the concrete window surround, and the other a new approach to the box form, pre-empting the final design in the way it stood forward of the building line.**

The Metropolitan's own Country Estates Company began to develop the area around Rayners Lane halt with its 'Harrow Garden Village' in 1929. In June of the same year the Underground's Managing Director Frank Pick proposed to the Metropolitan Railway that Rayners Lane be reconstructed as a joint station. After differences over funding of the project negotiations were restarted in 1931 when it was suggested that Rayners Lane have two 420ft island platforms and a single reversing spur. The station buildings would be designed by the Metropolitan's architect Charles W. Clark in similar style to his structures for the Stanmore branch. There were also some negotiations with the County Council over widening of the road bridge which delayed action beyond 1933.

House building around the station continued relentlessly and produced an enormous rise in passenger traffic which made reconstruction a necessity. On 14th March 1935 a temporary wooden booking office came into use and a brick footbridge and cycle store were erected for incorporation into the future building, whilst the old structures were demolished. Two preliminary schemes were devised by the London Transport architect's office. A December 1935 sketch shows a box-type ticket hall conforming to the building line with semi-circular window to the front and a high clerestory on the other three sides. A drawing of April 1936 shows another 'box' type ticket hall, this time projecting from the building line with entrances in the north and south walls. Reginald H. Uren produced the final design under the supervision of Adams, Holden and Pearson and the station opened on 8th August 1938.

The ticket hall tower was notable for the way in which it projected to straddle the pavement, maximising passenger access and making the station more prominent at this point where the road rises to cross the railway. Exterior walls were of dark red 'Old English' sand-faced brick and Buckinghamshire multi-coloured facings. Between the round-fronted kiosks was a backlit map of the Underground system. When a new booking office was built in 1987 the north entrance was bricked up, despite opposition from conservation groups. Blue-black enamelled bricks lined the ticket hall walls, with multi-coloured bricks above the ring beam. All visible concrete had a coarse aggregate of Portland stone. The arrangement of roof beams formed 110 small coffers in the ceiling.

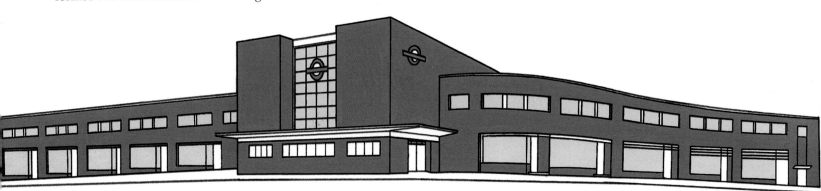

Rayners Lane station as built. Double-height shops were planned by the architects for each side of the main building but not started. Platform buildings were of red sandfaced brick, with round ended waiting rooms and staff facilities under the stairs. On the open sections of platform the concrete standards were spaced at closer intervals than was usual in railway practice to give better lighting.

View towards South Harrow. The ticket hall forms an imposing mass when seen from rail level.

As part of the Uxbridge line improvements it was decided to resite the terminal station closer to the town centre. Various schemes were drawn up for the design of the new station, which would be London Transport's last big terminus, and completion was delayed for some time. One 1934 plan was for a ticket hall midway between York Road and High Street with a short arcade and a direct approach from Belmont Road. A second scheme proposed a terminal on the eastern side of a circus in York Road, with a longer shop-lined arcade called 'Station Avenue' leading to a semi-circular parade – 'Market Circus' – and a bus station in the High Street opposite the Market House.

Plans for the building itself also underwent some development. A drawing dated 23rd March 1936 shows a two-storey façade with the first floor set back and a central glass-fronted ticket hall some two and a half storeys high. The hall would be arranged to a Y-plan with the fork of the Y forming a concourse to the trainshed. In a sketch made six months later a similar building has low wings extending from each end of the façade.[1]

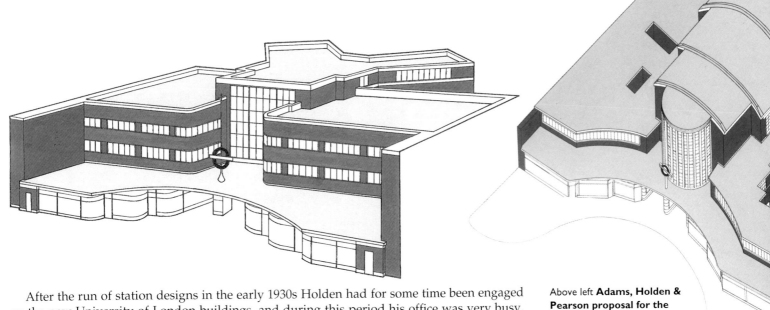

Above left **Adams, Holden & Pearson proposal for the terminus at Uxbridge of 1936.**

Above right **Leonard Bucknell's imposing but costly scheme of the following year – both prepared before economies in construction expenses and time became pressing.**

After the run of station designs in the early 1930s Holden had for some time been engaged on the new University of London buildings, and during this period his office was very busy, so the project was passed to Leonard H. Bucknell for completion and full design drawings were produced in January 1937. The low wings were now omitted and the ticket hall given a bow window with concrete mullions. The wide, arched trainshed had been a stipulation of the original requirements, and work was delayed because a decision could not be reached on the type of roof to be used for the 85ft span; laminated pine truss supports were considered, and reinforced concrete was another possibility.

The cost of Bucknell's design was found to be too high and upon looking into the matter Frank Pick found that the work had not been done by Holden's office – a condition of their original agreement. Pick wrote to Holden in April in 1937 expressing his concern that the design work had been 'farmed out' to other architects.[2] Pick proposed that if Holden could not supervise the work personally then no further work be passed to him. Holden conceded to Pick, indicating that he too was disappointed with the initial designs, but making the point that although other architects had undertaken the work he had himself set out the general guidelines to each and was still monitoring progress.[3] Pick then issued instructions that no new work be given to Holden's office unless he was to personally deal with it. After the resolution of this situation two new stations on the Northern line extension from Edgware to Aldenham (later called Bushey Heath) were entrusted to Adams, Holden and Pearson, namely the terminal itself and Elstree South. If Holden was unable to take on the work then it was to be passed to Raymond McGrath (1903-1977). In the event the war intervened and the extension was not made, although some designs had been completed.

By November 1937 Pick and Holden had reached an agreement, and in the meantime a new design for Uxbridge had been approved. The trainshed was now to be similar to that at Cockfosters, with the roof raised to accommodate the full-size loading gauge of the Metropolitan line rolling stock, and to give a more spacious interior.

The new station at Uxbridge opened to the public on 4th December 1938 and faced a forecourt which at the time of this view had been wired up as a trolleybus turning circle. The forecourt is now paved over for pedestrians.

Above **Forecourt sign.**

Above right **After the more expensive plans had been ruled out, the concourse and trainshed were based on an adaptation of the design at Cockfosters. Uxbridge station was sited in partial cutting to permit direct access on a single level from the street to the platforms.**

Below **Platform sign and first and second artworks for the stained glass panels (unused) by Ervin Bossányi.**

Below right **Centre of the façade, with gap to admit light to the stained glass above the canopy and large enamelled bronze letters for the station name.**

Bottom right **Full window installed in the ticket hall.**

Ground floor shopfronts were faced in light grey granite with a black granite skirting. Above a narrow canopy the first floor was of brown-grey brick, with a central opening which permitted light to reach stained glass panels set in the end wall of the ticket hall. Wing walls at each side of the opening on brick piers carried scuptures by Joseph Armitage based on stylised railway wheels and leafsprings. The spaces between the piers and the main walls were filled-in sometime before the early 1950s. In the forecourt stands an Underground sign bearing the station and line names in illuminated boxes; this distinctive design was newly introduced at this time. The station opened on 4th December 1938.

Charles Holden had first commissioned the stained glass artist Ervin Bossányi to produce windows for his University of London buildings in 1936-37. For Uxbridge Bossányi was again employed, and initially produced an intricate design criticised by Frank Pick as 'rather too modernistic.'[4] Pick suggested windows depicting a bridge and oxen, under the impression that the town's name was derived from this subject. A study was then submitted by the artist, but it was found that the subject had no connection with the town, and Frank Pick proposed that the coats of arms of Uxbridge Urban District Council and the counties of Middlesex and Buckinghamshire be used instead, having recently been impressed by a visit to see Bossányi's windows at the University of London. Bossányi was disappointed that the final form of the commission did not give him much scope for his creativity, but the richly coloured glasses do introduce a traditional element into the otherwise stark modernity of the board-marked concrete structure, and the installation of his work in a railway station was in keeping with Bossányi's ideal of public service. The windows were fitted some time after the station had opened, and for safety were removed during the War, being replaced in January 1949.[5]

By the 1930s sufficient residential growth had occurred at Ruislip Manor to warrant the halt of 1912 being rebuilt, and design work was begun in mid-1936 by Adams, Holden & Pearson who produced several preliminary schemes. Drawings showed curved or straight frontages set back behind bus pull-ins with the stairwells expressed in various ways. The extensive use of glass to give even greater lightness to structures appears in other contemporary designs by Adams, Holden & Pearson for East Finchley and Redbridge stations.

As built the ticket hall was within the bridge abutments and flanked by shop units. Beneath a canopy which projected but a few inches from the frontage, recesses with curved walls shelter triple swing doors into the hall. Multi-red wirecut bricks were used for the building exterior and bridge abutments.

Ticket hall walls were tiled to full height in alternate bands of different shades of cream. Direction signs and a clock face with bright orange discs for counters were fired into the tiles.

Double-height stairwells lit by side windows and clerestories from the ticket hall led up to the platforms. At the half-landings the less agile could rest on recessed wooden benches.

Above **Ruislip Manor exterior and ticket hall. The ceramic-faced clock can be seen on the right in the interior view.**

Below **One of several early suggestions for Ruislip Manor, here including glass-enclosed stairwells and the projecting canopy which was to have been a characteristic of other rebuilt stations on this line.**

Bottom **Scheme for the reconstruction of Hillingdon circa 1936-38, not carried out. The rebuilt station of 1993 is described in a later chapter.**

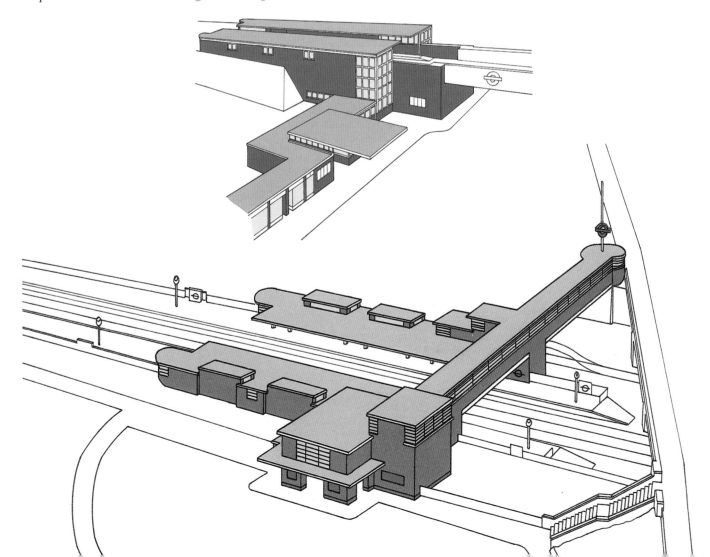

The north elevation of East Finchley was given over almost entirely to offices, the resulting mass contributing little to the design. Canopies appear thin and insubstantial in comparison to earlier examples, whilst redeeming features are the staircase enclosures and archer sculpture.

For the extension of the Northern line, East Finchley station was completely rebuilt to a design by Adams, Holden and Pearson with L. H. Bucknell. An early schematic for the station shows a main ticket hall on the north side of the railway with a single wide entrance; the hall would have been oblong with tapering sides. Staff facilities were to have adjoined the ticket hall at ground level facing onto a bus forecourt. At the other end of a subway to the platforms would be a second entrance for passengers from the general direction of Hampstead Garden Suburb, where Frank Pick himself lived at 15 Wildwood Road.

In a second plan the ticket hall was rectangular with an entrance offset to one side in a curved façade (see page 128). The yardmaster's office and trainmen's rooms were now to be housed in a large block on the south side. The third design, approved for construction in late 1938, also featured a curved frontage to the north and a small ticket hall to the south; staff accommodation was relocated to a bridge above the platforms. Most of the structures were finished in Buckinghamshire multi-coloured facings laid in staggered English bond to give a diaper effect; the south side building was faced in multi-red wirecut bricks.

As built the north façade was straight; to give the impression of a double-height ticket hall a small vestibule was provided behind the main window with its stained glass London Transport and LNER devices (the latter symbol has since been removed). The preliminary design sketch showed that a much larger area of glass had been proposed. Biscuit-cream tiles lined the interior up to door height with narrow bands of pale pinkish-brown tiles as a skirting and frieze. Offices and a kiosk were provided in the block next to the hall. In the octagonal south hall was a second passimeter, a bookstall and passengers' lavatories. A new subway built alongside the existing one linked the halls and stairways to the two island platforms. Despite the front vestibule, the low ceilings of the ticket hall and subway give a generally dark and cramped feeling to the interior, and the station is considered to be one of the less successful designs.

The single storey platform buildings were of concrete, clad to door height with biscuit-cream tiles skirted with a green band and capped with black and yellow bands. To protect passengers from the elements in this exposed location, brick screen walls were built with reinforced-concrete canopies across the outer tracks. The main canopies had an arrangement of clerestory windows. Spiral stairways enclosed in steel and glass towers led up to offices and a staff mess room on the overbridge. The stairways may be compared to those used by Walter Gropius for his factory building at the 1914 Werkbund exhibition.

The station came into use on 3rd July 1939. It is now a listed building; in 1989 the main ticket hall was rebuilt and the south hall passimeter removed.

Staff offices are suspended over the tracks. The smoke baffles for the then still running steam services can be seen between the towers.

Below left **Eric Aumonier at work on his archer sculpture for East Finchley. This figure formed part of a pre-war scheme to designate various new or rebuilt stations by the use of symbols referring to local historical associations. The scheme was stopped short by the war, leaving the archer as the sole completed work (see note 6 in appendix). The choice of this figure was a reference to the ancient hunting grounds in the district, and it is also an appropriate symbol for direct and speedy travel by electric train, pointing assertively towards the metropolis. The archer's angular forms are reminiscent of the carvings of ancient Asian and South American civilisations which had exerted a marked influence on progressive sculptors in the early part of this century. The statue was of sheet lead worked around Czechoslovakian beech supported internally by a steel and cast bronze armature; because of war-time materials restrictions the lead was recycled from salvaged scraps. The bow was of coppered and gilded English ash. In 1957, after damage from water seepage, the archer was recast (with minor changes in the modelling) and a new all-steel armature fitted. Below centre The second entrance on the Hampstead Garden Suburb** side of the station. Below right **Lamp standard and name sign.**

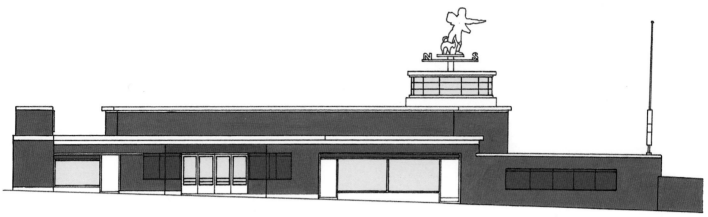

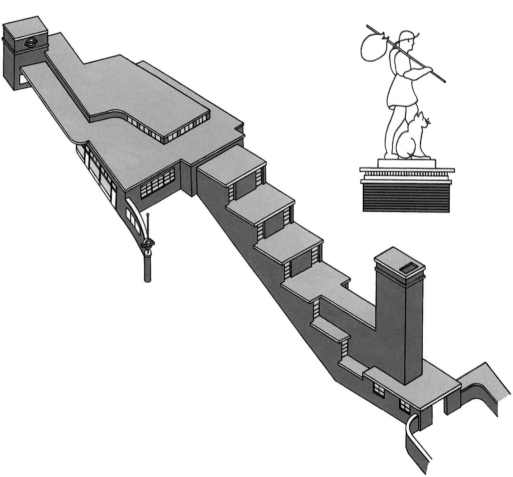

Above **Proposed elevation by Charles Holden of Archway Road entrance to Highgate with the figures of Dick Whittington and his cat on a weathervane.**

Right **Another scheme for the Archway Road entrance and escalator shaft with high vent tower which could have carried a sculpture group based on the Dick Whittington theme. The Priory Gardens entrance was planned to have been two storeys high with a kitchen and staff canteen on the first floor. The station opened on 19th January 1941. A single 'up' escalator to Archway Road was commissioned on 26th August 1957 in a simplified brick structure by Adams, Holden & Pearson.**

Below **Direction sign on escalator balustrade at platform level introduced circa 1935 and installed at certain sub-surface stations until the advent of fluorescent lighting.**

As the station at Highgate was to become an interchange point between the Northern line projected from Archway through East Finchley to High Barnet over the London & North Eastern Railway (LNER) and the extended Northern City line running over the LNER to Alexandra Palace, the surface buildings were reconstructed.

Early drawings made in 1935 by the London Transport architect's department proposed a hexagonal ticket hall below the LNER platforms with a long, sloping subway from Priory Gardens on the east side. A 1936 scheme included escalators descending at right-angles to Archway Road from a surface ticket hall. These plans were not considered satisfactory and the whole project was reviewed. During 1938 a new arrangement of ticket hall suspended over the surface lines with lifts down to the tube platforms was proposed, but in the executed design the architects returned to the layout of sub-surface ticket hall beneath the existing platforms, with escalators down to the tube platforms.

The old station was demolished and a waiting shelter erected on the island platform, with a central circulating area and stairs down to the new ticket hall.

Passengers from Archway Road could make their way to the station car park down a flight of steps built as a temporary measure when work on the upper escalator shaft was suspended, and in the car park there was an entrance stairwell.

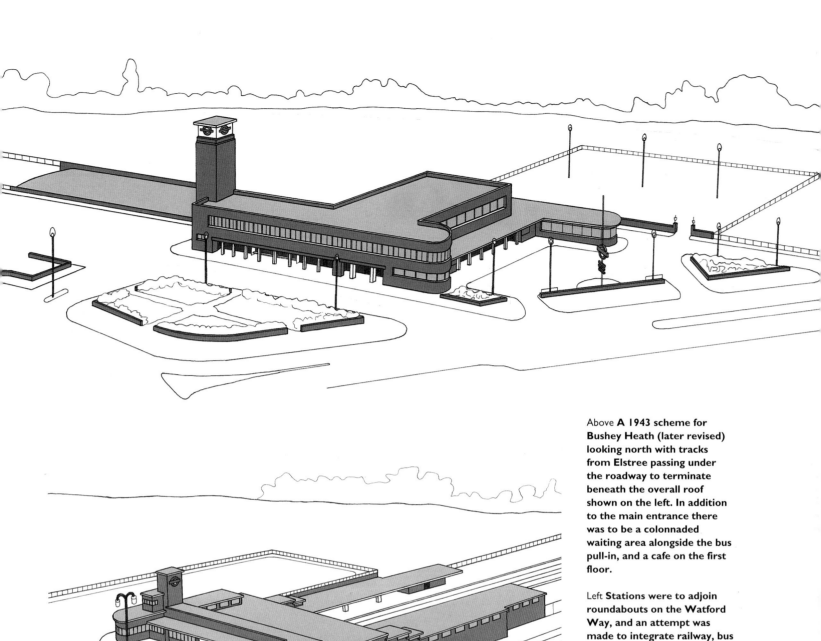

Above **A 1943 scheme for Bushey Heath (later revised) looking north with tracks from Elstree passing under the roadway to terminate beneath the overall roof shown on the left. In addition to the main entrance there was to be a colonnaded waiting area alongside the bus pull-in, and a cafe on the first floor.**

Left **Stations were to adjoin roundabouts on the Watford Way, and an attempt was made to integrate railway, bus and private car facilities. This is the second design for Elstree of 1944, enlarged from the original AHP scheme which had featured the sculpture of a roman soldier. The ticket hall would have been below road level to align it with a subway through the bridge to a bus shelter.**

Frank Pick charged Charles Holden with the design of Elstree South and Bushey Heath (initially Elstree and Aldenham) stations on the extension of the Northern line from Edgware due to be opened in 1940. Earthworks were in an advanced stage when development stopped after the outbreak of war. As it was intended to eventually complete the line, outline schemes continued to be prepared by the Underground architect (Holden's firm had ceased to be consulting architects in 1942), but the project was finally abandoned in the early 1950s in the light of continuing financial constraints and after Green Belt legislation prevented residential development of the area to be served. The building style proposed represented a late, if not the last, application of the general pattern established by Holden in the early 1930s, with the recurring motifs of towers, horizontal bands of windows, and round-ended waiting rooms.

Part of the 1935 New Works Programme included an extension of the Bakerloo tube from Baker Street to Finchley Road and on to Stanmore to relieve congestion on the Metropolitan main-line and the Edgware branch of the Northern line, facilitating through services to the West End from areas which had previously only had access to the City.

The two stations on the new tube were to be at St John's Wood and Swiss Cottage. Tunnelling was started in 1936, and the extension opened on 20th November 1939, when Bakerloo trains were projected through the new tube to Wembley Park and then over the former Metropolitan branch to Stanmore.

In compliance with a future road widening scheme, Stanley Heaps designed the new station for St John's Wood to be set back from the existing frontage lines, and the forecourt thus formed was given over to lawns and flower beds. Low wings containing a refreshment buffet and kiosks flanked the cylindrical ticket hall. The buffet later became a pub and after a period of disuse has now been rebuilt as a shop. A single entrance with swing doors was provided, although a 1936 schematic indicated twin entrances either side of a kiosk. The structural steel frame was designed to be strong enough to take a future superstructure. Exterior walls were of russet brown bricks on a plinth of polished black granite, and the entrance surround was faced with dark blue tiles.

Clerestory windows of thick glass lenses between concrete mullions lit the ticket hall. Faience slabs were carried up to the ring beam with golden brown bricks above. A feature in common with Heaps' ticket hall at Earl's Court was the ring beam inset; here the biscuit-cream tiles were edged in yellow and brown. Pale grey tiles were placed around the doorways and poster spaces and at skirting and door height. Instead of bronze, Queensland Silky Oak was used for shopfronts. The roof had a suspended ceiling of cream painted boards in a frame of metal T-sections painted apple green; this was an early application of such a ceiling in a London Underground station. The same finish was applied over the two escalators in an attempt to deal with problems of damp penetration. Spherical opal pendant lamps and 24in-diameter shallow opal dishes provided illumination at night. The difference in height between the front and rear of the escalator hall was accommodated by a sloping reinforced-concrete roof slab. Bullseye-shaped box lights mounted on columns served as direction signs as illustrated on page 136.

Platform tunnels incorporated an innovation: walls were finished in biscuit-cream tiles with the station name and a coloured bullseye symbol repeated in a continuous frieze at a height which could be seen from within the cars. Bands of yellow and brown tiles bordered the frieze. This feature was also employed at the new Swiss Cottage station, and subsequently at Highgate, King's Cross (Circle line), Bethnal Green, and the tube stations on the extension of the Central Line to Newbury Park. Bands of contrasting coloured tiles around archways were flush with the rest of the wall.

Above **A platform at St John's Wood showing the tiled name frieze introduced with this extension, and automatic vending machines set neatly into a recess.**

Left **Detail of tiled frieze: this feature may have derived from a similar idea used on the Berlin Underground in the 1920s. Such friezes were used at other sub-surface stations built over the next ten years including Highgate, King's Cross and those on the Central line extension to Newbury Park. The coloured bands were varied to suit individual decorative schemes.**

Right **Moulded low-relief tiles designed by Harold Stabler in 1936, and manufactured by Carter & Company of Poole. These were for random fixing to break up the monotony of plain tiled walls. Eighteen different patterns featured London Transport bullseye and griffin devices, historic landmarks, and heraldic emblems of the Home Counties. Their first application is believed to have been at Aldgate East, followed by St Paul's, the Bakerloo extension stations of 1939 and Bethnal Green, and they were used to a limited extent at Wanstead, Redbridge and Gants Hill after the war (see note 7 in the appendix).**

Below **Aldgate East, where rebuilding (completed 31st October 1938) to improve running on the District line required considerable engineering expertise.**

Above **Underground architect's impression of the proposed Harrow-on-the-Hill scheme, from the north.** Below left **North entrance as completed, with signal cabin towering above the shallow double-height entrance. Rationalisation through the austerity which was to affect much of the Underground's later pre-war extension plans has produced a more coherent – if less imposing – structure.** Below right **The ticket hall with built-in booking office on the right in place of a passimeter which had been the usual practice until this time.**

A surviving perspective illustration of Harrow-on-the-Hill station – served by both London Underground and British Rail services – shows a high tower to one side of the tracks and a signal cabin to the other, with a raised structure linking the two and serving as an integrated footbridge and ticket hall. The entrance façade may be compared with that at Uxbridge. In the final design the elements were combined and simplified, with the tower surmounted by the signal cabin as central feature, and the entrance structures much reduced in size for reasons of economy. In 1939 the south entrance was completed; here the narrow double-height vestibule was again used, this time rising clear of the main structure over the entrance stairs. Faience slabs lined the ticket hall, with bands of light green tiles as used at other Underground stations built during this period. Work at the station was completed in January 1943.

In 1938 London Transport expressed their concern at sluggish increases in traffic on the Piccadilly extensions and speculated that their expansion plans might be too optimistic.[8] Surviving records from 1939 show that the Underground wished to use simplified, plain block structures for future station developments. Delays to the new works caused by shortages of steel and labour during 1937 would have resulted in a congested programme for 1938-9, and some works were to be postponed until 1940; the intervention of the Second World War prevented these projects being started.

Below **Round ended waiting room at Kilburn, a feature first introduced at South Ealing in 1936 and employed throughout the reconstruction of the Metropolitan line in the late 1930s. The roof is of painted board – an economy measure which also made the canopies lighter. As part of the proposed Metropolitan line widening Pinner was to have been rebuilt circa 1939 with two island platforms featuring similar canopied structures, and a ticket hall within the bridge abutment. It was noted with some amusement in *The Builder* for 18th August 1939 that local residents had petitioned London Transport to ensure that the new station buildings conformed to the mediaeval character of this Middlesex village. In the event Pinner was spared this twentieth century intrusion – and improved railway facilities – when the war brought plans to a halt.**

Frank Pick retired prematurely from the London Passenger Transport Board in 1940 and died in 1941. In a letter written to Charles Holden in May 1940 he reflected on their past work and the future: 'It is indeed strange how the idea of a railway station still germinates to bring forth fresh flower and fruit. Just as you suppose you have analysed its functions and purposes completely and given them just expression, so something new springs into view and a fresh rationalisation of the elements in an architectural unity is demanded. We have not yet solved for example interchange in comfort and convenience between road and rail vehicles – Morden, Edgware, Osterley, South Harrow and Uxbridge are all deficient in this sense. So I can wish you joy as soon as this war is over in another attempt to catch up with requirements and add to the monuments of London suited to this industrial age.'[9]

Adams, Holden and Pearson had been retained as consulting architects to the Underground since the building of 55 Broadway. The arrangement was terminated in February 1942 because it was felt the expense could not be justified in wartime conditions. The Underground's own staff architect Stanley Heaps retired in 1943. After the war no appointment of a consulting architect was made although Adams, Holden and Pearson continued to be commissioned by the Underground for individual works, and for completion of projects started before the war.

CENTRAL LINE EXTENSIONS
EAST AND WEST

Opposite **General view of Loughton; although not part of the London Transport empire until the late 1940s, the styling is distinctly pre-war. A better understanding of the building's layout and construction of the false ceiling vault is given by the axonometric,** middle left, **based on the original plans. The low structure extending alongside the forecourt is the staff canteen. A footpath followed the railway at this point, and the designers neatly incorporated this into the new station by openings in the screen walls.**

Middle right **Ticket hall interior with subway to platforms behind the round vending machine, once a common feature of Underground ticket halls.**

Bottom left and right **The platform canopies and buildings. The light section of the canopy and the wide spacing of supports was achieved by deep reinforcing ribs on the upper surface. Pavement lights were let into the canopies.**

Between the wars rail transport in the area of expanding population in and east of the Lea Valley was mainly steam-worked and unable to meet the increasing demand for fast and reliable links with the City and through services to the West End. The London County Council's Becontree estate added to loadings on the main and Underground lines into London. Ilford station, the principal interchange point for road and rail services in the area, was inadequate for the volume of traffic using it. As early as the mid-1920s there had been moves to improve the transport situation, but it was only with the extension of the Central line as part of the New Works Programme 1935/40 that better conditions became a definite prospect. The 'North East London Electrification Scheme' and the 'Central London Railway North Eastern Extension' would see the Central line extended over existing LNER routes and new tube lines.

Stations in the centre were also to be rebuilt, the new St Paul's opening 1st January 1939. Work at Notting Hill Gate was stopped by the war.

John Murray Easton of the private practice Stanley Hall and Easton & Robertson was commissioned by the LNER on behalf of London Transport in September 1937 to redesign all stations north of Woodford to Ongar. Easton is not believed to have completed work for any stations other than Loughton. Both the LNER and London Transport supervised the design of this station, and the former company stipulated that whilst the building should embody the general spirit of London Transport style, it should have a character distinct from other Underground stations; the Underground's Frank Pick also had influence over the ultimate design. The station was set at the foot of the tree-lined railway embankment behind a large forecourt for buses. With a façade based on the theme of the then LNER London terminus of King's Cross, it was Easton's intention that a barrel vault would form the roof structure and be exposed; this was found to be impractical so a false ceiling of boards fixed to angle-iron brackets was enclosed in a steel, concrete and brick box. The original scheme had included a substation adjoining the building on the Buckhurst Hill side, but it was subsequently built a short distance from the Epping end of the platforms at the side of the tracks, as the original arrangement was considered unsuitable.

Specially made golden-brown bricks laid in monk bond were used for the walls with the upper edge of each brick rebated to give recessed joints; the same materials were used for the signal cabin and substation. The main window was of thick glass panels between concrete mullions in a reinforced concrete frame. Other windows were metal casements surrounded by a continuous concrete architrave – a design detail gaining popularity at this time. Low wings around a small courtyard on the south-east side of the station housed the train crew messroom, staff offices and cycle stores, and in the wing on the other side of the ticket hall was a railway telephone exchange. The vaulted ticket hall ceiling was rendered and was to have been fitted with a new type of sound-proofing tile introduced at the 1939 New York World's Fair (for which Easton and Robertson were the architects of the British Pavilion); these tiles were unavailable at the time of construction. It was a further stipulation of the LNER that ticket sales be made from a traditional wall-type booking office, and a passimeter was only installed after London Transport took control.

From the hall a subway led to stairs for the two island platforms. The distinctive concrete canopies with their rounded ends were cantilevered and had deep reinforcing webs on the upper side to support the curved profile. Pavement lights were set into the canopies. Casting of the canopies proved difficult because of the vibration caused by passing trains. The concrete work was finished in two shades of off-white 'Snowcem' cement paint tinted with grey and pink.

The station was opened by the LNER on 28th April 1940 but was not served by London Transport trains until 21st November 1948. London Transport redecorated the building upon taking it over, adding new signage and equipment. The Central line was further extended to Epping on 25th September 1949. A kitchen and canteen for busmen had been included in the original Loughton scheme and was later added on one side of the forecourt, built to a revised design.

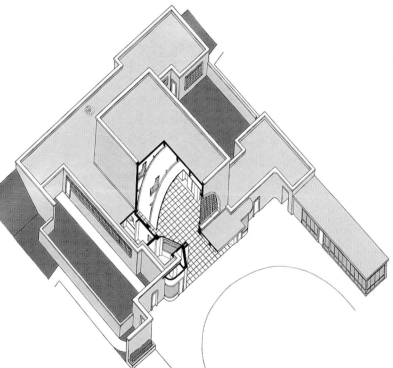

The eastern extensions would be balanced by a projection of the Central line from a junction with the Ealing Broadway branch at North Acton westward via GWR lines. The 'West London Electrification Scheme' would serve the developing factory and residential areas around Greenford and Ruislip, additionally taking some of the traffic which was by this time congesting the Piccadilly line. Design of the stations on the Central line western extension was the responsibility of the Great Western Railway's architecture department headed by Brian B. Lewis. In 1937 London Transport had approved the station schemes and were keen to press on with the work, but the Great Western delayed progress and plans were interrupted by the Second World War. The only structure completed to Lewis's original design was the small station at West Acton, which came into use in November 1940.

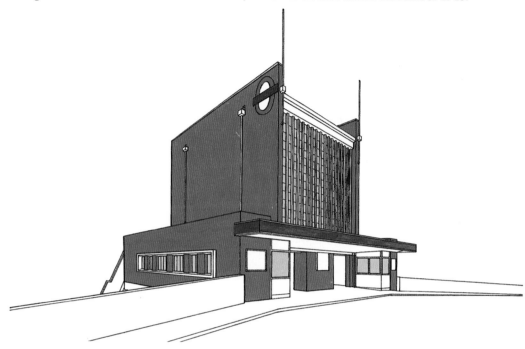

Perspective of Brian Lewis's West Acton – his only design completed in original form – full height glass and concrete windows between brick fin walls, looking a little lost in the leafy suburban surroundings.

In the immediate post-war period the need to rebuild and rehouse much of London placed a strain on the limited resources available. The cost of repairs after war damage to London Transport equipment reduced the funding for new works, and outstanding projects had to be assessed for priority. It was decided to complete the Central line extensions first, but with reductions made to the scale of the pre-war plans. This would be the last major London Transport project involving significant architectural work above ground and virtually the end of Adams, Holden & Pearson's relationship with the Underground. It was also the last work of the London Passenger Transport Board, which was nationalised from 1st January 1948, control passing to the London Transport Executive of the British Transport Commission.

From a junction with the existing line at Leytonstone some 2.5 miles of new tube were constructed beneath Eastern Avenue to join up with the LNER Hainault loop at Newbury Park. Works were suspended at the outbreak of war in 1939 and the tunnels under Eastern Avenue found alternative uses, partly as air-raid shelters, and from March 1942 as a tunnel factory for the manufacture of aircraft components.

The Newbury Park via Wanstead route had been planned to open in June 1941; platform tunnels and escalator shafts had been started, but no work had been done on the surface before the outbreak of war. Temporary surface buildings were erected for the use of the tunnel factory.

Plans for Redbridge station date from late 1935. At first it was to be named West Ilford, and then 'Red House' after a nearby tavern on Redbridge Lane. Subsequently the station took the name Red Bridge – after the crossing over the River Roding just outside Wanstead – and the name later became one word. Waste ground was used for the station site, and it was intended that the structure be set in a large forecourt bounded by a parade of shops to be continued into Redbridge Lane and Eastern Avenue. Work had not been started on the station buildings at the outbreak of war and facilities were erected over and around the platform stairwell to serve the tunnel factory. After the war steel shortages delayed construction of the permanent buildings. Work began in late 1946 and was completed towards the end of 1948, essentially to the pre-war Adams, Holden & Pearson design, but without the parade of shops.

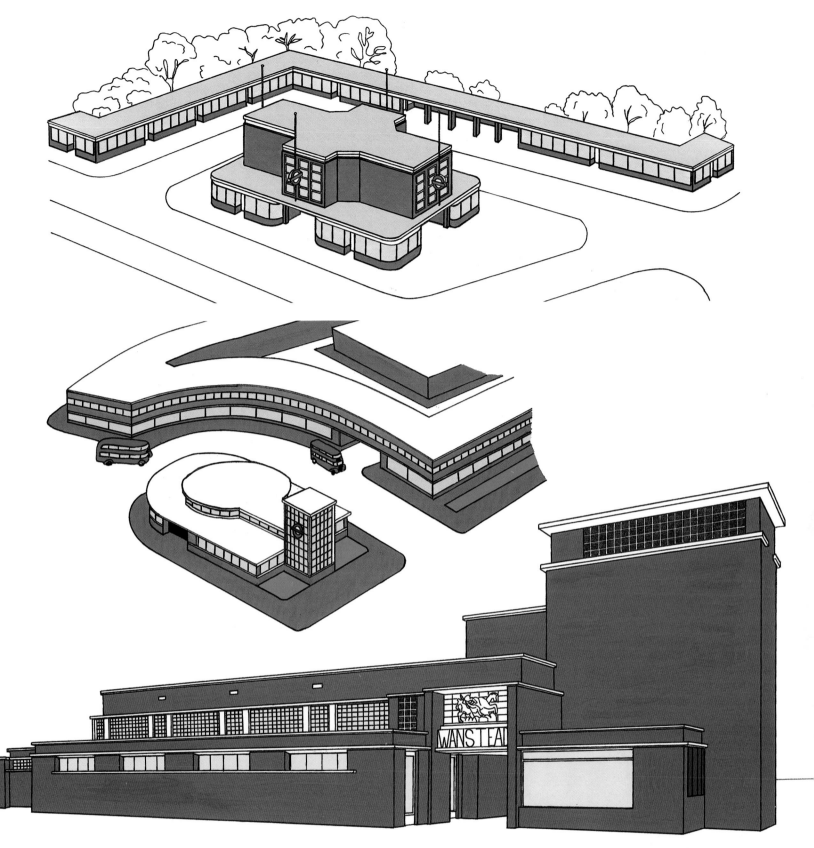

Top **This distinctive cruciform design was one of several schemes for Wanstead prepared during 1935-38. Other plans placed the station on the north-west corner of the Eastern Avenue/High Street intersection or included an integral cinema.** Middle **1937 Adams, Holden & Pearson proposal for Redbridge with an all-glass vent tower, which would have presented considerable cleaning problems in view of the dust blown up by passing trains. There was some mention of including a sculptured glass panel by Gertrude Hermes; this is further discussed in the section on Newbury Park. Another design utilised the stairwell roof as the podium for a footbridge over the main Eastern Avenue.** Above **Adams, Holden & Pearson design of 1939 for Wanstead, the first of four in which the final arrangement of tower and ticket hall was introduced. The grouped cubic forms and setbacks represent a move away from the simple block buildings of the early 1930s, and recall late works of H. P. Berlage such as the Gemeente Museum, The Hague. Above walls of Buckinghamshire facings a clerestory of glass blocks would light the hall, and over the entrances were to be placed carved and gilded mahogany signs depicting St George and the Dragon by Joseph Armitage. The composition was progressively simplified, and the final post-war scheme for a new structure had to be shelved, with the architects requested to use the shell of a building erected to serve the wartime tunnel factory – see page 147.**

Top left **Redbridge viewed from Eastern Avenue with the squat tower rising over the stairwell adjoining a circular ticket hall – similar in plan to Southgate – and staff rooms. This was one of the last Holden-designed stations, completed within economic restraints. The exterior was of Buckinghamshire facings on a plinth of concrete blocks, with a low percentage of red bricks to give a darker overall colour.**

Top right **Detail of decorative railings around stairwell roof, incorporating the bullseye symbol and 'LT' lettering.**

Middle left **A feature of the three tube stations on this extension were the clocks with bullseye symbols to mark the hours.**

Middle right **The island platform was just below the surface and excavated by cut-and-cover. Walls were faced with biscuit cream tiles and the frieze of bullseye symbols edged in bright blue bands, the bands being repeated on the trackside walls. A limited number of Harold Stabler's decorative tiles were fixed in the stairwell.**

Right **The ticket hall was lined with brindled Staffordshire bricks up to the ring beam and light-brown sand-lime bricks continued to the clerestory roof, with circular pavement lights set into the segmental recesses.**

Above **The relatively spartan Wanstead, looking east with the purpose built vent tower in the foreground flanked by low entrances and the adapted ticket hall behind. The exterior was faced in light grey granite aggregate render to sill level and cream spar above, with imitation joints hammered into the ticket hall walls to match the blocks forming the tower. A robust wall of steel louvres surrounds the upper escalator shaft beyond the hall.**

Left **Detail of the south entrance, clad in black frost-proof tiles. Between the entrances a vestibule led into the main hall, lined in biscuit-cream faience slabs with green tile bands.**

The Underground management had wished to include a 'Moscow'-type subsurface concourse at one of their stations since 1936 when the first part of the Moscow Metro opened. The aim was realised by Adams, Holden & Pearson at Gants Hill (referred to on original plans as 'North Ilford') where the lower escalator landing was enlarged between the platform tunnels to form a 150ft-long concourse with 20ft-high vaulted roof. Chrome yellow bands added colour to the biscuit-cream tiling. Construction began in 1937 and the station opened with the extension to Newbury Park on 14th December 1947, the platform-level concourse coming into use on 4th April 1948. The ticket hall was located beneath a roundabout on Eastern Avenue, and was to have been surmounted by a sizeable clock tower designed by the architects, but this was not carried out. The lower levels have recently been refurbished, with original finishings, fittings and furniture replaced. Right **A Moscow Metro station.**

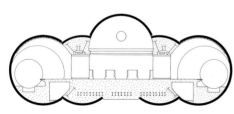

Diagram showing the intersection of cast-iron tunnels used to form the platform and 'Moscow' lower concourse spaces at Gants Hill.

After Gants Hill the new tube swung south-east away from Eastern Avenue, curving northward to surface either side of the LNER tracks of Newbury Park. This station had been opened on 1st May 1903 by the Great Eastern Railway on their Ilford-Woodford loop line. It was expected that the extension of the Central line would generate an enormous increase in traffic, and the station would become a focal point for the interchange of passengers between bus and rail. The LNER buildings on the road overbridge would have to be demolished so that Eastern Avenue could be widened and the existing facilities needed to be replaced by more modern and spacious accommodation.

Frank Pick met the architect Oliver Hill through their work for the Council of Art and Industry, and during 1936-37 they collaborated when Hill designed the British Pavilion for the Paris Exhibition of 1937. In the same year Hill was made consulting architect for all stations on the Central line extension from Stratford to Woodford via Newbury Park and Hainault. The only scheme known to be prepared by Hill and his assistant Edward Duley (1903-1984) was Newbury Park. Design of this integrated railway and bus station began in 1937, developed from a basic plan prepared by the Underground architect's department.[1]

The plan of the station was in the same spirit as that of Hill's British Pavilion at the 1937 Paris Exhibition, with much use made of sweeping curves. The front of the station would consist of shop units, with the bus stand and forecourt on the eastern side, and a large bullseye symbol mounted atop a high steel pylon would advertise the location for some distance around. The corner of the building below the pylon was to have concave walls faced with soldier bricks laid on-end (Hill used soldier bricks extensively in his 'Hill House' at Hampstead, 1936-38). A second group of shops would be added over the railway on the site of the old station buildings. The ticket hall would be laid out to a quadrant plan with a clerestory roof and circular toplight. A subway was to be built under Eastern Avenue with a spur rising directly into the ticket hall. At the rear of the development would stand a canteen for railway and bus staff.

Above **Perspective of Newbury Park by J D M Harvey, 1937. To the left are the curved shop units, and behind the pylon is the ticket hall clerestory roof, originally to have been of lozenge plan. The bus stand – 150 feet long and 30 feet high – was fabricated from reinforced concrete with an exposed aggregate of golden Chesil Beach shingle, and the roof clad in copper sheets with a salmon pink ceiling.**

Left **This plan view shows the layout of shops with footbridge and ticket hall behind, and bus stand on right. The curving frontage was echoed in the sweep of the low brick forecourt wall – to be planted with cotton lavender and catnip. Wall terminals were of spiral design. Road widening has resulted in the main portion of wall being demolished.**

The bus stand – reminiscent of certain airship hangars – has recently undergone substantial repairs.

The bus stand – reminiscent of certain airship hangars – has recently undergone substantial repairs.

Below **The Britannia Window designed by Gertrude Hermes for the Paris Exhibition of 1937 and proposed for re-use in either Newbury Park or Redbridge stations. It was placed into storage after the exhibition and is believed to have been lost during the war.**

A further connection with the 1937 Paris Exhibition is that Raymond McGrath, designer of one of the glass screens for the British Pavilion, suggested to the then London Transport Publicity Officer Christian Barman (1898-1980) that the screen might be re-used after the exhibition closed. Barman replied that the screen could be installed 'in one of the booking halls of the Board's new stations'.[2] McGrath then contacted Oliver Hill who accepted the idea subject to further approval. A second glass panel designed by Gertrude Hermes had the image of Britannia sandblasted into it; in a letter written to the artist in December 1937 Hill states that the window 'is to be re-erected in the new station I am doing at Newbury Park.'[3] As the window was 30ft-high it is difficult to see how it would have been used at the station. The matter is complicated further by a reference in *Passenger Transport Journal* (see note for East Finchley) to the installation of the Britannia window at Redbridge station; this would at one time have been practicable since Charles Holden originally intended Redbridge to have an all-glass tower.

Completion was projected for December 1940 but because of the war work stopped in July of that year before the buildings had been started. Due to the pressing need of providing interchange facilities the bus station was built after the war as soon as finances permitted, and was completed to Hill's design. The canteen was also constructed, but the rest of the project postponed. Although the extensive plans for reconstruction were still current in 1947 they had to be shelved due to the immediate post-war economic situation, and were never realised. Central line electric services commenced on 14th December 1947. The bus forecourt and stand, with 'temporary' ticket hall on its west side, came into use on 6th July 1949.

Ticket hall walls and ceiling were painted with white 'Snowcem', and the office interiors were yellow, white and grey. The structural steel frame was painted bright chrome orange

and poster panels violet-blue. Among the amenities provided was an office for bus inspectors which fronted onto the bus station.

The canteen was built to a revised design adjoining what was to have been a 'rush' exit from the permanent ticket hall, and opened in mid-1950. The structure was finished in two-inch high 'Danehill' red sand-faced bricks as specified by the architect. The interior was faced in egg-shell tiles and the kitchen tiled to full height. The seating area for 60-80 staff was originally hung with reproductions of Van Gogh paintings. A screen wall alongside the canteen is finished as the whole of the 'permanent' station building would have been – of red Danehill bricks with a skirting of Broughton Moor seagreen slate.

The old station on the Eastern Avenue overbridge had given direct access by separate stairways to the platforms, and a steel and concrete footbridge had to be constructed to link the platforms with the new facilities. The bridge and staircases were painted white, soft pink and lime green. Hill became known for his fabulous interior decorations during the 1930s, and the bright colours used at this station were characteristic of his work. The Great Eastern platform buildings were of red brick with stone dressings. These are little changed, and the original valanced wooden canopies supported by cast-iron columns may still be seen.

Country Life described the station as 'one of the most imaginative realisations of contemporary architecture'[4], and in Festival of Britain Year Oliver Hill was presented with a Special Architectural Award for his bus station design. The road-side buildings were demolished when Eastern Avenue was widened to four lanes of carriageway in 1956-57. On 2nd July 1979 the bus station became a listed structure. On 31st May 1948 the Central line was further extended to Hainault (rebuilt 1948-49), and thence round the loop to Woodford on 21st November that year.

Top **Spiral ends to the forecourt wall at Newbury Park.**

Above **Night view of the bus stand.**

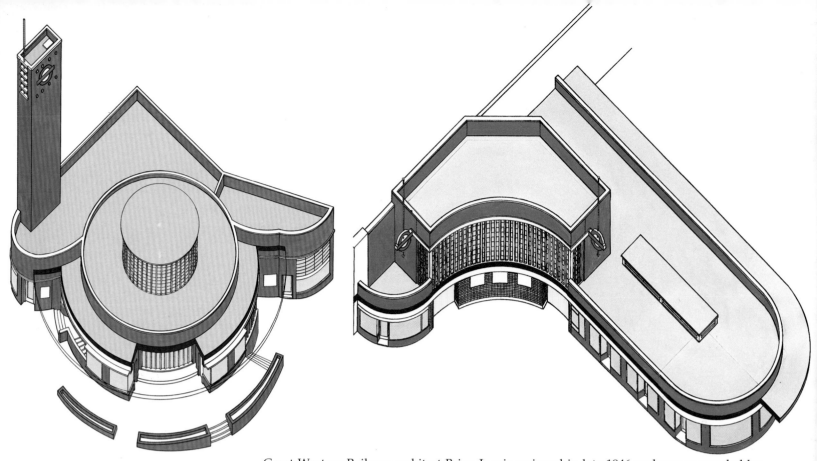

Original designs for Hanger
Lane left and Perivale right
showing Brian Lewis's
departure from the standard
Underground box form.

Below The spacious interior of
Hanger Lane achieved by
placing the ticket hall below
street level.

Great Western Railway architect Brian Lewis resigned in late 1946 and was succeeded by Dr Frederick Curtis, who had for a time worked in the office of Adams, Holden & Pearson. The number of engineering works on the western extension of the Central line, hampered by a bad winter and labour shortages, delayed progress and as the permanent buildings were not ready when the North Acton to Greenford section opened on 30th June 1947 temporary structures were put up. Following nationalisation, completion of the works was carried out by British Railways, Western Region architects under the supervision of Curtis and his assistant Howard Cavanagh.

Hanger Lane station – situated approximately half a mile from Park Royal Piccadilly line station – was opened as part of the Central line extension to Greenford on 30th June 1947, with a temporary building at the side of the Western Avenue near the west end of the island platform.

Lewis's designs for the first three stations on the extension departed from the usual pattern of Underground stations in the architect's combination of curvilinear and rectilinear forms. The 1937 scheme for Hanger Lane had included a 63ft-tower with illuminated bullseye signs and projecting concrete blocks. A parapet wall of soldier bricks surrounded a raised and continuously-glazed drum roof. At road level there was to be a cafe and shop in low wings on either side of the ticket hall. Kiosks over the two entrance stairwells flanked a waiting area for bus passengers.

Western Region architect Peter MacIver used the pre-war ground plan but revised the elevation in line with building restrictions and availability of materials. The permanent station opened on 2nd January 1949. The structure was placed at the side of the cutting with the ticket hall floor taken below pavement level to give additional height. The reinforced-concrete frame was infilled with cavity walls of red sandfaced bricks laid in English bond for the exterior and Sussex bond for the interior. A four inch-thick dome of reinforced concrete 44ft in diameter formed the roof, cast onto a permanent shuttering of wood-wool insulating slabs which was afterwards plastered over.

The ticket hall was faced in biscuit-cream tiles up to the ring beam. Around the walls were an auxiliary booking office, lavatories, two kiosks and a cycle store. Telephone booths were placed in the retaining wall between the stairs at basement level – this positioning of telephone booths between entrances was repeated by Lewis at Perivale, Greenford and West Acton.

At the time of completion the building was acclaimed in the architectural press for its design. When an underpass was constructed in 1960 for through traffic on Western Avenue, subways to each corner of the road intersection were excavated, radiating out from a central concourse with basement-level access into the station.

Above **Hanger Lane from the west, with the proposed cafe/kiosk in the foreground and an entrance stairwell behind. The weight of the concrete canopy was counterbalanced by an extension for staff rooms at the rear. This entrance has since been closed.**

Right **A box displaying the station name was left with its top open so that light was thrown upward to illuminate the immediate area by reflection. Stairwells were fitted with reeded glass panels in staggered rows.**

Until the early 1930s, when factories and small houses began to appear in the area, the hamlet of Perivale lay amidst fields on the slopes north of the River Brent. Mass concrete foundations for a new station to replace the halt of 1904 had been laid in 1938, and in 1946 work started on the station building. Unlike Hanger Lane, most of the building was completed to Brian Lewis's original design.

The structure was set against the railway viaduct with a curved red brick frontage and narrow ticket hall of quadrant plan and a sweeping canopy along the front of the deep ring beam. The large 'Glascrete' window with reinforced concrete mullions was to be found in several Underground stations designed during this period. Above the window were courses of soldier bricks forming a parapet wall. The right-hand wing of the building was to be extended some 50ft to accommodate three shop units. When the building was erected the end of the canopy was unfinished and provision made in the brickwork for bonding in the walls of the extension, but the work was not carried out, and the end wall still has an unfinished appearance.

As part of a scheme for the designation of stations announced in 1938 Perivale was to have been adorned with the symbol of a pear in some form; this proposal was not taken-up after the war.[5] The station is close to the famous Art-Deco Hoover Factory (1932-35) on Western Avenue, by Wallis, Gilbert and Partners, now a superstore.

Greenford station was built essentially to the pre-war design of Brian Lewis, who again employed a curving canopy here to give shelter over the entrances whilst following the pavement line. The narrow brick and reinforced concrete tower was built considerably lower than first planned. The ticket hall was laid-out parallel to the railway line, and in order to give access to the escalator approach it was curved around 90 degrees towards the rear, in which direction the floor sloped gently upwards.

Between the existing and new viaducts is the lower escalator landing, with a high ceiling rising some feet above rail level. From the landing a subway led to the British Railways steam platforms (blocked-off after the closure of the latter facility on 17th June 1963). A single 'up' escalator was installed alongside two fixed stairways – the first escalator at a London Underground station to carry passengers from ground level up to the platform, 33ft above the road. (An escalator removed from the Dome of Discovery on the Festival of Britain site was installed on the eastbound side at Alperton, Piccadilly line, in 1955 to perform the same function.) The island platform was given a central bay at its eastern end for use by British Railways trains working over the Castle Bar Park branch to West Ealing.

White City seen from the north, with the main entrance – a late application of the format begun by Charles Holden at Bond Street – standing beyond the low, rounded end of the former 'rush' ticket hall. Beyond the station entrance is the staff institute and canteen.

In 1908 the Franco-British Exhibition was established on ground at Wood Lane, Shepherds Bush, the exhibition running from 14th May to 31st October of that year. The exhibition buildings were painted white, and this led to the area becoming known as the 'White City'. The Central London Railway opened a station on Wood Lane to the designs of Harry Bell Measures on the opening day of the Exhibition.[6] This station occupied an awkward location on a loop and by 1920 had four platforms and a triangular arrangement which prevented their being extended to accommodate longer trains. For the western extension of the Central line a new station was built further north on Wood Lane, opposite the athletics stadium which had been opened for the 1908 Olympic Games. Completion of the construction was projected for April 1940, but because of the war development did not begin until May 1946.

Under the supervision of the then London Transport Chief Architect Thomas Bilbow, architects A.D. McGill and K.J.H. Seymour were given the brief of designing a station having a ticket hall which could handle normal traffic and also cope with the huge crowds attending the stadium when events were held. The solution was to incorporate an extension of the ticket hall to one side with three passimeters which could be used as a 'rush' hall. The main hall tapered from front to rear, and housed in a wing to the north of this was the second hall which curved round towards the road and was to have been continued as a subway, passing beneath Wood Lane and rising into the stadium grounds. To have been financed by the Greyhound Racing Association, the subway was never built.

The structural steel-frame was infilled with concrete blocks – to avoid placing a demand on domestic housing materials – with a facing of grey and buff multi-coloured bricks. A wide entrance gave access to the waiting area with phone lobby at the foot of a short flight of steps up to ticket hall level. Interior public areas were lined with biscuit-cream faience slabs up to door height with a capping of red and grey tiles; above this the walls were of exposed brick. From the outset the station was lit throughout by fluorescent tubes. At the rear of the hall was a wide gallery with staircases to the two island platforms and giving access to the 47-lever signal cabin on the east side of the station. Brick screen walls were built alongside the outer tracks. On the platforms, waiting rooms and staff offices were built under the stairs. Users of this station will notice that the running direction of trains is a reverse of the usual convention; this is a result of the way connections were taken off the former anti-clockwise terminal loop at Wood Lane. Adjacent to the ticket hall was the entrance to the first floor staff institute with a bar and recreational facilities; at the far end of the block is a kitchen and canteen for railway staff.

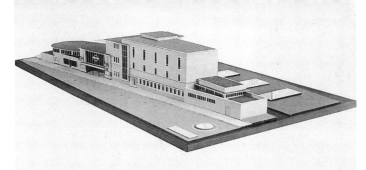

The first stage of the building opened on 23rd November 1947 with a temporary ticket hall in the partially completed rush exit; at this time the platforms were still unroofed. The Central line station at Wood Lane was closed on the same day. The main and rush ticket halls, staff facilities, canteen and platform canopies were finished in May 1950, along with the first part of the staff institute.

In Festival of Britain Year 1951 the designers of the station were presented with a Special Architectural Award for their work, and a plaque, which may be seen mounted on the front of the station next to the entrance, was given at a ceremony held on 12th July at the Royal Pavilion in the South Bank complex. Applications for the building to be listed have been unsuccessful. The former rush exit is now closed and has partially been rebuilt into offices.

Top left **This model by Kenneth Seymour of the station in a proposed form shows that offices were to have been extended over both ticket halls, with a larger staff institute on the first and second floors. Foundations and steelwork were designed to carry the additional loads, but the scheme was subsequently cut back to its existing size.**

Centre left and top right **The ticket hall flared towards the rear as a result of the adjoining rush hall. One wall was taken up by a ticket office of conventional form, advertised by large metal letters.**

Left **White City by night.**

Had the Northern line extensions set out in the 1935-40 New Works Programme not been halted by the Second World War and subsequently cut back for economic and other reasons, London Transport would have taken over a series of former LNER steam-operated branches in north London running from Finsbury Park via Highgate (High Level) and Muswell Hill to Alexandra Palace (opened by the Great Northern Railway, 1873), from the existing tube at Highgate (now Archway) via Finchley Central and Mill Hill East to Edgware (opened in August 1867), and to High Barnet (opened as a branch off the Edgware line, April 1872; West Finchley added March 1933). After expansion plans were finally shelved in 1954, the only sections to be retained comprised a stub to Mill Hill East and the High Barnet line. Apart from East Finchley and Highgate, already described on pages 134-5 and 136, the newly acquired stations remained in original form with minor building alterations and re-signing. John Murray Easton was appointed by the LNER to redesign stations north of Finchley in September 1937, but no details of any schemes he may have produced survive. Plans were made for the reconstruction of Finsbury Park, Finchley Central (by Reginald Uren with Adams, Holden & Pearson), High Barnet and Edgware (both by Underground architects), and some basic works started on the ground, but none completed.[1]

In the east the Central line also took in former LNER routes: the Stratford-Loughton section (Eastern Counties Railway, August 1856), the Great Eastern's Loughton-Ongar extension of April 1865, and the Ilford-Woodford loop of May 1903, which was severed between Ilford and Newbury Park after the construction of a new tube connecting the latter station and Leytonstone. Buildings between Leyton and Ongar were all originally of a standard pattern. South Woodford was provided with a new pavilion roofed ticket hall in 1883 and Buckhurst Hill similarly rebuilt in 1892, when additions were also made at Woodford.

For the Central line projection from Liverpool Street, Stratford was rebuilt in 1946, and minor alterations made during 1947-48 to the intermediate stations, with the exception of Leytonstone which was entirely redeveloped by London Transport architects. Loughton has already been described. A circular ticket hall and 'streamlined' waiting room was provided at Hainault (near to the new London County Council housing estate), and Grange Hill was completely rebuilt in 1949 following wartime damage. Roding Valley (opened 3rd February 1936) was reconstructed in the same year and a new ticket hall at Debden came into use in 1974, again serving a large housing estate. Blake Hall, the least-used station on the Underground, closed 31st October 1981 to be followed by closure of North Weald and Ongar on 30th September 1994. Woodford has recently been provided with a new canopied entrance area.

Below **Woodside Park circa 1936, built in a traditional railway style using cream facing bricks. For a time this station featured a colour scheme designed by the writer and comedian Spike Milligan in 1974. At the High Barnet terminus a virtually identical structure was provided, and there was once a bell which rang to announce train departures – this may now be seen in the town's local history museum. An additional ticket hall was opened at High Barnet in 1896, with a footpath towards the town.**

Segmental windows in walls of smooth red pressed bricks above a rough-hewn granite plinth set Barkingside apart from the other stations on the Hainault loop – see Chigwell below. The listed building entry attributes this station to one William Burgess, and states that as it served as a transfer point for the nobility travelling to the nearby Dr Barnardo's Home for Children a grander style was merited. No information is available on Burgess, and it is likely that the design was in fact prepared under the direction of W.N. Ashbee, Chief Architect to the Great Eastern Railway at this time. (See note 2 in Appendix). The building occupies some length of the down platform, with facilities ranged in a linear plan either side of the ticket hall. The ceiling has exposed beams.

Chigwell, with its twin pedimented gables and stairways expressed in the rear roofline, was similar to the old station at Newbury Park – also sited on a road overbridge.

Stations on the Loughton – Ongar branch were unassuming little dwellings for the stationmasters with single storey ticket offices attached, in the same style as those on the earlier Loughton line of 1856 with set-out string courses, architraves and quoins, here carried out in red brick. Debden, North Weald and Blake Hall were all of similar size. The original Loughton, Theydon Bois, Epping and Ongar (pictured) buildings had additional single storey structures and canopied entrances; the platforms were unsheltered. Blake Hall and Ongar were given a Grade II listing on 5th July 1984. Both stations are now closed.

POST-WAR DEVELOPMENTS

Above **Sloane Square after its
second rebuild in 12 years,
completed in time for the
Festival of Britain. A
superstructure has since been
added, overpowering the
uncomplicated design of the
station.**

Following the nationalisation of Britain's railways in 1948 the London Transport Executive of
the British Transport Commission (BTC) assumed control of the Underground, and the
London Plan Working Party was set up by the BTC to assess requirements for new lines.
Little money was available for building and when pre-war extension plans were reviewed,
only the completion of the Central line works was approved. In the mid-1950s, parliamentary
powers were given for the construction of a new deep-level tube which would become the
Victoria line, and soon after the completion of this project further tubes were built in the form
of the Piccadilly line extension to Heathrow Airport and the Jubilee line. At several sites
London Transport sought to make the most of their land assets by releasing the space over
stations for building; developments were completed at Morden, St John's Wood, Moorgate,
and Lancaster Gate but several schemes were not started.

Sloane Square station had been rebuilt with escalators in March 1940, but was hit by a
bomb the following November. Using the original contract drawings, reconstruction of the
station was completed on 3rd May 1951 under the supervision of London Transport's Chief
Architect Thomas Bilbow. An office development was added above the station in the 1960s.

In preparation for the Festival of Britain 1951 various works were carried out at Charing
Cross Underground station. The exterior was cleaned and the mosaic bullseyes removed. A
small hall faced in brick and Portland stone slabs was constructed on the south side of the
station for additional escalators commissioned on 3rd May 1951 to carry passengers down to
the lower levels, and it also served as a podium for new stairs up to the footway alongside
Hungerford Bridge. Architect and industrial designer Jack Howe RDI FRIBA FSIAD (b.1911)
worked on redecoration of the District line platforms, replacing the 1920s finishing with buff
tiles to the walls and eggshell blue tiles to the piers. This was the first use of the lighter weight
tiles which appeared in all new Underground works throughout the 1950s and 1960s. False
ceilings of asbestos board in aluminium frames were fitted with fluorescent tube lights in
aluminium holders. Howe redesigned platform kiosks with fronts of polished wood and
planned the Transport and Festival Information Centre which occupied the ticket hall
exhibition area during this period. Thomas Bilbow designed a new substation and control
room over the east end of the station which was completed in 1957. The exterior is of pinkish-
yellow Essex sandfaced brick with a decorative rendered panel over the main doorway.

Additional passenger facilities provided at Waterloo in 1951 were housed in a striking
building on the west side of York Road, with curving glass roof by Sir John Burnet, Tait and
Partners. Ticket hall fittings were of perspex or light-coloured materials – an unusual
treatment for a London Underground facility of the time.

Above **Across the river from Charing Cross stood Waterloo Station Gate by Sir John Burnet, Tait & Partners, serving as the entrance to the Festival of Britain for main-line and Underground railway passengers. Below the curved glass roof, suspended from laminated timber arches, were ticket halls, escalators, a restaurant and offices. After demolition of this trainshed-like structure, the Underground entrance was rebuilt as a permanent addition to Waterloo's Northern and Bakerloo line station.**

Left **Ticket hall at Notting Hill Gate of 1959 with green and buff floor tiles and newly introduced concealed lighting behind 'egg-crate' grilles.**

Reconstruction of the Central London line station at Notting Hill Gate was considered in the late 1920s, when Adams, Holden & Pearson designed a Portland stone façade similar to those at Bond Street and St Paul's. Widening of the busy thoroughfare was first mooted in 1936, and rebuilding of the Underground station started in 1937 with completion projected for December 1940.[1] Objections were made by the London County Council (LCC) to certain aspects of the scheme and delays occurred; work was stopped in late 1939 with the outbreak of war and the original street-level buildings remained.

Traffic increased rapidly after the war and the LCC commenced road widening in 1957 which required demolition of the existing separate station buildings erected by the former Metropolitan and Central London railways on opposite sides of the road. It was now possible to construct a subway and combined ticket hall beneath the roadway, thus saving interchange passengers the difficulty of negotiating the thoroughfare which had formerly been an obstacle between the Central and District/Circle stations. A.V. Elliott and A.D. McGill carried out the project for London Transport. The majority of the new facility came into use 1st March 1959, and the final pair of escalators in the lower flight was commissioned on 31st July 1960.

The subway was finished in mushroom coloured tiles and the hall in light blue. Extensive use was made of low-maintenance materials new to the Underground such as melamine laminate and aluminium which would see widespread application on the Victoria line.

Escalator shafts had suspended ceilings of laminate patterned in black, red, yellow and white. Escalators at this station were the first on the Underground to be fitted with aluminium side panels. Platforms were lined with mushroom coloured tiles and maroon at the entrances. Tiles used were of a lightweight type employed later throughout the Victoria line.

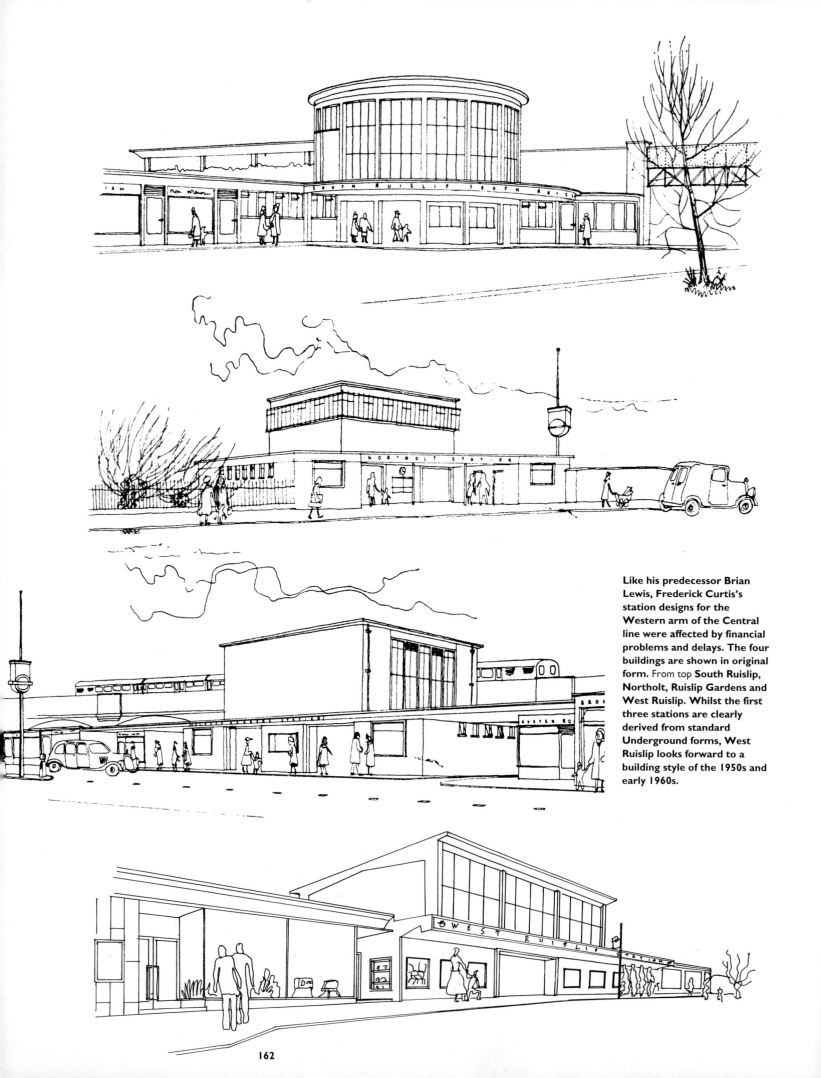

Like his predecessor Brian Lewis, Frederick Curtis's station designs for the Western arm of the Central line were affected by financial problems and delays. The four buildings are shown in original form. From top **South Ruislip, Northolt, Ruislip Gardens** and **West Ruislip.** Whilst the first three stations are clearly derived from standard Underground forms, **West Ruislip** looks forward to a building style of the 1950s and early 1960s.

Dr F. F. Curtis designed the four stations west of Greenford with Howard Cavanagh and R. H. Jones of the Architect's Office, British Railways (Western Region) immediately after the Second World War, but they could not be completed for some years because of the economic situation. Temporary passenger facilities were provided and the platforms completed in the short term, and the work on the road level station buildings continued sporadically throughout the 1950s until final completion in November 1961. By the time finance was available to erect permanent structures Curtis's designs had become outdated and they were restyled and simplified by John Kennett and Roy Turner. The reinforced concrete work at South Ruislip was started in the late 1940s but passengers used temporary facilities for some years. The circular tower had been designed with glazed panels set between the frame stanchions. As built, translucent panels were fixed around the outside of the tower. An abstract concrete frieze decorated the ring beam inside the hall. The concrete was inset with panels of multi-coloured ceramic and granite chips, and was intended to represent the flow of traffic through the station[2].

Above **South Ruislip's drum tower** was to have glazing set between the frame stanchions but in the unprecedented and innovative final design translucent laminated glass/glass fibre curtain walling was fixed around the outside. Lower walls were of dark blue-grey concrete brick – cheaper than the traditional clay variety, and at Ruislip Gardens brown brick was combined with Broughton Moor slate. Interior finishes were compatible with contemporary London Transport styling, with light-weight tiling similar to that introduced at Charing Cross, mainly in light blue or black, and mosaic tesserae.

Middle **Western Region** architects at this time made regular visits to the Continent and were particularly impressed by the reconstruction of the Dutch railway system. Despite the extremely restricted budget they wished to integrate a piece of art into the South Ruislip building, so an abstract cast concrete frieze by Henry Haig was fixed to the ring beam inside the hall, giving visual interest and concealing lighting units. The artist was influenced by the rhythms and patterns of traffic flow through the ticket hall.

Left **The terminus at West Ruislip**, carried out in yellow and white concrete brick, had a rendered ticket hall box supported by portal frames. The grooved soffit of the splayed canopy may be noted.

Top and above left **Both outside and within the small station provided at Moor Park, with its raking clerestory roof, the architects sought to create a feeling of warmth, covering concrete with mosaic, tiling and wood panels.**

Above right **The new Colindale ticket hall with lighting by fluorescent tubes arranged in continuous strips – a practice continued on the Victoria line.**

Four-tracking of the Metropolitan main line between Harrow-on-the-Hill and Watford South Junction was completed in 1962, a reconstructed station having been opened at Moor Park on 23rd April 1961. Mosaic came back into vogue with architects during the 1950s, promoted as a durable and attractive internal or external finish which required little or no maintenance, and limited use was made of it in Underground stations of the 1960s; at Moor Park it was combined with polished wood and metal. The art of fixing mosaic was not always familiar to contractors and incorrect cement mixes have resulted in some tesserae dropping off the walls. Northwood was also rebuilt in 1962, and the temporary facilities at Colindale which had been provided following destruction of the station by a bomb in September 1940 were replaced by a new ticket hall as part of an office block development.

At Waterloo an additional ticket hall on York Road with escalators to the Northern and Bakerloo lines was completed in May 1962 as part of the Shell Centre complex. Over the head of the escalators was fixed an illuminated mural on the theme of shells. Mushroom coloured tiles were used for the walls, and there were panels of mosaic flecked with metallic particles. New escalators and a small concourse below the British Railways subway at Waterloo opened on 6th September 1970, and a further ticket hall in 1973 replacing the old Bakerloo ticket hall and lifts from 17th March that year. Extension work carried out in conjunction with the International Terminal, opened in 1994, has resulted in a much enlarged main hall finished mostly in white.

Above **The erstwhile Festival of Britain Underground ticket hall reopened in 1962 beneath the Shell Centre on the South Bank. The exterior was faced in granite and dominated by an array of ventilation panels; the inside featured low maintenance aluminium, plastics and a large colour panel advertisement. Here the lighting has been concealed by grilles in the suspended ceiling.**

Centre and left **The terminus at High Barnet would have been submerged beneath an extensive development of tower blocks and car parking had either of the schemes shown here been carried out. From 1963 and 1964, these impressions were drawn up for architects Brian Calhoun and Parkins working for Winkfield Estates.**

This page **Preliminary sketches for Victoria line platforms and mock-up in the disused tunnel at Aldwych of experimental designs. The suspended ceiling was also installed at Gants Hill on the Central line in 1962, but found to be too expensive and difficult to maintain for general application, although it successfully reduced the sense of being in a tunnel – an effect which Underground designers have repeatedly sought to avoid.**

Opposite top left **Standard design of Victoria line platforms as first built. Cheaper, unclad, ceilings were provided at the northern end of the line. Grey tiling was relieved by coloured designs in the seat recesses at all stations. The motif by Abram Games OBE RDI FRCA (b.1914) for Stockwell was of a swan – referring to the nearby public house. Closed circuit television monitors were introduced for train operators – no guards were required on the trains. Illuminated signs were projected from the wall to enhance the integration of elements.**

Opposite top right **The finished design of platform headwall with all equipment in metal cabinets and signal lamps down one edge.**

Opposite centre **Typical Victoria line escalator shaft, with aluminium panelling throughout beneath a suspended melamine ceiling.**

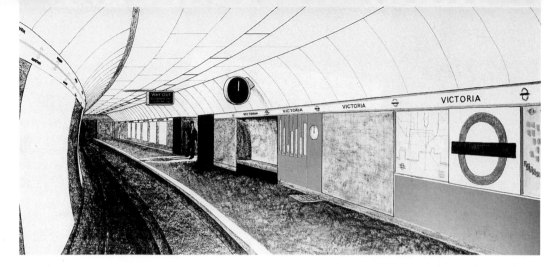

The route of the Victoria line had been considered as long ago as the 1930s: at the LPTB Second Annual Conference in 1937 the Railway General Manager J.P. Thomas had mentioned a tube 'from Victoria to Finsbury Park, to relieve the Northern and Piccadilly lines.' The London Plan Working Party Report was published in 1949 and amongst its first priority suggestions was a Route 'C' which would emerge as the Victoria line. Parliamentary approval for the project, with plans for a projection to Streatham and East Croydon omitted, was given in 1955. The line would link four busy main-line rail termini with the West End and north-east London, operated by automatic trains and signalling to offer much reduced journey times across central London.

Adams, Holden & Pearson completed their last work for the Underground in 1961 with the reconstruction of Mansion House station and London Transport undertook to design the Victoria line wholly 'in-house', under the direction of the London Transport Design Panel, whose members included Chief Architect Kenneth J.H. Seymour and Misha Black (later Sir Misha, 1910-77). Design Research Unit (DRU) – a sizeable industrial design organisation of which Misha Black was a founder – acted as design consultants to London Transport until the early 1980s. A mile of experimental twin tunnels was excavated between Finsbury Park and Seven Sisters in 1960-61 and the project began fully in August 1962; five years later an extension to Brixton was given financial approval.

Above **Model of Blackhorse Road, the only completely new surface station on the line, showing the ticket hall clerestory roof and vent tower which hints at a flirtation with Brutalist architecture. Dark brickwork is contrasted with white mosaic and exposed textured concrete containing shiny mineral particles. The rear of the station features a canopy for bus passengers above an area paved with hexagonal slabs and pebbles, with concrete plant tubs shaped to match. The line opened in stages between 1968 and 1971. Pimlico was added in 1972.**

The Northern line (City branch) station at Old Street was rebuilt during this period with finishes similar to the Victoria line platforms.

Existing stations were reconstructed with interchange facilities, the new tunnels being arranged to give direct cross-platform interchange wherever possible. The heavily trafficked Oxford Circus was rebuilt during 1963-8 with a concourse ticket hall beneath the circus itself, and Stockwell was provided with a new surface building. Bus stations were built at Tottenham Hale and Walthamstow Central to enhance transport connections at street level.

All the new station ticket halls except Blackhorse Road were below ground which limited the architectural possibilities, but a uniform scheme of platform finishes was adopted throughout the line. Walls were finished in light grey 6in-square tiles with dark grey tiles around the platform archways and dark blue, black or grey tiles around poster panels. Grey tiles were chosen to provide a neutral background for posters and signage, and being a standard colour would be easy to replace if damaged. Grey appears to have been the suggestion of Misha Black; it has since been said that it gives the stations a somewhat clinical and drab appearance, but the designers themselves commented: 'the stations may be criticised for appearing visually unexciting, but we consider that preferable to a transient popularity without lasting qualities.'[3] Square and rectangular tiles in light and dark blue, dusky pink, olive green, dark turquoise and other colours were used in ticket halls to give an individual appearance to each station; 'accent' colours – orange, yellow – helped to make elements such as columns stand out for safety amongst the moving crowds.

Mosaic tesserae were used as an alternative to tiling for some areas and brushed metal introduced for trimmings and nosings to protect the corners of walls and piers. In recent years the tile mortar appears to have failed, aided by vandals, and some tiles have parted company with the walls. The thin tiles used during this period are more prone to damage than the heavier weight examples of earlier works. Mosaic tends to be vulnerable to graffiti because of the relatively large areas of porous grouting which are difficult to clean. Suspended ceilings were installed in all areas and doors were faced with melamine laminate in various colours: dark blue, buff, olive green and salmon pink. Melamine laminate was chosen for its durability and cost but there have been doubts expressed about its fire-resistance when certain grades are used. Platform walls were built out from the tunnel lining in order that they might be vertical rather than curved. A deep enamelled-iron frieze ran the length of every platform showing the station name in white on a blue ground with exit directions on a black band above. The first colour selected to identify the new line on signs and publicity material was royal purple; this colour was not easy to achieve successfully in vitreous enamel and so Cambridge blue was chosen instead[4].

Bullseye symbols bearing the station name were displayed on back-lit panels at most stations (some have since been replaced with vitreous enamel signs), whilst those at Walthamstow, Blackhorse Road and Tottenham Hale were made as enamelled signs lit from a concealed source above. Fluorescent lights were fitted in a single strip suspended from the false ceiling. Illuminated signs had white lettering on a black ground; there were also new style bifurcation and line diagrams. Litterbins were recessed below the nameboards. Ticket halls were fitted with automatic fare collection gates and an innovation was the use of closed circuit television screens to give train operators a view of the further ends of platforms. For the platform headwalls all equipment was contained in polished metal cabinets, with signal lamps mounted neatly on one edge.

The fibreglass relief of a black stallion by David McFall RA (1919-1988) with mosaic by Trata Drescha (b.1928) embellished the exterior of Blackhorse Road, opened with the first section of line from Walthamstow to Highbury & Islington on 1st September 1968. In the ticket hall exposed stanchions clad in bright metal and gold-flecked mosaic panels created a light interior. The passimeter booking office – one of the last of its kind – was removed in 1988.

Below The tile designs at the 12 original Victoria line stations (see note 5 in appendix).

Hatton Cross – serving the engineering area on the south-east perimeter of the airport – was provided with a substantial surface building clad in three shades of light brown tile, beneath an overhanging canopy faced in textured concrete which forms a sheltered walkway on three sides. It has been suggested that the roof was at one time to have formed a car park. An array of slit windows lights the hall. The designers continued to use materials introduced with the Victoria line such as laminated plastic for panelling and stainless steel for trimmings, but they abandoned the neutral grey scheme in favour of a range of colours – purple, green, brown, red and blue, with beige and off-white – reflecting another change of direction for interior design. The platforms had a suspended ceiling of corrugated metal, and the soffit of the central beam was faced in mosaic, carried down the sides of piers and decorated with the former Imperial Airways 'speedbird' motif. A revised form of station name frieze included the silhouette roundel developed by Design Research Unit. Multicoloured terrazzo in large panels was used as an alternative to the usual concrete flooring.

Upon the retirement of Kenneth Seymour, Sydney Hardy was appointed to take over as head of the London Transport Architects' department. He set about restructuring the office and introducing working practices more in line with those in the private sector, seeking to improve cost efficiency under the constraints of continuing budget problems.

A project already under way when Hardy joined London Transport, and which in some respects represents the end of an era in Underground station design, was the projection of the Piccadilly line from Hounslow West to Heathrow Airport, giving the first direct rail access from the centre of London. Hounslow West was rebuilt as a through station and the first wholly new Underground stations for several years built at Hatton Cross and Heathrow Central (both predominantly subsurface works). The cut and cover excavation at the station sites had the benefit of making flat ceilings possible, so that greater space was available for the platform tunnels, and the usual 'tube' effect could be avoided. For Hatton Cross and Heathrow Central the new sites gave the architects the freedom to design all the elements of the stations together instead of having to add sections piecemeal as was the case with alterations to existing facilities.

The line from Hounslow West to Hatton Cross came into use 19th July 1975, and the second portion to Heathrow Central (now Heathrow Terminals 1, 2, 3) was opened by Her Majesty the Queen on 16th December 1977. At Heathrow Central two escalators linking the concourse with the surface were commissioned on 17th July 1978. Buildings were specially sound insulated to reduce noise from aircraft passing overhead.

Limited space at Heathrow Central (now Heathrow Terminals 1,2,3) restricted the architectural possibilities, and the surface structure – in its cramped and somewhat messy location – was little more than an enclosure for escalators and the head of a ventilation plant – hence the smooth band of louvres in the rounded box form. A port-cochére outside the station narrowly misses the end of an unfinished footbridge. Escalators descend to a subsurface ticket hall and concourse with various facilities for the traveller, and further escalators – in separate flights for arriving and departing passengers – connect with a wide concourse between the platforms below. From the ticket hall travolators link with the three terminals. For the first time on London Underground, internationally recognised pictograms were included in signage. Piers were faced with extra durable, bright-orange tiles, and tinted glass screens enclose the escalator well. The travolator wall murals are by Minale Tattersfield.

At rail level the suspended ceiling was curved down to finish at the platform edge, noted by one critic as a useful counter to a fear of falling. A further feature carried over from the Victoria line was the provision of murals for the seat recesses, and Tom Eckersley produced a design based on the tailfins of 'Concorde'. A preliminary design by David Gentleman RDI Hon FRCA (b.1930) had used the enlarged image of a feather as a metaphor for flight and to suggest a pattern of airflow. This is illustrated below. (Please see note 6 in appendix.)

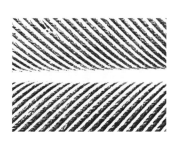

Mock-up on disused platform at Aldwych prepared by DRU in 1971 for possible use in the reconstruction of South Kensington Piccadilly line platforms, representing a transition between the Victoria and Jubilee line styles. Actual work contemporary with this time included the subsurface passages at South Kensington (1974), and platforms at Moorgate (Northern line), both featuring a rectangular tile replacing the square type which had been common in the 1960s. Features of this experimental design such as the laminated plastics and metal-trimmed edges found their way into the Heathrow extension stations of 1975-78, but the silhouette roundel device developed by DRU was never used in this application. A few years later a design for Bond Street (Jubilee line) was installed at Aldwych, and this incorporated many of the elements which would be employed on the new line.

The Jubilee line had also been discussed in the London Plan Working Party Report of 1949 but was not considered practicable at the time. In the mid-1960s the 'Fleet line' was proposed as a new cross-town route, to run over the Bakerloo line from Stanmore to Baker Street, and thence in new tube via Bond Street, Green Park, Strand (now Charing Cross), Aldwych, Ludgate Circus, Cannon Street and Fenchurch Street, crossing the River Thames to join the East London line between Surrey Docks and New Cross/New Cross Gate. It was hoped that the tube would stimulate development in south-east London and serve the newly planned schemes at Covent Garden and St Katharine's Dock. The full-length route was postponed in 1968 but government approval for the first stage – to terminate at Charing Cross – was given in 1971 and construction began the following year. The project was renamed the Jubilee line in 1977 to commemorate the Queen's Silver Jubilee, and opened officially by HRH Prince Charles on 30th April 1979; it represented the last major tunnelling scheme for some years.

As with the Victoria line the new works were mostly below ground. Under the supervision of the Design Panel with Chief Architect Sydney Hardy and Design Research Unit, a move was made away from the austere tiling of the Victoria line: the four new sets of platforms were to be tiled in flame red. Roundel station nameboards would be displayed on grey vitreous-enamelled units (grey being the chosen colour for the line), and bright yellow plastic panels would give emphasis to the exit archways; the yellow and grey panels were carried round the tunnel barrel as bands. Platform walls were concave. A new type of name frieze was introduced to conceal cabling and indirect down-lighting. After Sir Misha Black reviewed the scheme two of the stations were given different colours: for Bond Street a deep cobalt blue, and for Charing Cross ermin lime green.

Top left **June Fraser ARCA PPCSD (b.1930), a partner at DRU, designed the decorative panels for Green Park, and decided to use a pattern of leaves which she collected and photographed, the images afterwards being fired onto tiles by Michael Douglas. The red tiles had already been ordered and there was no possibility of choosing a colour more sympathetic to the subject as the designer requested, so the olive green motif appears almost black against the red background, and the leaves are more dead than alive. In the attempt to give the station a uniform image the architects chose to reproduce the leaf pattern in green on a grey background for the Victoria line platforms, replacing Hans Unger's original panels which had faded badly.**

Above left **Much use was made of green, yellow and blue moulded plastic for the ticket hall at Charing Cross – designed in-house by London Transport architects as the first of a series of new projects.**

Top right **Charing Cross Northern line platforms (formerly Strand station) were decorated with murals by David Gentleman (b.1930) depicting a sequence of scenes from the building of the mediaeval Eleanor Cross from which the area takes its name. The artist made small engravings on boxwood blocks, and the printed images were then enlarged photographically for silk-screening onto the laminated panels. Gentleman took great care that all architectural and operational elements were integrated into the design, including the placing of station name roundels, seats and litter bins concealed behind slots in the panelling. As with the best of the works commissioned by the Underground, the murals have a timeless quality, and, whilst functioning well as a coherent whole, the individual elements also provide a great deal to engage the eye of the waiting passenger on any part of the platform. Unfortunately, the loss of revenue through reduced advertising space prevented full platform-length murals being introduced on a wider scale.**

Centre right **For the Jubilee platforms David Gentleman took a more graphic approach, using eight different images of Nelson's Column derived from photographs he had taken specially. Pigeons in flight add an unmistakable reference to Trafalgar Square and indeed London itself.**

Above right **The Bakerloo platforms (formerly named Trafalgar Square) were decorated by Richard Dragun and June Fraser of DRU with images from the National and National Portrait galleries, selected in consultation with the galleries themselves. The 350ft-long melamine laminate murals were planned during 1978-79 but no money was available at the time and the works were not completed until 1983. The designers enhanced the mural effect of the images by reproducing them in monochrome and adding selected areas of colour. Included among the designs are Sandro Botticelli's 'Venus and Mars', Paolo Uccello's 'The Battle of San Romano', Henri Rousseau's 'Tropical Storm with a Tiger', and portraits of Henry VIII, William Shakespeare and Sir Christopher Wren.**

THE 1980s AND 1990s

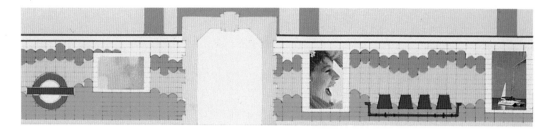

Above **Film stars were to provide an appropriate theme at Leicester Square. Only the 'sprocket hole' bands were used in the final design.**

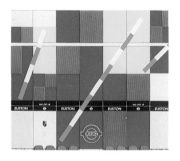

Above **Artwork for the enamelled panels at Euston by David Hamilton and Robert Cooper, based on the arms of Henry Fitzroy, first Earl of Euston. Work was completed in 1987.**

Towards the end of the 1970s GLC money was promised to London Transport for the refurbishment of stations neglected during the Victoria and Jubilee line works. The 'Station Update Policy Report' of 1979 considered proposals for the improvement of Central and Bakerloo line facilities. Soon after this London Transport architects under the leadership of the then Chief Architect Sydney Hardy drew up the 'Initial Design Strategy for the Rail System', a report which set out to address the state of decay on the Underground system and the means of dealing with it in a comprehensive station modernisation programme. New guidelines would facilitate the better co-ordinated management of new works and evolve as experience was gained[1].

The report commented on the 'visual chaos' which had resulted from the piecemeal alterations and addition of equipment with little consideration for its environment or compatibility with other fittings. For example, stations had been defaced by the super-imposition of services such as security video cameras and 'off the shelf' lighting units, with no attempt to integrate them into the overall design. Vandalism and litter added to the state of decay after years of use with little maintenance.

A design strategy was felt to be essential to link the disparate elements present on the system and to reconcile the various departments involved in station refurbishment who often worked without consulting each other. The aims were to improve passenger confidence, maximise use of the Underground – during a period when traffic levels were declining – and available resources, and improve the environmental and safety standards for both passengers and staff.

Three levels of station identification were defined. Moving away from the long-established practice of overall uniformity in use of material and colour, each station would have a unique decorative scheme inspired by the associations and activities of the locality to give it a distinctive identity; a particular 'theme' colour might also be allocated. The line as a whole would be represented by the use of the line colour – as shown on the Underground line diagram – in the frieze, furniture and fittings. Corporate identity would be maintained by the continued use of the roundel (in appropriate applications), and the line diagram, but would not be allowed to dominate the station's own theme. Money would be spent where it would see the biggest return in increased passenger numbers. Conservation of historic features was to be balanced with modern needs where possible.

A grant was won from the Greater London Council on the basis of the strategy report and a team of architects established to direct the projects; outside practices including Chapman Lisle and Hulme Chadwick were commissioned as consultants. In early 1980 the GLC imposed cuts which resulted in internal redundancies and the consultancies being terminated. However, after political changes within the GLC, finance was made available in 1981, but as it fell short of the original requirement it had to be employed in a manner which would be mainly cosmetic: facelifts rather than complete refurbishment. Money would be used to achieve the greatest visual effect, although this was contrary to public surveys which suggested general improvements to lighting, cleanliness and safety would be more welcome. A major implication of this spending policy has been that with a few exceptions – Baker Street, Charing Cross, Tottenham Court Road and Piccadilly Circus – new works stopped at platform level, emphasising the contrast between new and old.

Stations to benefit would be mainly in the central area on the Northern and Central lines where facilities had been missed by the improvement programmes of the 1930s, the heavily used locations receiving the fullest attention. Artists and students at the Royal College of Art collaborated with the architects on individual schemes.

Above **At Surrey Docks (now Surrey Quays) and Shadwell on the East London line, new station buildings by the Underground's own architects were completed in 1983.**

Centre **The basis of platform modernisations was to be a 'kit of parts' – seen in this 1979 mock-up at Aldwych – consisting of tubular steel rails fixed at intervals around the platform tunnels to break up the monotony of the walls and emphasise the barrel shape. From these rails would be suspended equipment, signage, and poster panels, thus giving a degree of flexibility and freeing the wall area for finishing as required. An extruded aluminium duct would run the length of the platform, serving the dual purpose of enclosing services and carrying the station name on a continuous frieze in the line colour. The rails were found to interfere with the rolling stock loading gauge and were abandoned at the trial stage, so that all equipment would now be mounted directly on the walls. The aluminium duct was too large and expensive, and in its place the architects chose post-formed melamine laminate on plywood for economy and durability. Following the Oxford Circus fire in 1984, materials came under close scrutiny and vitreous enamel was re-introduced for ducting and cladding.**

Left **A preliminary scheme prepared before the grant cuts were imposed was for a 'nightlife' theme at Queensway, with dark colours and violet filters to some of the lights.**

The platform works were completed with varying degrees of success, benefiting at least from being completely refinished, but work was hampered by the requirement that it be carried out in the few hours when trains did not run, and projects often overran completion dates. Sydney Hardy's argument in favour of a committed long-term investment programme and a better overall view of projects had been taken up by his successor Donald Hall (as Director of the restructured Department of Architectural Design), but repeated difficulties in funding and political changes continued to affect schemes adversely. Unco-ordination of projects remained a problem during the decade, a major example being the rebuilding of ticket halls for the installation of Underground Ticketing System (UTS) equipment which was carried out separately from modernisation works.

Above **Bond Street was the first station in the Central line programme to be completed in 1982. London Transport architects chose a 'wrapping paper' motif, with the station name silk-screened onto tiles laid in panels and bands. Work was begun at several other sites in this year.**

Right **In conjunction with the Jubilee line works the lower levels at Baker Street were refurbished. Robin Jacques prepared murals depicting scenes from Sir Arthur Conan Doyle's Sherlock Holmes detective stories, and Michael Douglas designed motifs and patterns based on miniature silhouettes of the fictional detective, printed onto tiles by Pamela Moreton.**

Sculptor Eduardo Paolozzi (b. 1924) had been commissioned in 1979 to design murals for Tottenham Court Road. He used as a basis for his design the activities for which the street of the same name has become known – music, photography and electronic equipment, fast-food and nightlife. The colour scheme was varied according to the lines: brighter hues with some metallic glass for the Central platforms, and more muted, 'digital' decorations with a thread of black or grey throughout on the Northern. Designs were applied using mosaic tesserae and smalti. Murals were continued throughout the station from platform to street, decorations in the 'rotunda' (a disused lift shaft) and escalator approaches being made more effective by the polished metal ceilings.

Central line platforms were completed in 1983, and the Northern line murals in 1985 forming one of the most impressive and complete (if not universally acclaimed) schemes executed during this programme, giving the station a strong identity through the use of vibrant colour, pattern and rhythm – a myriad of literal and metaphorical images which bring the fast-moving world above ground down to meet arriving passengers. In 1985 the work received a Silver Medal in the British Architectural Design Awards, and an exhibition was held at the Royal Academy in the following year.

Above **Abstract painter Paul Huxley ARA (b.1938) was commissioned in 1984 to produce designs for the Northern and Piccadilly platforms at King's Cross St Pancras. Huxley selected tiles as a suitably traditional material. The murals are effectively individual panels – each a complete image in itself – sharing related forms and colours, with the arrangement of elements varied to suggest transition and movement: a visual pun on the letters K and X may also be perceived. As in his paintings, Huxley juxtaposes colour and monochrome forms in the same or adjoining panels. Each platform is given a separate overall colour – turquoise, green, brown, and violet – graduated in intensity, and linking the mural panels into a whole. One difficulty in all work in this scale is that the overall effect cannot be appreciated except from a moving train, and will often be obscured by passengers; the platform width also limits a panoramic view.**

Centre and right **The Shepherd's Bush scheme by Chapman Lisle Associates (completed 1985) was based on a countryside theme. Julia King provided a mural entitled 'Town and Country' for the ticket hall, in which urban images are hidden in the shadows on the landscape. The ceiling was painted to suggest a blue sky.**

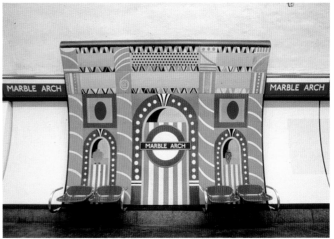

Annabel Grey decorated the panels at Marble Arch (1985) with colourful representations of arches, and designed murals depicting hot-air balloons in mosaic for the Finsbury Park platforms (1986).

For Oxford Circus Nicholas Munro, a student at the Royal College of Art, provided the initial artworks based on his impressions of the station, and these were developed by the architects using glass mosaics. The Central line platforms (completed 1983) were given a motif of 'snakes and ladders' – suggesting passageways (the snakes), escalators and stairs. Bakerloo platforms (completed 1985) had 'maze' panels – a literal, if not wholly complimentary, interpretation of the station plan. Following the fire in 1984 the damaged Victoria line platform was refinished in white vitreous enamelled panelling with decorative sections incorporating elements from the murals on the other two lines.

Piccadilly Circus was completely refurbished between 1984 and 1986 by London Transport architects whose tiling scheme (first drawn-up in 1978-79) was inspired by the bright lights and lively atmosphere of the Circus. New high-gloss glazes were developed especially for the project by the German manufacturers, and many tiles specially handcut, representing a considerable accomplishment by the craftsmen who carried out the fixing. Green and rust-red bands can be found throughout the network of tunnels, with the addition of the line colours where appropriate, combined in many different patterns.

Tiling at Leicester Square was given a border of film sprocket holes – the remaining feature of a rejected scheme to depict the images of personalities from the world of cinema. Robert Cooper (b.1949) designed the enamelled doorway surrounds to suggest proscenium arches and neon lighting (completed 1985).

Allan Drummond's vitreous enamel panels for Holborn show near life-size objects of antiquity from the British Museum, and huge trompe l'oeil columns flank the escalators. At Waterloo (completed 1988) Christopher Tipping worked on the theme of theatre and music to design tiled panels with mediaeval minstrels, dancers and other figures. The panels terminate above frieze level with rosette devices.

Robert Cooper assisted David Hamilton with designs for Euston (1987), using abstract images based on the coat of arms of Henry Charles Fitzroy, first Earl of Euston, arranged in various changing scales and repeating patterns.

Embankment was completed in 1988, with murals in vitreous enamel by Robyn Denny (b.1930), who was commissioned through consulting architects Arup Associates. A theme for the murals was suggested by an evening walk across the River Thames on Hungerford Bridge – a point at which the curve of the river gives superb views of the Thames and the activities which occur on its margins in this area. Coloured lights, banners and bunting created a feeling of celebration and recalled the Festival of Britain held on the South Bank in 1951. Denny broke down the curving shape of the river into a series of lines, which when given colour became ribbons. The colours correspond to those of each of the station's four lines as they appear on the Underground map, with the addition of blue to indicate the river itself and red for the tube trains. The bright images of the riverside are displayed on each platform, creating a cheerful atmosphere in what could otherwise be a threatening labyrinthine environment. Large areas of white enamel enhance the lighting levels and deter graffiti artists. The project was commended under the Brunel Awards Scheme for 'Outstanding Visual Design of Public Railway Transport' for 1989.

In conjunction with a £6 million scheme at Paddington during 1984-87 a new Bakerloo/Circle/District ticket hall was excavated and the old facility rebuilt. New tiling in the subways and Bakerloo platforms was decorated by David Hamilton with part and whole images of early tunnelling machines, including Marc Brunel's design of 1818 in the new ticket hall.

Terminal 4 station at Heathrow Airport (opened 1986) was designed by LUL Architectural Services with cream coloured reconstructed marble as the predominant material, in a restrained style – for the period – looking ahead to the move away from decoration which emerged at the end of the decade. The numeral '4' was cut into the platform walls, and inlaid with its mirror image into the floor to form an arrow at the exit. Much of the signage was fabricated from laminated plastic. This station is unique in that the spacious underground concourse with services and travel shops immediately adoins the single platform. The concourse plan is based on two adjoining half octagons, and it is lit both directly from the ceiling and by uplighters around the access gallery.

Monument has been rebuilt in connection with the extension of the Docklands Light Railway to Bank. A 1930s-inspired concourse adjoins the westbound platform.

On Hammersmith's platforms, butterfly canopies are suspended from curved trusses painted pastel green. Conduits carrying lamps are colour coded for the District and Piccadilly lines, and station clocks incorporate motifs based on the line diagram. There are glass cabins in the spirit of Holden's 'streamlined' waiting rooms, and surfaces are clad with neutral grey vitreous enamel. Whilst there is space and light on the upper levels, the platforms seem overcrowded with structures and equipment.

The area centred around Hammersmith Broadway and the District/Piccadilly station has frequently been considered for redevelopment. In 1962 there were plans to cover the whole station site with a raised platform supporting four tower blocks and a series of garden areas[2]. Foster Associates were commissioned in 1977 and produced a scheme for a large shopping, office and transport area enclosed beneath a fibreglass canopy between four towers (illustrated in introductory pages)[3]. Foster Associates were taken off the project in 1979 and the following year the developers Bredero announced a new scheme designed by Elsom Pack Roberts Partnership, the Foster plans being rejected in spite of strong local public support as they were not thought to be commercially viable[4]. No work was carried out on the revised proposal.

Deterioration of the island site increased over some years, and demolition started in earnest in late 1988. By March 1990 most of the site had been cleared except for the façade of the former Riverside bus garage which has been restored to resemble its original form as Bradmore House, now serving as a restaurant[5]. The scheme was completed in 1994. Hammersmith Broadway is now dominated by the massive pink, grey, cream and brown bulk of the 'Centrewest' office complex, forming a perimeter enclosing the Underground and bus stations. Two ticket halls are provided, and in the main one Harry Ford's 1906 façade has been partially re-erected around a tiled mural suggesting the reflection of Hammersmith Bridge in the River Thames. Finishes are predominantly white tile and glass block in the ticket halls.

The new station at Angel, rebuilt as part of an office development and completed in 1992. The platforms and other subsurface areas are a showpiece of the early 1990s design philosophy on the Underground.

At Angel, T. P. Figgis's 1901 station, with its narrow single island platform and lifts, had become overcrowded and shabby. A comprehensive reconstruction has been undertaken by YRM Architects to provide a spacious new ticket hall on Upper Street and escalators down to the trains, with a new northbound platform tunnel excavated and the island filled-in to become the wide southbound platform. It is now policy to create a calming visual environment of neutral colours and rationalised signage. Reduced budgets are now available for decoration, and there has been a shift away from giving stations an individual local identity towards a single corporate style. That ticket halls and platforms may be entirely devoid of decoration is perhaps a questionable improvement, but the subtle detailing of some recent works does add points of interest. Materials in 'minimal intervention' schemes, dictated partly by fire safety requirements, include stone, ceramics and exposed metal and vitreous enamel. Colour palettes tend to consist of white, grey, cream and natural stone hues. Lighting has been augmented in conjunction with more reflective surfaces.

Realignment of the A40 Western Avenue required that the wooden halt at Hillingdon – some of it comprising the original Metropolitan structure – be demolished and a completely new facility provided. A limited competition was held after LUL Architectural Services Group had submitted a proposal, and in 1987 Cassidy Taggart Partnership were commissioned to build their design as part of a sizeable civil engineering programme. It was completed in 1994.

A scheme is currently under way to improve London Underground access to central Watford. A link will be made between the Metropolitan branch north of Croxley (the present terminus is to be abandoned) and the British Rail Croxley Green branch to Watford Junction via the High Street station. Alan Brookes Associates[6] are designing new stations for Ascot Road and Watford West. A halt may be provided at Cardiff Road for football traffic. The main feature of the designs is the overall canopy of profiled metal sheeting intended to provide an effective shelter zone for passengers and facilities. In the contour of the canopy is expressed the direct flow of passengers from street to train.

At Hillingdon walkways and stairs connect with a central ticket hall which contains free-standing cabins for staff and equipment beneath a low pitched roof with fritted glass varied in a pattern corresponding to sun diagrams, providing equipment with maximum protection from the sun whilst still flooding the station with light. Air moves freely in the upper space and roof panels can be opened. The roof is stepped down to a lower level over the platforms – reminiscent of the Victorian trainsheds – and there are waiting shelters with glass block walls.

Left **For Ascot Road, where the line is on a viaduct, the shelter concept is taken a stage further and the canopy wraps down to envelop the station and form a portal through which trains pass. For Watford West, with its platforms in cutting, the canopy instead rises up to oversail the building line. These features, combined with carefully planned internal lighting, will ensure that the stations, if built, will form focal points in the urban environment both by day and by night.**

185

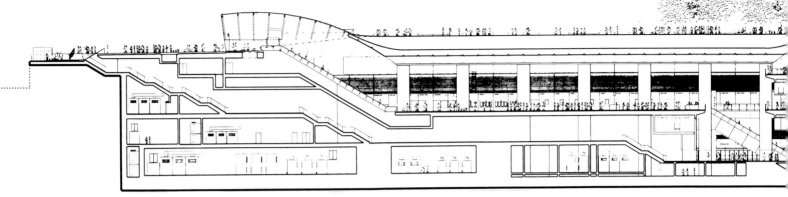

Sir Norman Foster & Partners were required to design Canary Wharf station within the basin of the former West India Dock. Access to the sub-surface concourse is via three glass domes set within a landscaped park over the station. Intended to be unobtrusive, and yet easily recognised, they were developed from station entrances designed by the same architects for the Bilbao Metro system – as structures which clearly express the termination of the escalator shaft at the surface. An important factor which influenced the design was that the station would most frequently be seen from above by occupants of the surrounding buildings: careful consideration was given to this aerial view to ensure a satisfactory aspect. Inside the lengthy concourse – with a ticket hall at each end – direct lighting is reflected off the twin concrete vaults.

A major project is the extension of the Jubilee line. An underground railway to serve south-east London had been proposed for many years, and was included in the 'Fleet line' proposal of the early 1970s, but it was only with development of the former docklands areas that the need for a direct link between the Canary Wharf site on the Isle of Dogs, the City, West End and main-line termini provided sufficient impetus and financial backing to build the line.

As an incentive to public funding the new line will also aid the regeneration of the East End and improve transport for the inner south and south-east areas hitherto neglected because the civil engineering technology was not available. The line will relieve the Docklands Light Railway (DLR), and make possible interchange with a future Channel Tunnel Rail Link and CrossRail line at Stratford.

The 10-mile railway leaves the present Jubilee line at Green Park (the Charing Cross terminus is to be 'mothballed'), crossing the River Thames between Westminster and Waterloo, continuing via Southwark, London Bridge, Bermondsey, Canada Water (Rotherhithe), and passing under the Thames twice more to reach Canary Wharf and North Greenwich, making a final river crossing northward to run alongside the North London Railways' line from Canning Town through West Ham to the terminus at Stratford. Almost all the new stations will have interchange facilities with local transport infrastructures. Royal assent was given in March 1992, and the line is expected to open in 1998.

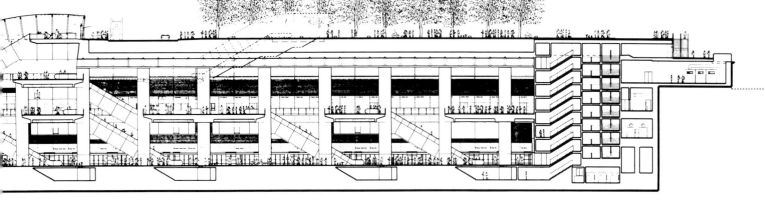

For North Greenwich William Alsop and Jan Störmer wanted to make the station an object visible in the ground – announcing its presence and revealing the activities of the railway below. Floors in the initial cut and cover design left were stripped away and a linear garden created through which passengers would pass on their way to the trains. Underneath the planted concourse, suspended so as to free the platform from obstacles, would be an oval section cabin for staff. The developers required that the site be covered over and the design had to be reworked within a concrete box above with a roof carried on two rows of bifurcated columns. Within the box is placed a passenger concourse and ventilation duct; 'wings' form a smoke hood should a fire occur. Three platforms are provided as this will be a train reversing point.

Above **Ian Ritchie Architects** have enclosed **Bermondsey** station within a glass and metal carapace, so that residents can see into the station as an integral part of their environment, and arriving passengers are greeted with a view of the outside. By carefully grading the translucency of the glass, daylight can filter down to platform level creating areas of light and shadow which contrast the scale of human and engineering forms. At night the interior lighting shines out to impart a welcoming glow. Platforms are contained partly within the diaphram wall box and partly in cast-iron tunnels.

Right **MacCormac Jamieson Prichard's Southwark** comprises several different spaces. The main drum ticket hall on Blackfriars Road will have a glass block lantern over the double-height space, suggestive of a Holden station of the 1930s. Escalators carry passengers to an intermediate concourse where they are joined by those from a second ticket hall at Waterloo East, and the lower levels are reached by escalators descending under a sweeping concrete ceiling. Light is admitted to the escalator shaft through the planar-glazed roof of the upper concourse. It was proposed that a computer controlled mirror would track the path of the sun and reflect the light to other mirrors and down the escalators.

The Jubilee Line Extension Project Office was set up in 1989, with Roland Paoletti (formerly of the Hong Kong Mass Transit Railway) as Architect-in-charge. Paoletti saw a great opportunity for using innovative architecture to realise the full potential of the project as an enhancement to the existing system through the provision of high-quality stations which looked toward travel in the next century. In common with LRT and LUL design managements, Paoletti has set aside recent Underground practice, and selected 11 like-minded architectural teams to develop the schemes and generate further ideas. The important considerations were safety, comfort – escalators in banks of three instead of the usual two – and direct passenger routes, disabled access via lifts, and as much natural lighting as practicable. The designers' brief was to expose as much of the infrastructure and its fabric as possible, concentrating resources on the planning of spatial form rather than applied decoration. This they have done by taking the basic working elements and exploiting modern engineering technology to create true architecture throughout the station levels, in structures which are derived from a common approach, but sensitive to the character of their individual environments. A limited range of durable and fireproof materials such as natural metal, concrete, glass (used extensively for its light transmitting and graffiti-resisting properties) and ceramics have been specified. Platform finishes will be standardised for every station to maintain a single line identity.

Recognition of the achievement so far is well illustrated by the report of the Royal Fine Arts Commission: "an example of patronage at its best – and most enlightened . . . the Commission finds these proposals very exciting and congratulates London Regional Transport for their inspired efforts . . . this programme recalls the remarkable pre-war developments of the Underground under the leadership of Frank Pick.[7]"

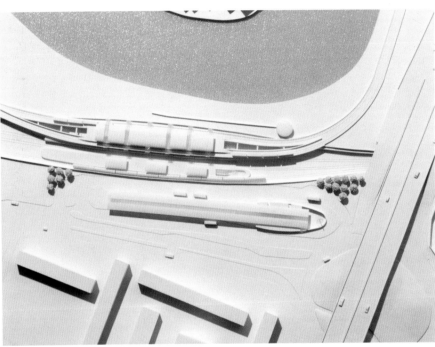

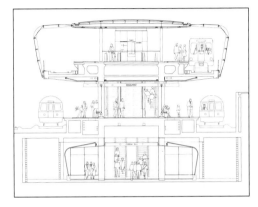

Top **West Ham station by van Heyningen & Haward Architects** will form an interchange with the District and North London lines. Within the brick-clad building several elements are combined as a linear matrix: ticket hall, bridge and concourse areas each flowing into the next. The design has been developed so that the spacing of a standard column is utilised to produce a regulating unitary grid, carried right through from the entrance colonnade to the platform canopy supports. The roof of the overbridge is continued over a spacious escalator and ticket hall. By night the glass-block walls form a band of white light, animated by the passengers within.

Centre and above **For Canning Town, Troughton McAslan** were presented with a restricted site in which to provide three island platforms and a bus station. The station comprises a series of clearly expressed exposed structures set against the arid environment alongside Bow Creek. The sweep of the river and the proximity of the Canning Town flyover were factors influencing the design, and the plan view is suggestive of moored vessels. Space constraints were solved by placing the DLR platforms above the Jubilee line on vee-shaped trusses echoing the escalators. Voids between the tracks allow light to reach the glazed roof panels of the single sub-surface ticket hall, and afford a view of the platform above. Street access is via the adjacent bus station.

Left **Canada Water**, where a glazed drum serves as an atrium over the ticket hall, and a bus station adjoins the entrance.

THE HERITAGE

Many of the Underground's 'listed' stations come from the adventurous decade of the 1930s. The escalator at Southgate and the westbound platform at Sudbury Town are illustrated on this page.

The need to introduce modern railway technology into outdated and inadequate station buildings, to universal standards and at low cost, resulted in original ticket windows, tiling, and fittings being removed and destroyed, and replaced by items insensitive to their surrounds or a pastiche of the original. Tiled murals have been drilled through and conduit added where it had previously been tidied away. Replacement of almost all the bronze escalator uplighters on the system by lighting engineers who saw them as inefficient (increased lighting levels were required for safety) and dirt-collecting is another example. Through the pressure of both internal and external agencies the Underground has once again become more aware of heritage; this has led to refurbishments being carried out with greater regard for the retention and restoration of historic features wherever possible.

Pleasing all interested parties is not an easy matter: conservation pressure groups, design managers, architects and external consultants all have their own view on what is required, and perhaps their own agendas. Each site requires decisions on its individual merits and

change is difficult to control at 'ground level'. Increasingly complex safety regulations add further restrictions for planners. The link between good intention and actual work is where things can go wrong; the very act of *design* can have unsatisfactory results when it imposes the designer's own ideas on the work. Furniture, equipment and finishes can be unsympathetic to the structure and space, dominating instead of complementing the environment and altering its character. Designers may make too many assumptions concerning the authenticity of the features they have been asked to replace or add to, and need to maintain a consideration for the past in responding to the needs of the present.

Whilst sustained investment and political will has still to be assured, London Underground is working to recapture the spirit and dynamism of the 1920s and 1930s which made the system it has inherited an example to others around the world. Just as the great pre-war achievements were planned with future traffics in mind, so we too need to be aware of our responsibility to the next generation in caring for the Underground's heritage.

Above **Kilburn Park (Grade II listed)** Below **Colliers Wood (Grade II listed)** and **Arsenal.**

Below **Wood Green (local listing)** and **Gants Hill.**

A number of stations are 'listed' – all Grade II status – as follows:

Architect	Station	Year Built	List Date	Notes
Holden	Acton Town	1932	17.5.94	
Holden	Arnos Grove	1932	19.2.71	
Fowler	Baker Street	1863	26.3.87	Platforms 5 and 6
Holden	Balham	1926	16.6.87	
Great Eastern Railway	Barkingside	1903	22.2.79	See p159 note 2
Ford	Barons Court	1905	14.2.85	
Great Eastern Railway	Blake Hall	1865	11.4.84	Closed 1982
Whitechapel & Bow Railway	Bow Road	1902	27.9.73	C.A. Brereton, engineer
Holden	Chiswick Park	1932	18.2.87	
Holden	Clapham Common	1924	27.3.81	Surface structure
Holden	Clapham South	1926	16.6.87	
Holden	Cockfosters	1933	26.5.87	
Holden	Colliers Wood	1926	25.6.87	
Holden/Heaps	Ealing Common	1931	17.5.94	
Barry/Ford	Earl's Court	1878/1906	7.11.84	
Holden	Eastcote	1939	17.5.94	
Holden/Bucknell	East Finchley	1939	22.7.87	
Clark/Fowler	Farringdon	1923	17.5.94	
Ford	Fulham Broadway	1910	14.2.85	
Fowler	Gloucester Road	1868	7.11.84	
Clark/Fowler	Great Portland Street	1930	19.1.87	
Green	Holloway Road	1906	17.5.94	
Holden/Heaps	Hounslow West	1931	17.5.94	Main building
Figgis	Kennington	1890	21.8.74	Altered 1922-24
Heaps	Kilburn Park	1915	15.3.79	
Easton	Loughton	1940	17.5.94	
Heaps	Maida Vale	1915	26.3.87	
Figgis	Moorgate	1900	10.11.77	C&SLR structure
Green	Mornington Crescent	1907	24.4.87	
Hill	Newbury Park (bus stand)	1949	19.1.81	
Holden	Northfields	1932	17.5.94	
Fowler	Notting Hill Gate	1868	7.11.84	Subsurface trainshed
Holden/James	Oakwood	1933	19.2.71	
Great Eastern Railway	Ongar	1865	11.4.84	Closed 1994
Holden	Osterley	1934	26.5.87	
Welch & Lander	Park Royal	1936	28.1.87	
Holden	Piccadilly Circus	1928	7.3.84	
Holden/Uren	Rayners Lane	1938	17.5.94	
Holden	South Wimbledon	1926	25.6.87	
Holden	Southgate	1933	19.2.71	
Holden	Southgate station parade	1933	11.3.85	
Holden	St James's Park/55 Broadway	1929	9.1.70	
Holden	Sudbury Hill	1932	17.5.94	Including substation
Holden	Sudbury Town	1931	19.2.71	
Holden	Tooting Bec	1926	16.6.87	
Holden	Tooting Broadway	1926	16.6.87	
Holden	Turnpike Lane	1932	17.5.94	
Holden/Bucknell	Uxbridge	1938	12.1.83	
Hawkshaw	Wapping	1869	27.9.73	Listing covers staircases to platforms and tunnel portal dating from 1824-43

Stations with local listing are:

Architect	Station	Year Built	Borough	Notes
Holden/James	Bounds Green	1932	Haringey	
Great Northern Railway	Mill Hill East	1867	Barnet	
London, Tilbury & Southend Rly	Plaistow	1903-05	Newham	Second building
Harrow & Uxbridge Railway	Ruislip	1904	Hillingdon	
Holden	Ruislip Manor	1938	Hillingdon	
London, Tilbury & Southend Rly	Upton Park	1902-03	Newham	Second building
London & North Eastern Railway	West Finchley	1933	Barnet	Platforms
Holden	Wood Green	1932	Haringey	
Great Northern Railway	Woodside Park	1872	Barnet	

CHAPTER NOTES

The First Underground Railways pp10-25

p10 1 *The Building News* 10 October 1862, p268.

p10 2 *The Builder* 10 January 1863, p23.

p11 3 *The Building News* 10 October 1862, p268. The original Circle line surface buildings were demolished circa 1910-12.

p13 4 *The Builder* 3 October 1868, p726.

p17 5 *The Builder* 22 February 1873, p140.

p18 6 *The Builder* 6 March 1880, p296.

p24 7 From 'Design of Stations', a paper given by Stanley Heaps and reproduced in *T.O.T. Magazine* (the Underground Group staff magazine) February 1927, p36.

p25 8 *The Builder's Journal and Architectural Record* 4 July 1900, p405. Influenced by the work of George & Peto and others, Harry Bell Measures was particularly keen on extensive detailing in terracotta, and he frequently combined an array of shaped gables and turrets with grotesques and finials to produce exciting rooflines.

p25 9 *The Builder's Journal and Architectural Record* 7 May 1902, p181.

Towards a Uniform Architecture pp26-39

p28 1 From 'Design of Stations', a paper given by Stanley Heaps and reproduced in *T.O.T. Magazine* February 1927, p36.

p28 2 ibid. Heaps does not discuss to what extent the contractors or architects were responsible for the original conception of the façades. Detailed Underground drawings showing the arrangement of blockwork indicate that each site was very carefully worked out.

p35 3 *The Electrical Times*, 27 June 1907.

Metropolitan and District Reconstructions pp40-45

No notes

Suburban Classical pp46-49

p46 1   From 'Design of Stations', a paper given by Stanley Heaps and reproduced in *T.O.T. Magazine* February 1927, p36.

Developing a Corporate Style pp50-59

P50 1   From *The Morden Extension and the Kennington Loop,* Underground Group, 1926.

p52 2   From an undated note by Charles Holden circa 1941.

p58 3   *The Architectural Review* November 1929, p218.

C.W. Clark and the Metropolitan pp60-65

p65 1   *Building* February 1927, p64.

Hubs of Empire pp66-75

p66 1   From *London – The Unique City* Steen Eiler Rasmussen, London, 1934.

p68 2   *Journal of the Royal Institute of British Architects* 24 January 1931, p167.

p70 3   A similar outcry occurred when Eric Gill's 'Prospero and Ariel' over the entrance to BBC Broadcasting House in London was revealed to the public in 1931.

p70 4   From a note by Charles Holden, 3 December 1940.

p71 5   *Building* September 1929.

A New Architecture in Suburbia pp76-113

p78 1   *The Journal of the Royal Institute of British Architects* 24 January 1931, p168.

p78 2   From a draft of Charles Holden's Royal Gold Medal acceptance speech. *British Architectural Library reference HoC 1/4/iv.*

p78 3   From a draft paper by Charles Holden entitled *Aesthetic Aspects of Civil Engineering* 26 April 1944.

p79 4   ibid.

p79 5   ibid.

p80 6   ibid.

p82 7   *Design for Today* August 1933, p135.

p86 8   ibid, p137.

p86 9   *The Observer* 25 September 1932, p25.

p86 10   *The Architect and Building News* 23 September 1932, p386.

p97 11   Harold Stabler (1872-1945) also designed the first official seal of the London Passenger Transport Board, a cap badge for its uniformed staff, decorative tiles (see page 139), posters, and a radiator mascot for certain of the Underground Group's buses. Stabler was associated with Carter and Co. of Poole who supplied many of the tiles and faience used in Underground stations from the 1920s onwards.

p102 12   Southgate Borough Council petitioned the LPTB to change the name, proposing the alternative of 'Merryhills' (a local stream) or 'Oakwood Park'. It was also suggested that 'Southgate North' would have been more appropriate and geographically accurate. The LPTB felt that these suggestions might cause confusion and refused to change the name on the grounds of costs incurred in replacing all the signs, stating that 'the public will quickly realise the area which is served by this station'. On 3 May 1934 the LPTB compromised by adding the suffix '(Oakwood)', and the reference to Enfield was dropped altogether on 1 September 1946, by which time the area was sufficiently developed to be an entity on its own.

p103 13   In his essay *Charles Holden – the enigma,* D.F. Anstis stated that the architect Harold G. Cherry FRIBA (1880-1961) assisted with the design of certain stations. Cherry lived in the same village as Holden, and Adams, Holden & Pearson were consulting architects for his Welwyn Cottage Hospital, but the only

Underground work definitely attributed to him is the signal cabin at Oakwood (now closed). Other work by Cherry included houses and schools in Buckinghamshire and Hertfordshire.

p105 14   *The Architect and Building News* 10 November 1933, p167.

p106 15   *Journal of the Royal Institute of British Architects* 11 November 1933, p28.

p109 16   Gordon Russell (1892-1980) is said to have worked on prototype designs for the combined seat/sign units at Hammersmith, Earl's Court and elsewhere. It has not so far been possible to substantiate this assertion.

p110 17   A similar illuminated sky sign had been used by Percy J. Bartlett for his Boots the Chemist store in Coventry completed in late 1931/early 1932 – see *The Architect & Building News,* 30 December 1932.

Night Architecture p114-119

No notes

Building for the Board pp120-127

p120 1   *Shelf Appeal,* October 1936, p46.

The New Works Programme 1935-40 pp128-141

p130 1   *The Railway Gazette* 26 March 1937

p131 2   Noted in a letter from Frank Pick to Charles Holden 13 April 1937 concerning the decline in standard of station design, with Pick's comments relating to Uxbridge, Rayners Lane and Eastcote stations. Soon after this a representative of Adam's, Holden and Pearson visited Leonard Bucknell's office and insisted on taking away all the drawings connected with the East Finchley project; Rayners Lane was carried out by Reginald Uren under Holden's direction.

p131 3   Noted in a letter from Charles Holden to Frank Pick 20 April 1937. Holden was prepared to accept that other architects could be brought in by Pick to design station, and stated that it might be 'breaking fresh ground'. In 1936 it had been announced that three further new stations would be opened as part of the extension plans: 'North Circular Road' between Finchley Central and East Finchley, 'Watford Way' between Mill Hill and Mill Hill East, and 'Willenhall Park' south of High Barnet. Another document mentions a station called 'Edgebury' (Edgewarebury is an area north of Edgware near the site of the proposed Brockley Hill station) to be designed by the 'Architect for All Soul's' – this may have been C.H. James who submitted designs for a new building at All Soul's College, Oxford in 1946.

p132 4   Noted in a letter from Charles Holden to Ervin Bossányi, 10 February 1938.

p132 5   *Ruislip & Eastcote Tribune,* 11 January 1950.

p135 6   The addition of artistic devices with local or symbolic references to public buildings was particularly popular on the continent at this time, and suited Pick's interest in the integration of art and design for the benefit of all. The symbols would take the form of sculptures, murals or other decorations. One published reference to such symbols during this period is in *Pennyfare* for March 1938, p49, which notes the display of a silhouette of Dick Whittington and his Cat at the new Highgate station. Designs for this feature in drawings by Holden and have been shown on page 136 of this book. Also mentioned is the inclusion of an image of St George and the Dragon at Wanstead to identify with the nearby public house and George Green; an early Charles Holden design for Wanstead does show the symbol – see page 145. The third device was that of a Ball and Cross to indicate the dome of St. Paul's for the station of the corresponding name; this was subsequently installed using carborundum material inlaid in the floor paving, and is featured in *Pennyfare* for May 1940, p60.

A paragraph in *Passenger Transport Journal* for 25 February 1938 gave further details of the scheme: Barnet – a mural commemorating the Wars of the Roses; Denham proposed western terminus of the Central line – an angler; Elstree, the site of a post on the Roman Watling Street was to have displayed a Roman soldier; Fairlop, which was at one time to have been the station for a new City of London Airport – an aeroplane; Woodford, an ancient crossing place – an heraldic tree or river; Mill Hill East – the crest of the Middlesex Regiment; Mill Hill (The Hale) –a windmill; Perivale – a pear; Redbridge – the Britannia window by Gertrude Hermes for Oliver Hill's Pavilion at the 1937 Paris Exhibition, and South Ruislip, with either Ruislip Gardens or West Ruislip – bullrushes. This particular scheme petered out with the start of the war and was never resumed, but the practice of referring to local or historical associations has been continued by London Underground until recent years. In addition to the East Finchley archer, Joseph Armitage carved a transformer in low-relief to embellish the electrical substation on Archway Road, and some years after the war James Walker FRBS carved a 'chef tasting food' for Adams, Holden & Pearson's staff canteen at Uxbridge (1952, demolished). For the Baker Street staff canteen and training centre Edward Bainbridge-Copnall MBE FRBS (1903-1973) provided a bas-relief of Diana as Goddess of the Harvest (1949).

p139　7　*Note to caption for decorative tiles*

Biscuit-cream glazed tiles commissioned from Harold Stabler in 1936 used at several Underground stations between 1938 and 1947. The tiles were also shown in the 'Exhibition of Tiles and Tilework, old and new' held at the Victoria and Albert Museum in 1939. The full list of subjects depicted on the tiles is as follows: Surrey (coronet& oak); Middlesex (crown and three seaxes or swords); Bedfordshire (eagle); Kent (horse);London County Council (lion against cross above river); Sussex (martlets); Berkshire (princesses); Buckinghamshire (swan); Hertfordshire (stag); Essex (three seaxes); the Crystal Palace; London Transport (griffin); Houses of Parliament (including a bowler hat and two coronets); London's River (five seagulls over water); St Paul's Cathedral; Thomas Lord; London Transport (bullseye symbol); 55 Broadway.

p140　8　The Underground's expansion programme was subject to difficulties in the latter part of the 1930s; at an official dinner for Charles Holden in 1936 for the presentation

of his Royal Gold Medal, Frank Pick mentioned the many ambitious schemes produced for the Underground by the architect which could not be realised because 'our resources were not as extensive as his imagination' (*Journal of the R.I.B.A., 25 April 1936, p625*). The policy of building extensions which justified themselves by subsequent house-building came under attack, and Pick himself stated that the Piccadilly extensions had not generated the projected volume of traffic: 'the evidence of the last two years shows that this expectation was too optimistic'. In 1937 Lord Ashfield, the LPTB Chairman, commented that 'traffics are not showing that liveliness to which we had hitherto become accustomed: capital expenditure is perhaps too adventuresome'. *Report of the Second Conference of the London Passenger Transport Board 1937, p3*. Pick followed this by saying that 'progress which is not self-remunerative and appearance which does not enlarge custom are luxuries not to be afforded', *ibid, p23*. In retrospect, traffic from housing development in areas served by the Underground has followed, and indeed additional lines have required to be constructed.

p141　9　Noted in a letter from Frank Pick to Charles Holden, 9 May 1940. In February 1940 Holden had queried Pick's recommendation that consulting fees be reduced, and Pick suggested that the arrangement be terminated altogether. Despite Pick's abrupt manner, to which Holden generally responded with patience and co-operation, their work was founded on a great friendship, and both individuals valued the other's opinions and criticism.

Central Line Extensions East and West pp142-157

p148　1　*General Manager (Railways) Letter to Outdoor Administrative Staff, number 21*, 1 March 1937.

p150　2　Noted in a letter from Raymond McGrath to Oliver Hill, 8 October 1937. *British Architectural Library reference HiO/67/2/-.*

p150　3　Noted in a letter from Oliver Hill to Gertrude Hermes, 15 December 1937. *British Architectural Library reference HiO/67/2/-.*
　　　　Gertrude Hermes OBE RA 1901-83, was a sculptor and printmaker.

p151　4　*Country Life* 11 November 1949, p1451.

p154　5　See note 6 for page 135

p156　6　Measures' Wood Lane was reconstructed by Stanley Heaps c.1915.

Inheritances from the Main Lines pp158-159

p158　1　A scheme was considered in 1936 for the extension of the Barnet line to an Underground station called simply 'Barnet' in the town centre, see *Modern Transport*, 19 December 1936. London Transport drawings from April 1939 show a new concrete and brick ticket hall suspended over the existing High Barnet platforms, and escalators connecting with the main road. The 1938 station designation scheme included a mural at the station to commemorate a decisive battle in the Wars of the Roses that took place at nearby Monken Hadley. Apart from the construction of a new signal cabin work was halted by World War II. Extensive redevelopment plans were proposed in the early 1960s – see page 165.

　　　　2　The styling of other buildings at Hertford East, Wolferton, Colchester and Felixstowe, all with the cupola lantern feature, supports this assumption. William Neville Ashbee FRIBA (1852-1919) joined the office of Edward Wilson, Chief Engineer to the Great Eastern Railway in 1874. Made head of architectural department 1883 and retired 1916.
　　　　For further reading see *A Pictorial Survey of Railway Stations, Gordon A. Buck, SPARKFORD 1992; Dictionary of Architects of Suffolk Buildings 1800-1914, Brown, Haward and Kindred, IPSWICH 1991.*

Post-War Developments pp160-173

p161   1   *General Manager (Railways) Letter to Outdoor Administrative Staff, number 21, 1 March 1937.*

p163   2   The South Ruislip frieze was the first large public work of Henry Haig ARCA (b.1930). The economic restrictions of the period precluded any commissioned decoration, and the frieze panels had to be purchased as 'off the shelf' items from a precast concrete works where the artist fabricated them in specially devised moulds. This arrangement meant that the artist's name was not recorded at the time, and consequently the work has until now remained anonymous. There was some discussion about a similar frieze for the new concourse at Euston, then under reconstruction, but this was not taken any further. Henry Haig went on to carry out many large-scale commissions in enamelled steel, sculpture and stained glass, including Clifton Cathedral; Lloyds Bank Regional HQ, Bristol; J.C.B. Rocester; Stewarts Construction, Milton Keynes, and churches, convents, medical centres and private residences.

P168   3   From *Notes on the design of stations on the Victoria Line,* Kenneth Seymour and Misha Black, March 1969.

p168   4   The original alternative was grey but this was felt to be too dull; it was later adopted for the Fleet line which became the Jubilee line. From *Victoria line – some propositions for the Design Panel,* London Transport Publicity Office, 2 October 1963.

p169   5   *Victoria line tiled seat recess designs.*
      To add a 'touch of interest and humanity to the rather severe platforms' – to quote the Victoria line opening booklet – several graphic designers and artists were commissioned to produce panels of coloured tiling for the seat recesses, continuing a long-standing Underground tradition of using artists to add decorations related to the locality. Tiles were manufactured by Carter & Co. of Poole.

      Walthamstow by Julia Black was based on a print by designer William Morris who once lived in the area; the tile makers were unable to reproduce the fuschia pink specified by the artist. *Blackhorse Road* by Hans Unger (1915-75) shows a black horse. *Tottenham Hale* by Edward Bawden RA (1903-89) represents the former ferry. *Seven Sisters* by Hans Unger. *Finsbury Park* by Tom Eckersley recalls the duelling grounds of former times. Edward Bawden's *Highbury & Islington* depicts a castle keep atop a hill or 'bury'. *King's Cross St Pancras* by Tom Eckersley is a visual pun on the name, and the same artist selected the Doric portico of the original *Euston* main-line terminus. *Warren Street* is a play on the station name by Alan Fletcher (b.1931) of Crosby/Fletcher/Forbes (forerunner of Pentagram Design Ltd), who chose a maze for passengers to while away the time until the next train. The artist noted that the average train interval was three minutes, and he tried to create a labyrinth which would be difficult to do in under four. *Oxford Circus* by Hans Unger suggests the intersection of routes and the circus itself (panels replaced in 1984). *Green Park* was also by Unger, with an abstract representation of the park (panels replaced in 1979, by this time badly faded). A silhouette of Queen Victoria was produced for the station of the same name by Edward Bawden, his first proposal having been to use a gold sovereign.

      On the southern extension of the Victoria line, George Smith of Design Research Unit prepared the *Vauxhall* panels, based on the theme suggested by the tile manufacturers of Vauxhall Gardens and the River Thames. Abram Games' design for *Stockwell* depicts a swan as a reference to the nearby public house and local landmark, and Hans Unger's *Brixton* makes play of reversing the station name to a 'ton of bricks'.

      For *Pimlico,* Misha Black felt a contemporary artist would be appropriate for the station serving the Tate Gallery and commissioned Peter Sedgley (b.1930) to produce an op-art design of yellow spray bursts on a white ground, inspired by his painting "Go" of 1968. At the time Sedgley was exploring the possibilities of optical art, and the work made use of simultaneous contrast and after images. The dusty atmosphere has blackened the tile grouting (the artist's request for a washable grout was not taken up) and the overall effect is not as originally envisaged.

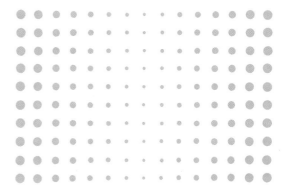

p171   6   Tom Eckersley also prepared a mural based on the theme of military tents for Hounslow West station in 1975, but this was not used.

The 1980s and 1990s pp174-189

p174   1   for a fuller comment see Sydney Hardy's article 'Underground Update' in *Building,* 20 June 1980 p50.

p183   2   (1962 scheme for Hammersmith) *The Architect's Journal,* December 1962 p1255.

p183   3   (Foster scheme) *The Architect's Journal,* 31 October 1979 p915

p183   4   Elsom Pack Roberts Partnership/Bredero scheme included office blocks on four sides, with an opening to the west giving access to a 'new town park'. The station would be submerged below ground. For details see *Building Design,* 30 May 1980, p1, and *The Architect's Journal,* 4 June 1980 p1090. There was considerable local opposition and the plans caused controversy within the Council.

p183   5   The present frontage was in fact the garden or east façade; it was re-erected to face the west in 1913 when Bradmore House was incorporated into the bus garage site.

p188   6   Recent works by the partnership include a new station at East Croydon, and refurbishments at Truro, Penzance and Gloucester. Design proposals have been submitted for Central line platform canopies, Croydon Tramlink Interchange and a new station to serve London Luton Airport.

p188   7   *Royal Fine Arts Commission Twenty-Ninth Report,* January – December 1991, HMSO, London.

APPENDIX ONE
THE PASSIMETER

Above left **The Kilburn Park passimeter was of a unique design, but soon afterwards a standard type was established** above right **based on a rectangular plan with wood and glass sides. The lower part of the booth was sometimes faced in the same tiles as the ticket hall walls.**

A particular feature of Underground station ticket halls from the late 1920s to the early 1980s was the 'Passimeter' – a free-standing booking office developed in America, so-called because of the metering devices which counted passengers through the turnstile or flipper arm outside the ticket window. The first passimeter on the London Underground came into use at Kilburn Park on 16th December 1921. The booths were subsequently installed at new and reconstructed stations throughout the system, and by the end of the 1930s were to predominate on the Underground, with traditional wall-type booking offices for auxiliary use only. The Metropolitan Railway and certain main-line companies also introduced passimeters at some of their suburban stations towards the end of the 1920s.

The passimeter could be used for both the issue and collection of tickets, eliminating the employment of a separate ticket collector at times of light traffic in the smaller stations, and its advantage over the wall-type office was that it could be placed in the direct line of passenger flow, but was of a sufficiently compact size that it did not obstruct the circulating area. A speed trial conducted at Piccadilly Circus during October 1922 recorded the issue of 809 tickets in one hour of the evening peak. It was also considered that the working conditions and attitude of booking clerks could be improved by bringing them into closer proximity with the public.

In January 1932 a new prototype passimeter was evaluated and approved for installation at all the new stations then being built. By the mid-1930s the passimeter had been more or less standardised, with variations to suit the individual location.

Below left **A prototype passimeter by Adams, Holden & Pearson in the ticket hall at St James's Park, with real travertine marble sides. Later examples had chamfered instead of rounded corners.** Below right **The booking clerk's view.**

Their use was reduced from the 1980s because of the higher level of security required for booking offices, combined with the need to improve the clerks' working conditions. As the Underground Ticketing System was introduced from 1986 onwards the old auxiliary booking offices were rebuilt to modern standards and most of the passimeters removed, although some examples have been preserved in-situ or found new uses.

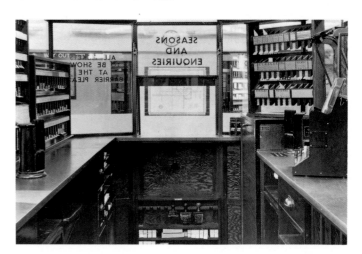

APPENDIX TWO

BIOGRAPHICAL DETAILS OF ARCHITECTS AND ARTISTS

Included here are biographical details for most of the architects in private practice who have worked for the Underground, the senior Architects employed by London Transport and its predecessors, and artists who have contributed work to London Underground buildings. Some individuals are well documented in other works and are briefly mentioned in the main text.

Joseph Armitage (1880-1945). Born in the West Riding of Yorkshire. Articled to York architects Penty and Penty, and later Assistant to the Hull City Architect. Moved to Leicester to lecture at the School of Art, moving again to London in 1914. Workshops in various London locations after World War One. *Works for Charles Holden at: 1920 New College, Oxford; 1927 Torbay Hospital; 1929 55 Broadway; 1932-6 National Library of Wales; 1936-8 new University of London buildings; 1938 Uxbridge Underground station; 1937-8 Westminster Hospital; 1937-8 lamp standards at each end of Chelsea Bridge; 1939 Underground electrical substation on Archway Road.*

Aubrey Eric Stacey Aumonier ARBS (1899-1974). Born at Northwood, Middlesex, the grandson of William Aumonier (1839-1913) - a wood and stone carver of Huguenot descent - who had started the firm of William Aumonier & Son in 1876, specialising in architectural and ecclesiastical carving, sculpture and statuary, and fibrous plaster. Aumonier & Son first worked for Charles Holden on the Incorporated Law Society extension in 1903. The firm also made many architectural models including that of 55 Broadway. Eric Aumonier trained at the Central School of Arts and Crafts and joined the firm on a full-time basis in the early 1920s. After World War II Aumonier worked on his own and with sculptors Esmond Burton, Philip Bentham and Cecil Thomas. He also made stage sets for most of the major English film studios. Retired to New Zealand 1968. *1924 reproduction of artefacts from the tomb of Tutankamun for the British Empire Exhibition; 1928-9 South Wind sculpture, 55 Broadway; 1930 Sheen Kinema, Surrey; 1931 BBC Broadcasting House, Portland Place; 1932 foyer murals, Daily Express building, Fleet Street; 1938 Norwich City Hall; 1939 Acton Railway Works canteen; 1939 Royal Arms for the British Pavilion at the New York World's Fair; 1939 Archer figure, East Finchley Underground station; 1940 School of Oriental Studies, University of London; 1951 White Knight statue at the Festival of Britain; 1959 Quaglino's Restaurant, Jermyn Street; 1959 Diamond Trading Company, Holborn Circus (for Esmond Burton); 1959-62 'Shell Ball' - Shell upstream building; 1964 figures and detailing on the Fortnum & Mason clock.*

Christian August Barman OBE RDI FRIBA (1898-1980) Industrial designer, poet. Studied architecture at Liverpool University. Assistant Secretary to the Society of Architects from 1922 and joint editor of the Architectural Review 1927-33. Worked for Frank Pick as Publicity Officer to the London Passenger Transport Board 1935-41. In 1942 he became Assistant Director of Post-War Building at the Ministry of Works. Chief Publicity Officer to the British Transport Commission 1947-62. Established the Railway Design Panel 1953.

Thomas Robert Bilbow FRIBA MSA (1893-1983). Born North London. In the office of Ernest Newton 1911, Alick Horsnell 1914, and Henry Hare 1915, subsequently with Ralph Low, Frank Matcham and Peter Dollar & Mather. Having found little employment during the slump of the early 1920s Bilbow joined the Underground as a temporary assistant to Stanley Heaps 1922, working on the designs for stations on the Edgware extension. Appointed Deputy Architect to the LPTB 1933 in charge of railway work. Made Assistant Architect in 1938, taking over from Stanley Heaps with the title of Architectural Assistant 1943; appointed Architect two years later. Retired 1960. *Works completed under his supervision include: 1946-50 White City Underground station; 1949 Baker Street Training Centre & Canteen; 1951 Sloane Square Underground station; 1959 Notting Hill Gate Underground station.*

Ervin Bossányi Hon.FMGP (1891-1975). Born Regöce, Southern Hungary and studied painting at the Budapest Academy of Arts and Crafts. After internment 1915-19, he returned to Budapest and then moved to Lübeck, Northern Germany. His first stained glass panel is believed to have been made in 1926. By 1929 when he moved to Hamburg Bossányi had achieved a high reputation as a stained glass artist. However, in 1934 he fled the Nazis and came to live in England. An exhibition of Bossányi's work was held at the Beaux Arts Gallery, London 1935, and his introduction to Charles Holden at the time the new University of London buildings were being designed resulted in a commission to make three windows for the Goldsmith's Library and the Senate House Assembly Room lobbies (1936-7). *Some main works at the following locations: 1937-45 Tate Gallery; 1938 Uxbridge station; 1938 Middlesex Library, University of London; 1948 Victoria and Albert Museum; 1949-50 Christ Church, Port Sunlight, Merseyside; 1950-53 Sanctuary, Chapel of Michaelhouse School near Durban, South Africa; 1954-61 Anglican Cathedral, Washington DC; 1956-60 Canterbury Cathedral. After 1965 Bossányi concentrated on painting, but produced two windows depicting St Francis for the Zouche Chapel at York Minster (completed 1974).*

Leonard Holcombe Bucknell FRIBA (1887-1963). Born at Chippenham. Attended the Royal Academy Schools. Worked in the office of C. M. Hennell and Ralph Low, and afterwards for H. V. Lanchester and E. A. Rickards. President of the Architectural Association 1936-8, and a founder member of the Building Centre. In private practice he worked on his own, and later in partnership with his wife Ruth Ellis.

Howard Ernest Bernard Cavanagh ARIBA AADip (1909-1960). Born in India. Attended Architectural Association Schools 1925-30. Worked in the office of Graham Dawbarn and subsequently H. Barnes & Partners and Morris de Metz. Joined the Great Western Railway architect's office in 1945. In 1946 Assistant to Brian Lewis, and appointed Assistant Architect to Frederick Curtis 1947. Supervised the design and later completion of stations on the Central line West Ruislip extension. Became Architect to British Railways (Western Region) 1949.

Charles Walter Clark FRIBA ARICS (1885-1972). Born at Wandsworth. Articled to Henry J. Snell of Plymouth 1901. Assistant to Walter Burrows and worked one year in London, Brighton & South Coast Railway Architect's office. Appointed Architectural Assistant to Metropolitan Railway 1910, and Architect in 1921. After some negotiation Clark was retired with a pension by the LPTB in December 1933 and is not believed to have continued a full time practice. *Works in addition to those in the main text: 1920 war memorial Baker Street station; 1922 house in Grange Gardens, Pinner; 1925 Watford High Street Station (never served by trains); 1931 Preston Road and Northwick Park; signal boxes for the Watford branch and some 130 Railway cottages and private houses for the Metropolitan Railway's speculative residential estates. After retirement designed a series of yachts for his own use.*

Dr Frederick Francis Charles Curtis DrIng FRIBA (1903-1975). Born at Darmstadt, Germany. Studied at the Technische Hochschule 1922-7, remaining to lecture until coming to England in 1933. Assistant Architect to the Southern Railway 1934, and in the office of Adams, Holden and Pearson 1935-6. Lectured at Liverpool School of Architecture 1936-42. In private practice from 1945 until appointed Architect to the Great Western Railway in 1947 after Brian Lewis's resignation. First Chief Architect for the Western Region of the Railway Executive in 1948, and subsequently Chief Architect to the British Transport Commission (BTC). Retired 1968. *c.1947-49 Reading Signal Works; 1958 passenger terminal at Hull and BTC Staff College, Woking; 1959-60 interior of the Channel Islands ship "Caesarea"; 1962 Engineering Research Laboratories of the British Railways Technical Centre, Derby.*

John Murray Easton FRIBA (1889-1975). Born in Aberdeen and articled to G. Bennett Mitchell. Worked in the offices of Collcutt & Hamp, Raymond Unwin and Wimperis & Simpson. Formed partnership with Howard (later Sir) Robertson 1919. Easton & Robertson joined practice with Edwin Stanley Hall 1929. In 1937 Easton was appointed consulting architect to the London & North Eastern Railway for the rebuilding of stations from Buckhurst Hill to Ongar and north of Finchley Central to High Barnet, but the only work to be completed was the station at Loughton (1940). In 1955 Easton was awarded the Royal Gold Medal for Architecture. Retired 1962. *Works with Robertson include: 1925 British Pavilion, Paris Exposition; 1927-28 New*

Horticultural Hall, Westminster (awarded the London Architecture Bronze Medal); reconstruction of Sadler's Wells Theatre and the Savoy Hotel, London; 1932 Royal Bank of Canada; 1935 Zoological and other laboratories at Cambridge; Hospital for Sick Children, Great Ormond Street (awarded the London Architecture Bronze Medal for 1936); 1937 new buildings for Gonville and Caius College and the Pitt Press, Cambridge (awarded the RIBA Medal for best building in Cambridge); 1938 Metropolitan Water Board Laboratories at New River Head, Finsbury; 1939 British Pavilion, New York World Fair; 1939 Queen Charlotte's Maternity Hospital, Hammersmith; 1950 Student's hostel, St Bartholomew's Hospital Medical School, for which Easton was presented with the Annual Gold Medal of the Worshipful Company of Tylers and Bricklayers in 1954; many other buildings for universities and hospitals, hotels and houses.

Sir Jacob Epstein KBE, Hon. LLD (Aberdeen), Hon. DCL (Oxford), LG (1880-1959), sculptor. Born in New York of Polish-Jewish parents. Studied at Art Students League and Ecole de Beaux Arts, Paris from 1902. Moved to London 1905 and after a recommendation by (Sir) Francis Dodd gained his first commission from Charles Holden to provide eighteen figures for the exterior of the British Medical Association building (now Zimbabwe House) the Strand (completed 1907-8). *Subsequent works include sculpture for the Oscar Wilde memorial at Père Lachaise, Paris (1909-12); 'Rock Drill' (1913); 'Rima' - a memorial to the naturalist W.H. Hudson - Hyde Park (1925), the commission having been given to Charles Holden's partner Lionel Pearson who designed the surround; 'Night' and 'Day' for the Underground building (1928-9); a poster for London Transport - "Epping Forest" (1934); Epstein made many other sculptures and portrait busts on public display and in private collections. Knighted in 1954.*

Thomas Phillips Figgis FRIBA (1858-1948). Born in Dublin and articled to A. Gresham Jones 1873. Came to London and worked in the office of A. E. Street 1881, and from 1882-5 under John Belcher. Studied at RA Schools. Commenced private practice 1885, working on his own and with H. Ibbotson, A. Needham Wilson, Alan E. Munby and H. Wilson. *1890 six stations for the City & South London Railway; Stockwell, Oval, Kennington, Elephant & Castle, Borough, King William Street. 1900-01 seven stations for C & SLR extensions: London Bridge, Moorgate (including company HQ), Old Street, City Road, Angel, Clapham North, Clapham Common; 1897 two houses at Harrow; the Radium Institute, Portland Place; Cassel Hospital, Penshurst; conversion of St John's Lodge, Regents Park to the Sir John Ellerman Hospital for Officers, a Training Colony at Lingfield and Farm Training School at Wallingford; St Columba's Chapel, Oxford;*

St Ninian's Church, Golders Green; St Aidan's Church, West Ealing; Vicat Cole Art School, Kensington; Ladbroke Grove public library; Coopers' Company School, Bow; five stations for London & South Western Railway's Meon Valley line, Hampshire; Woolwich and Borough polytechnic institutes; houses at Letchworth and Hampstead Garden cities. Official architectural adviser to the Presbyterian Church of England.

Henry Louis Florence RA VPRIBA FGS (1843-1916). Born at Streatham. Articled c.1860 to E. C. Robins, subsequently assistant to J. R. Hakewill and F. P. Cockerell. Studied at Atelier Questel, Paris. Commenced practice 1871. Between 1877 and 1887 worked in partnership with Lewis H. Isaacs, architect and a director of the District Railway. *1871 King Lud Tavern, Ludgate Circus; 1874 Cadby's Piano Factory, Olympia; 1876 Holborn Viaduct Hotel and Station; 1879 Holborn Town Hall; restoration of Gray's Inn Hall; Queen Victoria Memorial, Kensington High Street; the Institute of Journalists, Whitefriars; various hotels including the Carlton, Haymarket (1897-9); 1899-1900 Underground railway offices and station at St James's Park.*

Harry Wharton Ford FRIBA (1875-1947) Born at Hampstead. Attended Architectural Association Schools. Articled to F. W. Hunt and subsequently assistant to T. W. Aldwinckle, J. T. Bressey and T. Dighton Pearson. Appointed resident architect to the District Railway 1900, resigned 1911, but continued to design for the District Railway whilst in private practice 1911-16. Temporary Assistant Civil Engineer to the Admiralty 1916, working on the conversion of Ditton Park, Datchet, into the Admiralty Compass Observatory. Returned to private practice 1919 and was architect and surveyor to the United Synagogue 1920-36. Retired 1945. *Designed new or reconstructed stations and other buildings following electrification of the system at Acton Town, Aldgate East, Barons Court, Blackfriars, Cannon Street, Charing Cross, Ealing Broadway, Earl's Court, Hammersmith, Northfields, St James's Park, South Kensington, Temple, Walham Green, Westminster and Victoria. Ford also claimed to have designed the District Railway bullseye station nameboard (later reproportioned by Edward Johnston) and styled the word 'UndergrounD' with larger initial and final letters. 1924 East Ham Jewish Cemetery - for which he was awarded a 'Mention d'Honneur' at the Budapest International Exhibition; Borough, Mile End and Bow Synagogues; alterations and additions to eighteen other London synagogues.*

Sir John Fowler KCMG LLD DL (1817-1899) Engineer-in-chief to the Metropolitan and District Railways, supervising the design of their early stations to 1870. Consultant to the City & South London Railway, Central London Railway, and many other concerns.

Alfred Horrace Gerrard (b.1899) Born at Hartford, Cheshire. Attended Manchester School of Art 1919 and subsequently the Slade School. As well as the commission for 55 Broadway in 1928 Gerrard carried out sculpture for St Anselm's Church, Kennington and various memorials, murals and woodcuts, including work for the Selfridge store, Oxford Street. After serving as a War Artist 1944-5, Gerrard returned to the Slade and was appointed Professor of Sculpture 1949. Awarded the Silver Medal of the Royal Society of British Sculptors 1960. Retired in 1968 as Emeritus Professor and was made a Fellow of University College, London 1969.

Leslie William Green FRIBA (1875-1908). Born at Maida Vale, London. Apprenticed to his father Arthur C. Green 1891. Attended the Arts School, South Kensington 1892-3, and studied in Paris 1894-5. Independent practice 1897. Appointed architect to the three Yerkes' tube companies in 1903, designing more than forty stations and other buildings. Also an electrical transformer station at South Kensington on Pelham Street, and supervised other works for the District Railway, possibly including the generating station at Chelsea. After a period of convalescence in Switzerland returned to England and died at Mundesley, Norfolk from tuberculosis. *Other work includes a block of flats, Buckingham Palace Road; 26 Kensington Palace Gardens; Pall Mall Safe Deposit (before 1897); 1904-05 buildings at 29-30 St James Street and 27-29 Bury Street; extension to his own house at 50 Maida Vale.*

William Donald Campbell Hall B.Arch (Dunelm) RIBA FCSD. Studied at the University of Durham. Architect to Cumberland County Council; in private practice at Newcastle; Assistant County Architect for Surrey; Deputy County Architect for East Sussex; joined London Transport 1975 as Deputy Chief Architect; Director of Architecture and Design 1981-86; latterly in private practice.

Sydney Hardy Dipl Arch RIBA (b.1923). Born at Castleford, Yorkshire. Assistant to N. R. Paxton 1941-42; Assistant architect to West Riding County Council 1951-53; joined British Railways North Eastern Region (subsequently merged with the Eastern Region) 1954 and Regional Architect 1961-74; Chief Architect to London Transport 1974-81.

Stanley Arthur Heaps FRIBA (1880-1962). Articled to Latham A. Withall 1896-9, continuing as junior assistant until 1901; attended AA Evening Schools. Architectural Assistant to Admiralty at Greenwich Hospital 1901-3, in the latter year joining Leslie Green as assistant. Worked on the construction of stations, depots and other buildings for the three Underground group tube railways. After Green's death Heaps was retained by the Underground and appointed architect 1910, subsequently also being appointed to the Underground group's constituent companies. Throughout the 1920s and 1930s Heaps worked with Charles Holden on the large building programme, was responsible for the platform and tunnel architecture and some buildings at new stations, and designed the railway depots at Hainault, Neasden, Aldenham and Acton Overhaul Works. From 1925 also supervised the design of bus garages and trolleybus depots. In July 1940 Heaps was seconded to the Ministry of Aircraft Production for the construction of an aircraft factory at Birmingham. Retired 1943.

Oliver Hill MBE FRIBA (1887-1968). Articled to William Flockhart 1907-10, setting up his own practice in the latter year. Studied at the AA Evening School. Returned to private practice 1919, designing many private houses and other buildings in the British Isles and elsewhere, and working on the design of exhibition displays. In 1937 Hill was appointed consultant architect to the London & North Eastern Railway to work on the rebuilding of stations between Stratford and Newbury Park via Woodford and Hainault; the only work to be completed was the bus station and canteen at Newbury Park (1949-50), with assistant Edward Duley FRIBA (1903 -1985). Hill was greatly interested in interior decoration and furnishing and produced lavish designs using materials such as silver foil, chrome, marble, engraved glass and exotic woods.

Charles Henry Holden RDI FRIBA MTPI (1875-1960). Born at Bolton, Lancashire. Articled to E. W. Leeson of Manchester 1892-96; attended evening classes at Manchester School of Art 1893-94, and Manchester Technical College 1894-96. Worked in the Bolton office of Jonathan Simpson 1896, moved to London 1897 as assistant to C. R. Ashbee; attended the RA School of Architecture. Joined H. Percy Adams as Chief Assistant in 1899 and became a partner in 1907. Served as Lieutenant and Major in the Imperial War Graves Commission, travelling to France in 1917 and appointed as one of the four Principal Architects to the Commission 1920. Made sole architect for the new University of London buildings in 1931, after which time his work was mainly concerned with that project until 1937; he considered the

completed buildings to be the peak of his achievement. Awarded the Royal Gold Medal in Architecture and an Honorary Doctorate from the University of Manchester in 1936; a decade later he received an Honorary Doctorate from the University of London. Appointed town planning consultant to the City of Canterbury in 1943. Worked on the City of London Reconstruction Plan with Sir William Holford 1946-47, and on the South Bank reconstruction scheme 1947-48. *Holden's many buildings have been well documented in other works, and only those for the Underground Group are listed here. 1924 London General bus station and Underground Pavilion at Wembley for the British Empire Exhibition; 1923-24 Westminster station, side entrance; 1924 rebuilding of stations on the former C & SLR, 1925-27 Bond Street Underground station; 1925-61 many stations as discussed in the main text; Acton Works offices (1931-39). Holden also designed many items of street furniture and other equipment for the Underground Group and London Transport.*

Charles Holloway James RA FRIBA (1893-1953). Born at Gloucester. Articled to W. B. Wood. Assistant in the office of Sir Edwin Lutyens, and subsequently with Barry Parker and Raymond Unwin. After World War One set up practice with H. R. Thompson and later C. M. Hennell. Went into partnership with surveyor Stuart Frank Bywaters 1925, and additionally with S. Rowland Pierce 1933-48. Awarded the RIBA London Architecture Medal and a Ministry of Housing Medal for his Wells House at Hampstead 1949. *Worked on the restoration of the Goldsmith's Hall, and submitted plans for additions to All Souls' College, Oxford 1946-7. 1919-21 Swanpool Garden Suburb, Hull, and houses at Thorpe Bay, Essex; 1920-23 various houses at Second Garden City, Welwyn; the layout and design of public housing schemes in various parts of the country; several private houses (including his own) in Hampstead Garden Suburb; 1931 the Empire Marketing Board stand at Olympia (with Charles Holden); 1932 Bounds Green and Enfield West (now Oakwood) Underground stations. 1932-38 Norwich City Hall; 1934-36 Slough Municipal Offices; 1935-37 Hertford County Hall (all with Pierce).*

Felix James Lander FRIBA (1897-1960). Born at Newbury. Worked for Barry Parker and Raymond Unwin and subsequently Louis de Soissons where he met N. F. Cachemaille-Day (1896-1976), and Adams, Holden and Pearson. In partnership with

Cachemaille-Day from 1928 and joined Herbert A. Welch (1889-1953) in 1930. After Cachemaille-Day left in 1935 Lander continued to work with Welch until the latter's death. Lander was involved in church architecture and did much work for the Diocese of St Albans, designing several post-war churches in the area including St Barnabas, Adeyfield (1953) and the West Hertfordshire Crematorium. *Works by the partnership include: 1932 St Nicholas's Church, Burnage, Manchester; 1933 St Saviour's Church, Eltham, awarded the RIBA London Architecture Bronze Medal; 1933 Midland Bank Record Office, Colindale; 1936 Park Royal station and the Hanger Hill Estate and other housing schemes; 1939 Kingsbourne House, High Holborn. Sean Lander recalls that the architects were considered for the design of Hanger Lane at one point.*

Brian Bannatyne Lewis MA PhD BArch FRIBA LFRAIA (1906-1991). Born at Lottah, Tasmania; studied at Melbourne University, Australia. Articled to A. J. Ainslie of Melbourne 1924-7 and worked in Singapore as a mining engineer and architect 1928, moving to England to attend Liverpool School of Architecture in the latter year. Joined the Great Western Railway architectural staff 1930 and made Assistant Architect 1938. Also in private practice with his wife 1932-40. Released from war service in 1943 to return to the GWR; appointed Chief Architect to the company in 1944 and worked on designs for Central line stations at Denham, Harefield and points to Hanger Lane, a proposed new station and hotel at Swindon and proposed hotels at Swansea, Bristol, Birmingham and elsewhere. In 1946 resigned his post to take up the newly created Professorship of Architecture at the University of Melbourne where he remained until 1955. Awarded the Royal Australian Institute of Architects' Sulman Medal in 1953 for his University House at the Australian National University, Canberra. A late work was the new School of Architecture buildings at Melbourne University 1964.

Harry Bell Measures FRIBA (1862-1940). Born at Richmond, Surrey. Articled to Arthur Loader of Brighton 1877; student at Brighton School of Science and Art 1877-82 assistant to Loader 1879-83 and commenced independent practice 1883. Architect to father and son builders William Willett, carrying out housing schemes in Brighton, Kensington, Chelsea, Hampstead and elsewhere. Subsequently architect to various organisations concerned with providing improved housing for the poor, and through these philanthropic connections received the commission to design the original stations for the Central London Railway (completed 1900), and Wood Lane (1908). Built a series of 'Rowton House' hostels 1895-1905, and Gordon Mansions, WC1. Latterly designed the Union Jack Club, and Director of Barrack Construction to the War Office.

Samuel Rabinovitch (b.1903). Born at Cheetham, north Manchester. Attended Manchester School of Art from 1919 and the Slade School 1921-4. Commissioned to produce a Sculpture for 55 Broadway 1928-29; giant heads 'Youth' and 'Age' for the Telegraph newspaper offices, Fleet Street 1930. Rabinovitch has also had a lifelong interest in sport, and won a Bronze Medal for wrestling at the 1928 Amsterdam Olympics. Unable to gain a teaching post, he took up wrestling and sparring with professional boxers to support his art and changed his name to Sam Rabin, also fighting under the name of Sam Radnor. His series of boxing paintings is particularly well known. Rabinovitch had a successful wrestling career throughout the 1930s, and appeared in the Alexander Korda films 'Henry VIII and his Wives' (1933) and 'The Scarlet Pimpernel' (1934). Rabinovitch trained as a singer, entertaining troops during World War II and singing for BBC radio. Appointed drawing teacher at Goldsmith's College, London 1949, continuing to paint, design posters and illustrate. Rabinovitch taught at Bournemouth College of Art 1965-85, and Poole Arts Centre 1985-9. Won prizes at the Second and Sixth Biennales of Sport in Fine Art (1969 and 1977). His name was incorrectly shown as 'F. Rabinovitch' in reports of the Underground headquarters building and subsequent accounts of the work.

Kenneth James Hyde Seymour AFC FRIBA (b. 1910). Born at Brentford. Pupil Architect to Louis D. Blanc; studied at Northern Polytechnic School. Joined the Underground Architect's office 1931 and remained there until 1940 except for the period 1934-6 when in the architect's office of Thomas Tilling. Rejoined London Transport as one of two Principal Assistant Architects in 1946; Chief Architect 1960; retired 1974. *1946-50 White City station; 1946-52 Garston garage; 1950-55 bus overhaul works, Aldenham; from 1962 supervision of architecture and design for the Victoria line; 1963 White City Railway Staff Training Centre.*

George Campbell Sherrin FRIBA (1843-1909). Born London. Articled to H. E. Kendall, and subsequently in the offices of S. J. Nicholl, John Taylor jnr. and Frederick Chancellor. Commenced independent practice 1887. Consulting Architect to the Metropolitan Railway from 1893. *1880-92 Woburn Park School, Weybridge; 1886-97 reconstruction of Spitalfields Market; 1892-96 Moorgate Street station; 1895-96 dome of Brompton Oratory Church; 1897 Farnborough Town Hall; 1898-1902 Kursaal fairground, circus and other buildings, Southend; 1898 additions at Liverpool Street (Metropolitan Railway); 1899-1902 St Mary's Roman Catholic Church, Eldon Street, London; 1900-03 superstructure of Moorgate Station Chambers; 1903-4 Alexandra Hotel, Dovercourt; 1906-7 High Street, Gloucester Road and South Kensington stations; 1909-10 Monument and Victoria Underground stations; many houses. Rebuilding of Edgware Road (Metropolitan), with a new entrance on Marylebone Road, was completed in 1911, the arcade at Liverpool Street (Metropolitan) and reconstruction of King's Cross (Metropolitan) were completed by his son Frank (1879-1953) in 1912 and 1912-13 respectively, and Finchley Road in 1915.*

Sidney Robert James Smith FRIBA FSI (1858-1913). Born at Southampton and articled to Alfred Bedborough, subsequently assistant to Coe & Robinson, and in partnership with Coe after Robinson's death. Commenced independent practice 1879. Architect to Sir Henry Tate and also to the Lambeth Board of Guardians from 1899. *1887-1898 various public libraries and schools in south London; 1897 Tate Gallery, Millbank; 1900 frontage of City & South London Railway Bank station; 1901 additions to the Royal College of Music; 1907 Euston station, City & South London Railway; Private houses in Mayfair.*

John Hargrave Stevens (1832/3-1875) Pupil of William Wilkins - architect of the National Gallery and St George's Hospital. Stevens was District Surveyor of Bethnal Green and surveyor to the Western District of the City. He worked in partnership with George Alexander, designing the church of St John the Evangelist, Ladbroke Grove (1844) and houses in the area. Surveyor to the City Terminus Company and Bayswater, Paddington and Holborn Bridge Railway - subsequently the North Metropolitan Railway. Appointed architect and assistant engineer to John Fowler 1853, holding this post until 1857.

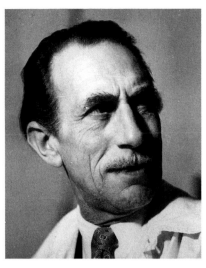

Reginald Harold Uren FRIBA ANZIA (1903-1988). New Zealander of Cornish descent who came to England 1930. Won the competition for a new Hornsey Town Hall (1933, completed 1936), which gained him the RIBA London Architecture Bronze Medal; at thirty years of age Uren was the youngest architect to have received the award. The design of the town hall set a new style for municipal buildings in England. Associated with Adams, Holden and Pearson for a time. In 1936 joined practice with J. Alan Slater and A.H. Moberly, continuing the practice of Slater and Uren until retiring to New Zealand in 1968. *Town halls for Southall and Ruislip-Northwood (neither was built); 1937 Granada Cinema, Woolwich (with Cecil Masey), 1936-40 Finchley Central station (not built); 1938 Rayners Lane station; two houses for himself at Stanmore, Middlesex; 1939 John Lewis department store, Oxford Street, London; 1957-60 Sanderson's building, Berners Street, London; Bridge Hall housing, Southall (awarded the London Regional Architecture Medal); 1968 Norfolk County Hall, Norwich.*

Frederick (James or Jabez) Ward Little is known of this architect, except that he carried out a number of buildings in the newly developed Queen Victoria Street during 1870-74, including: 1870 Blackfriars District Railway station; 1873 Albert Buildings; c.1874 Imperial Buildings & Poultry Chambers (the latter exhibited at the Royal Academy).

Sir John Wolfe Wolfe-Barry KCB FRS LLD (1836-1918). Born in London, the younger son of Sir Charles Barry, architect of the Houses of Parliament. Barry began his career in 1867, and was the engineer for Earl's Court station, the District Railway's Putney and Ealing extensions, and the completion of the Inner Circle line. Appointed consulting engineer to the Metropolitan 1895 with partner Cuthbert A. Brereton, and was responsible for encouraging the District and Metropolitan railways to undertake trials with electric traction in 1899. *Other works include Tower Bridge (with Sir Horace Jones and subsequently H.M.Brunel), Blackfriars Bridge and the King Edward VII Bridge at Kew. Consultant and engineer to several railway companies and dock authorities in the U.K. and overseas.*

The Reverend Allan Gairdner Wyon FRBS (1882-1962). Sculptor and medallist. Studied sculpture at the RA Schools. Received into Holy Orders 1933. Vicar at St Peter's, Newlyn, Cornwall 1936-55. Designed many ecclesiastical sculptures and memorials, and had works in several major collections.

PRIMARY SOURCES AND FURTHER READING

Company board minutes: Great Northern, Piccadilly & Brompton Railway 1897-1909; Charing Cross, Euston & Hampstead Railway 1900-1909; Metropolitan District Railway 1853-1917; Underground Railways Traffic Circulars 1926-33; London Passenger Transport Board 1933-42; London Transport Annual Reports 1934-47; New Works Committee 1936-8; Southgate Urban District Council Minutes.

Periodicals: Academy Architecture; The Architect & Building News; The Architect's Journal; The Architectural Review; Arkitekten; Bauwelt; The Builder; Building; Building Design; Building News; Commercial Art; Concrete Quarterly; Country Life; Crafts; Design; Design & Construction; Designer; Designer's Journal; The Electrical Times; International Architect; The Journal of the RIBA; Novum Gebrauchsgraphik; Official Architect; The Railway Gazette; Railway Magazine; The Studio.

Publications

Reconstruction and enlargement at Baker Street Station		Metropolitan Railway	1912
The new Piccadilly Circus Station		Underground	1928
Handling London's Underground Traffic	J P Thomas	Underground	1928
A Note on Contemporary Architecture in Northern Europe (1930 Tour)	W P N Edwards	(private)	1931
London: The Unique City	S E Rasmussen	Jonathan Cape	1934
An Enquiry into Industrial Art in England	N Pevsner	Cambridge University Press	1937
Art & Industry No.244 – Special Transport Issue		The Studio	1946
London Plan Working Party Report 1949		HMSO	1949
The History of The Metropolitan District Railway to June 1908	A Edmonds (prepared for publication by Charles E Lee)	London Transport	1973
Reconstructing London's Underground	H G Follenfant	London Transport	1974
Industrial Design in Britain	Noel Carrington	Allen & Unwin	1976
Initial Design Strategy for the Rail System	Department of the Chief Architect, LTE	London Transport	1980
London's Underground Stations	Laurence Menear	Midas Books	1983
Contemporary Designers	(ed.) Ann Lee Morgan		1984
Edwardian Architecture	A Stuart Gray	Duckworth	1986
ABC of London Underground Stations	David Leboff	Ian Allan	1994
Designed for London	J Rewse-Davies Oliver Green	Laurence King	1995

The RIBA British Architectural Library provided access to the private papers of Charles Holden and Oliver Hill; Charles Hutton to his collection of Holden material; the London Transport Museum Library to documents relating to Frank Pick; the Trustees of the Bossányi Archives to Ervin Bossányi's papers and Edward Armitage access to his father's papers.

INDEX
Page numbers in brackets indicate illustrations

REPRODUCTION CREDITS

Unless otherwise stated below, all black and white photographs are copyright the London Transport Museum, all colour photographs are copyright Capital Transport Publishing, and all illustrations are copyright David Lawrence. Some illustrations have been prepared from poor or damaged drawings by kind permission of AHP Partnership (successors to Adams, Holden & Pearson) and/or LUL Architectural Services Group.

Other material is reproduced by kind permission of the following:

AHP Partnership 54/ 66/ 131 above left
William Alsop and Jan Störmer 187 middle, lower
Elizabeth Argent 201 (C.H. James)
Edward Armitage 198
Freda Aumonier 198
Nick Bailey 31 centre left
Bauwelt magazine 110 lower right
Alan Brookes Associates 185 middle, lower (rendering David Lawrence)
Ruth Bucknell 131 above right/ 199
Vivien Castle 200 (H.W. Ford)
John Cornforth 199 (C.W. Clark)
Philip Coverdale 202 (G.C. Sherrin)
Design Research Unit 166/ 169 lower/ 172 top, lower left
David Easton 199
Dr M. M. Figgis 199
Margaret Foreman 199 (F. F. C. Curtis)
Sir Norman Foster & Partners 5/ 186 photography Richard Davies/187 top
June Fraser 173 top left, lower right
David Gentleman 171 lower right/ 173 centre right
Sydney Hardy 200
Paul Huxley 178 top
Sean Lander 201
The Guildhall Library 11 lower
Hendon Library 165
Quentin Houlder 7
Charles Hutton 201 (Charles Holden)
Jubilee Line Extension Project Office 189 lower
John Kennett 163 middle
David Lawrence 1/ 22 top right, bottom right/ 25 above/31 centre/36 lower right/ 40 top right/ 41 top left/ 43 centre left/ 74 lower/ 84 lower/ 100 lower left/ 101 lower/ 110 lower left/ 111 lower/ 143 bottom right/ 146 top right/ 170 lower left
John Gillham 91 bottom
London Transport Museum 34 lower left/ 45 centre/ 61 top right/ 125 lower left
London Underground Limited 3
LUL Architectural Services Group 57 lower/ 86 lower left/ 140 upper/ 174/ 175 centre, lower/ 176 above, lower left/ 177/ 178 middle, lower/ 179/ 180/ 181/ 182 top, centre
MacCormac Jamieson Prichard 188 right
Sam Rabin 202
RIBA – British Architectural Library 2/ 9/ 22 lower left/ 38 top left/ 77/ 80-81/ 93 top right/ 149 upper/ 201 (Oliver Hill)/ 202 (R.H. Uren)
Ian Ritchie Architects (photography Jocelyn van den Bossche) 188 above
Judy Russell 149 lower left
Science Museum 13
Peter Sedgley 196
John See 75 upper/ 132 top left
Margery and Gordon Stewart 201 (H.B. Measures)
Vera L. Stubbs 200 (L.W. Green)
David Stuttard 159 middle
Troughton McAslan 189 above
The Trustees of the Bossányi Archives (photography Keith Waters) 132 lower left/ 198
van Heyningen and Haward Architects (photography Putler/Armiger) 189 top
The Worshipful Company of Goldsmiths 97